T0335218

WHAT THE BEST LAW TEACHERS DO

WHAT THE BEST LAW TEACHERS DO

Michael Hunter Schwartz

Gerald F. Hess

Sophie M. Sparrow

HARVARD UNIVERSITY PRESS

Cambridge, Massachusetts, and London, England

2013

Library of Congress Cataloging-in-Publication Data

Schwartz, Michael Hunter.
What the best law teachers do / Michael Hunter Schwartz,
Gerald F. Hess, Sophie M. Sparrow.
pages cm
Includes index.
ISBN 978-0-674-04914-7 (alk. paper)
1. Law—Study and teaching.   2. Law teachers.   I. Hess, Gerald F., 1952–
II. Sparrow, Sophie.   III. Title.
K100.S39 2013
340.071—dc23   2013005272

To the twenty-six extraordinary law teachers we studied
and their students for their time, inspiration,
and insight.

To our spouses, Stacey, Layne, and Chris, and to our
children, Samantha, Kendra, Mike, Amanda, Kai,
and Silas, for your love, support, patience, and
inspiration.

—Michael Hunter Schwartz, Gerry F. Hess,
Sophie M. Sparrow

Contents

WHAT THE BEST LAW TEACHERS DO

I

Introduction

Who was your best teacher, law or otherwise? What made that teacher so effective?

For the past four years, we have posed these questions at conferences, law schools, and to groups of Chilean, Georgian, Iranian, and Turkish law teachers. In response, law teachers have described their best teachers' attitudes, expectations, teaching methods, mental habits, beliefs about students and learning, personal qualities, teaching emphases, and anything else that made their teachers so noteworthy. The results have been strikingly similar. Across cultures and schools, the best teachers distinguish themselves by their thoughtfulness, caring about their students, high expectations, commitment to student learning, and ability to engage their students.

Those same qualities distinguish the twenty-six law teachers we have written about in this book.

Starting in spring 2008, we sought to study extraordinary law teachers, teachers who have a significant, positive, and long-term effect on their students. Our goal was to create the first systematic, rigorous study of excellent law teaching. We have written and read a number of scholarly efforts at synthesizing the teaching and learning research from other fields; we wanted to contribute something new that would be credible to our colleagues. We also were cognizant that other works have identified many ways legal education and law teachers need to change; we wanted to offer something different.

This book is the product of that four and-a-half-year study. In the process, we have reviewed hundreds of nominations and visited the law schools where the subjects of this book were teaching. We observed each subject teach, interviewed their students, and scrutinized thousands of pages of interview transcripts, student evaluations, testimonial letters, and teaching materials.

We recognize that the term "best" is hard to define, as we explain below. However, we believe that we have identified twenty-six great US law teachers. We chose the title for this book, *What the Best Law Teachers Do,* for several reasons. First, it echoes the title of its predecessor book, Ken Bain's *What the Best College Teachers Do.* Second, we believe that our results also reflect not only what excellent law teachers do, but also what excellent teachers in other fields do.

Studying and describing the complex phenomena that make up these twenty-six professors' teaching was challenging and inspiring. To the extent readers find some of our descriptions and explanations unconvincing, we, not the twenty-six teachers, are responsible. And even though trying to capture teachers' practices was challenging, we each were enormously inspired by the teachers we studied. In speaking with them, watching them teach, reading their materials, and talking to their students, we had an incredible opportunity to learn. We are deeply grateful for the time and energy they put into this project.

The book consists of ten chapters. The rest of this chapter includes a description of our methodology, biographical data about the twenty-six subjects of the book, and an executive summary. Chapter 2 presents the results of a foundational study we conducted in which we asked people who nominated candidates for this book to define "extraordinary learning" in law school.

Chapter 3 focuses on the teachers' common personal qualities and attitudes. Chapter 4 describes the nature of their relationships with their students, and Chapter 5 focuses on their expectations of their students and themselves. Chapter 6 details how they prepare for class. Chapter 7 describes what happens in their classrooms. Chapter 8 illustrates how they assess students and provide them with feedback. Chapter 9 focuses on the lasting lessons students learn from these teachers.

In Chapters 3 through 9, we chose to extensively rely on teachers' own words and on the words of their current and former students. Given the volume of material, we only had space to include a very small portion of the quotes. In choosing material, we sought to provide a balance among somewhat competing goals: presenting evidence to justify our conclusions, sharing the teachers' numerous explanations of their teaching insights, giving representative and instructive samples of teachers' practices, and producing a book of suitable length to be a useful tool for law teachers.

Some teaching practices and attitudes are true for all the twenty-six law teachers we studied. Many more are overwhelmingly common. A few are shared by the majority of the teachers, and some are idiosyncratic. Where feasible, we tried to note those distinctions. Each interview, however, reflects individual facets of our subjects' teaching. Because of the variety in interviews, more teachers may engage in particular behaviors than we have noted. In other words, even if a teacher is not described as adopting a particular approach, that teacher may engage in it anyway; we just didn't learn of it.

Chapter 10 concludes the book and suggests how individuals and law schools might use the book to promote good teaching practices at their law schools.

Methodology

We began this project with three goals: (1) identify outstanding law teachers in the United States, (2) synthesize the principles by which they teach, and (3) document those principles in a way that is useful to others.

Our process involved sifting through hundreds of nominations, carefully studying more than 110 nominee files, conducting twenty-six visits to the law schools of the subjects, interviewing people for dozens of hours, reading thousands of pages of interview transcripts, and spending countless hours analyzing, discussing, and writing about what we had learned.

Description of the Study Process

This project consisted of five phases, each of which is explained in greater depth below. The five phases were: (1) an initial phase, during which we solicited, accepted, and publicized nominations; (2) a paring-down phase, in which we solicited additional evidence that we used to select teachers who would become the subjects of in-depth study; (3) a study phase, in which we visited the law schools where the subjects were teaching; (4) an analysis phase, during which we reviewed the material we had gathered, looking for common themes; and (5) a final phase in which we organized the themes and practices, selected evidence, and wrote the book. While this description suggests that the process was linear, the phases overlapped considerably. We began soliciting nominations in early spring 2008 and conducted the first study of a subject in March 2008. We continued to take nominations through March 2010, made final decisions as to subjects in summer 2010, and conducted the last visit of a subject in fall 2011.

Phase I: Soliciting Nominations

The goal of the first phase was to gather as many nominations from as many sources as possible. We sought nominations from law students, law professors, law school deans, and law school alumni. We solicited the nominations by creating a website for the study, http://washburnlaw.edu/bestlawteachers/, and submitting requests to a number of listservs, including the lawprof listserv, the associate deans' listserv, the deans' listserv, the clinic listserv, the legal writing listserv, the teaching methods listserv, and the academic support listserv. In each solicitation, we asked for nominations of outstanding teachers and asked that our request be forwarded to law school colleagues, students, and alumni. Appendix A includes the text of this solicitation. The solicitation included a link to a nomination form, which provided a working definition of "exceptional learning" (see Chapter 2) and asked the nominator to provide information about the nominee and nominator. The form asked for the nominee's name, title, institutional affiliation, courses, and teaching awards. The form also asked for the nominator's name and contact information, relation to the nominee, the nominator's own definition of exceptional learning, and the nominator's basis for believing the nominee produced exceptional learning.

We received more than 250 nominations. More than 230 came through this nomination form: http://washburnlaw.edu/bestlaw teachers/. Approximately thirty nominations came through e-mails or in-person discussions. Many of the people who became subjects of the study received multiple nominations. The project website includes the names of all the nominees and the nominators' explanation as to why the nominator believed the nominee produces extraordinary learning: http://washburnlaw.edu/bestlawteachers /nominees/index.php. Two examples, drawn from outstanding candidates, illustrate the extraordinary teachers whom we were unable to include as subjects.

ANGELA UPCHURCH, *Capital University School of Law,*

> engages students in active learning during every class session, and
> commands the attention of every single student in the room. She
> also constantly explores new and different teaching methods to
> teach complex legal concepts. Professor Upchurch demonstrates
> an extensive knowledge of the subjects she teaches, but she
> uses it to push students in their own exploration of law, instead
> of coming off as pretentious or lofty. She can read students
> extremely well, and always adjusts during class to get at what
> students are struggling with so that everyone is keeping up. . . .
> She very clearly is concerned about us outside of the classroom.
> She realizes what concerns and issues students are having,
> especially first year students, and she makes a point of being

available outside of class. Despite her extremely busy schedule, she makes a point of getting to know her students outside of class and is very supportive in helping everyone with questions or concerns about being a law student in general.

—MARY NIENABER-FOSTER, STUDENT,
CAPITAL UNIVERSITY LAW SCHOOL

STEPHEN R. LAZARUS, *Cleveland Marshall College of Law:*

The students at Cleveland-Marshall quite simply adore Professor Lazarus. . . . Several common themes emerge from [his] student evaluations. "Professor Lazarus is an amazing professor." "Best professor at Cleveland State University." "Excellent instructor! I would take Lazarus for every law school course if at all possible." "I would recommend Professor Lazarus for all bar courses. You walk away well prepared." "This professor is excellent—THE BEST. I've taken him 5 times now. Explains things clearly and in an interesting manner. Great sense of humor, seems to really enjoy teaching." "TAKE LAZARUS. YOU WILL LEARN." . . .

He is a demanding instructor, insisting that students master the materials. . . . [A student wrote]: "You probably could get a better grade with a different professor, but Lazarus is a must." . . . Professor Lazarus gives multiple quizzes throughout the semester. According to his teaching philosophy . . . students need to master the material as they progress through the course rather than wait until the end of the semester to begin studying. . . . He is smart, dedicated, kind, and a man of impeccable reputation.

We asked all nominees for permission to include them on the website. Nearly all agreed. About twenty-five did not respond to the request; a half dozen declined their nominations.

Phase 2: Selecting Subjects

We asked nominees who were interested in being considered for the project to submit (1) evidence that they had an extraordinary, sustained, salutary effect on students, (2) a statement of their teaching philosophy ("Why do you teach the way you teach?"), and (3) two years' worth of student evaluations. Approximately 110 nominees chose to submit materials by e-mail or regular mail.

In requesting additional materials, we made it clear that the most important part would be the evidence that the nominees produced "extraordinary learning." We did not prescribe what might constitute adequate evidence of extraordinary learning, explaining, "We are not wed to any particular form of evidence and will consider anything you submit." We did, however, provide a list of items that we believed might help with our deliberations:

- Testimonials from colleagues who teach your students later in the curriculum
- Testimonials from students and alumni
- Testimonials from practicing attorneys who hire your former students
- Examples of your students' work products in your classes
- Syllabi, learning objectives, assignments, and similar course materials
- Results of surveys of students attending your law school
- Teaching awards
- Student performance on exams, even including the bar exam
- Anything else you believe demonstrates your effect on students

One of the three coauthors closely reviewed each file. A few nominees so clearly warranted study that we immediately decided to do so. Many other nominees were teachers whom we would have studied if we had had more time and space. Those files were evaluated by a second coauthor. Particularly at the end, we had to make very fine distinctions in deciding whom to include in the study.

The subjects we chose submitted a wide variety of evidence, and, during our study visits and interviews with students and alumni, we developed additional evidence of their effect on their students. Many subjects submitted moving testimonial letters. For example, one subject submitted more than one hundred letters from current and former students. Another nominee submitted a series of letters written by former students (some more than ten years after law school), who all wrote that the nominee not only had been the greatest influence among their law professors on how they practice law but also hugely influenced them to balance their personal and professional lives in a healthy way. Three of the subjects submitted evidence from their current and former students who said they hoped to live their lives and treat their clients and colleagues in a way that imitated their professors. Another subject submitted the results of a class-wide statutory drafting project. We heard from a hiring partner at a law firm practicing in a specialty area, who reported that he gave preferential consideration to students who had taken a course with one of these teachers, a professor who had taught the foundational course in that hiring partner's field.

Most of the subjects had won multiple teaching awards. Two received such an award on more than twenty occasions; another received a teaching award more than a dozen times. The subjects' teaching evaluations were also impressive. One literally received the highest possible score in each category from every student in a large, first-year class.

While this book details our observations regarding twenty-six law teachers, we originally had twenty-nine excellent teachers to study, including Gerry Hess who became a coauthor. The two selected subjects whom we did not study both declined after initially agreeing to participate in the study. One of the two, Elizabeth Warren of Harvard Law School, declined because she had accepted a position as the chair of the Congressional Oversight Panel for the Troubled Asset Relief Program. The other declined to participate and asked not to be included in the book.

Phase 3: Visiting Subjects

We visited subjects between spring 2008 and fall 2011. Most visits required multiple days; all the visits, except one, were conducted by a single author. For each subject, we observed one or more class sessions (a few by videotape) and observed some subjects' interactions with students out of class. We interviewed the subjects and met with students and alumni. On several trips, we met with faculty colleagues or associate deans. We also interacted with students and alumni by phone and e-mail.

During class observations, we each kept a running record of what was happening in the classroom every minute or two. We noted how frequently and how much students were speaking, whether students were paying attention, and which students participated. We often tracked the number and types of questions the subjects asked. We noted teachers' behaviors and teaching techniques. We structured student/alumni and subject interviews around a series of questions. The questions we asked of the subjects appear in Appendix B; the questions we asked of the students and alumni appear in Appendix C. In both contexts, we asked follow-up questions requesting the speakers to elaborate on or provide a more concrete example of their statements. The subject interviews required a minimum of two hours and often took longer. The student/alumni interviews generally took an hour. The subjects signed informed-consent forms, as required by Washburn's Human Subjects Committee. We recorded most student, alumni, and subject interviews. If we were unable to record, we took extensive notes during and after interviews.

Phase 4: Analyzing Data

The goal in this phase was to identify themes from the data we generated during our visits—hours of audiotaped interviews, materials that subjects submitted, student evaluations, and our classroom observation notes.

We used a qualitative approach to reviewing and analyzing the data. Qualitative research is an effort to understand a particular human behavior and the reasons that underlie it without imposing the researcher's preconceptions about that behavior. As Aida Alaka explains in connection with her own qualitative study of student error in legal writing papers,

> [Qualitative research is] commonplace in education research. . . .
> Qualitative research collects and analyzes nonstatistical data
> using methods such as interviews, case studies, ethnographic field
> work, and comparative historical analysis, and is not reliant
> on gathering systematic information from a large number of
> cases. . . . Qualitative research is particularly appropriate for
> decoding and interpreting the meaning of observable phenomena.
> —AIDA ALAKA, THE PHENOMENOLOGY OF ERROR IN
> LEGAL WRITING, 28 QUINNIPIAC L. REV. I (2009)

To facilitate our analysis of the data, we created a web page to which we uploaded all materials for each subject. We each read through materials, identified core themes, organized the themes, and divided them into a proposed list of chapters, topics, and subtopics.

Phase 5: Organizing and Writing

Once we identified topics and subtopics, we each took a third of the subjects and carefully reviewed all their materials. We created new files that organized the data according to the chapters and lists of tentative topics and subtopics. We also trained research assistants to similarly review and organize subjects' testimonial letters and student evaluations. Finally, we selected data, synthesized it, and wrote the chapters.

Most recently, we asked the subjects to provide examples of difficulties they had experienced as teachers. We incorporated many of those examples throughout the book.

Biographical Information about the Subjects

We are grateful to the twenty-six subjects whose names and institutional affiliations as of the time of writing are below:

Patti Alleva, University of North Dakota School of Law
Rory Bahadur, Washburn University School of Law
Cary Bricker, University of the Pacific, McGeorge School of Law
Roberto Corrada, University of Denver, Sturm College of Law
Bridget Crawford, Pace University School of Law
Meredith Duncan, University of Houston Law Center
Beth Enos, retired, Lewis & Clark Law School
Paula Franzese, Seton Hall University School of Law

Steve Friedland, Elon University School of Law

Heather Gerken, Yale Law School

Ingrid Hillinger, Boston College Law School

Steven Homer, University of New Mexico School of Law

Don Hornstein, University of North Carolina School of Law

Nancy Knauer, Temple University, James E. Beasley School
of Law

Larry Krieger, Florida State University College of Law

Susan Kuo, University of South Carolina School of Law

Andy Leipold, University of Illinois College of Law

Nancy Levit, UMKC School of Law

Paula Lustbader, Seattle University School of Law

Nelson Miller, Thomas M. Cooley Law School

Hiroshi Motomura, UCLA School of Law

Julie Nice, University of San Francisco School of Law

Philip Prygoski, Thomas M. Cooley Law School

Ruthann Robson, CUNY School of Law

Tina Stark, retired, Boston University School of Law

Andy Taslitz, American University Washington College of
Law (formerly of Howard University School of Law)

The twenty-six teachers represent a wide array of personal, professional, and intellectual backgrounds. Nearly 60 percent (fifteen) of the twenty-six subjects are women. One fifth (19 percent) self-identify as racial minorities, and a little more than 15 percent (4) self-identify as members of the LGBT community. We based these conclusions and nearly all of the data that follows on our reviews of the subjects' law school faculty pages, the *2011–2012 Association of American Law Schools Directory of Law Teachers,* and *US News and World Report* law school rankings.

Though a majority of the subjects attended upper-tier law schools, the group as a whole represents the entire *US News* spectrum of law schools as Fig. 1 shows.

The subjects teach at law schools in every region in the country and, in very rough terms, they teach at law schools distributed equally throughout the *US News* rankings as Fig. 2 shows.

Collectively, the subjects are very experienced law teachers with more than 530 years of legal teaching experience. Sixty-one percent have taught for twenty years or more, and a large majority have tenure at their current institutions.

The subjects' course loads include everything from foundational doctrinal courses, to legal writing, to advanced seminars that focus on social movements affecting the law. Nearly a third of the professors in the study include nondoctrinal courses among the subjects they teach. However, most (77 percent) teach doctrinal

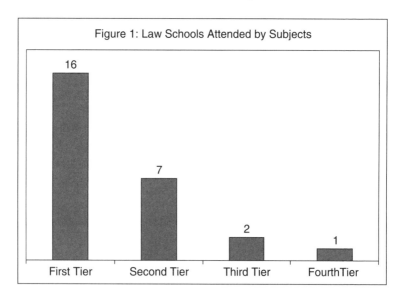

courses. Three teach legal writing; two teach in the externship/clinical/trial practice sphere; and one is an academic support professor. As Table 1 shows, three-quarters of the professors teach or have taught first-year courses.

Finally, as a whole, subjects' scholarly publications and presentations indicate their passion for their areas of concentration, and their particular commitment to improving law teaching and learning. As a group, the subjects have published a great deal; of their more than 440 law review articles, subjects have authored approximately 100 articles that were published in highly ranked law reviews, including papers in the law journals of William & Mary, Harvard, Yale, Columbia, Michigan, Vanderbilt, Northwestern, and Cornell. Additionally, the professors have published papers focusing on law teaching and learning topics on more than 110 occasions.

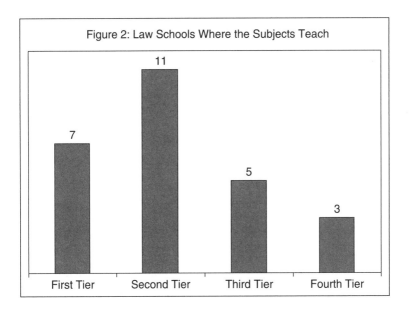

Figure 2: Law Schools Where the Subjects Teach

| First Tier | Second Tier | Third Tier | Fourth Tier |
| 7 | 11 | 5 | 3 |

Table 1. First-Year Teaching

Professor	Course
Alleva	Civil Procedure
Bahadur	Torts, Civil Procedure
Corrada	Contracts
Duncan	Criminal Law, Torts
Kuo	Criminal Law
Enos	Contracts
Franzese	Property
Friedland	Criminal Law, Property
Gerken	Constitutional Law
Hillinger	Contracts
Homer	Legal Reasoning, Research, and Writing
Knauer	Property
Leipold	Criminal Law
Levit	Torts
Lustbader	Criminal Law
Miller	Torts
Motomura	Civil Procedure
Prygoski	Constitutional Law
Robson	Law and Family Relations
Taslitz	Criminal Law

Several of the professors have also written casebooks and casebook chapters in their areas of expertise. Appendix D lists the subjects' scholarship addressing teaching and learning topics.

Executive Summary

The heart of this section is a reductionist report of a complex phenomenon—the myriad behaviors, thinking processes, philosophies, and goals of twenty-six extraordinary law teachers. While there is great variation among the teachers studied, their commonalities outweigh their differences and fit into the categories identified below, which also define the chapters of this book: personal qualities, relational behaviors, expectations of their students and themselves, class preparation, teaching activities, assessment efforts, and long-term effects.

Exceptional Learning

When soliciting nominations of outstanding law teachers, the coauthors prompted nominators with a definition of exceptional learning in legal education. Nominators were asked to articulate their definitions of exceptional learning. The coauthors synthesized their working definition of exceptional learning with the nominators' definitions. The resulting definition includes both exceptional intellectual development and exceptional personal development. Intellectual development includes deep, nuanced doctrinal understanding, synthesis of doctrine and legal theory, analytical and cognitive skills, law practice skills, and judgment. Personal development includes emotional maturation, self-awareness, motivation, compassion, professionalism, and professional identity development.

Personal Qualities

In *The Courage to Teach* (1998), Parker Palmer made two points that relate personal qualities to exceptional teaching. Palmer explained that "we teach who we are" and "good teaching cannot be reduced to technique; good teaching comes from the identity and integrity of the teacher." The personal qualities of the exceptional teachers in this study play an important role in their success. Certain personal qualities are particularly noteworthy. These teachers are thoughtful about their teaching in every way, from setting goals to coming up with effective and creative ways to achieve those goals. They take responsibility; if their students are not learning, the teachers usually blame themselves. They are expert in their fields and in their students' learning needs. They are also passionate, enthusiastic, positive, energetic, authentic, expressive, and creative. They have superb listening skills, exude empathy, and are very good at what they do. They are committed to continuously improving themselves as teachers. Finally, their students find them to be inspiring and, in most instances, humble.

Like many professionals, the teachers struggle to find appropriate work-life balance. A few feel so devoted to their work as teachers and scholars that they have little time for much else. Most, however, find the time to have close relationships with their significant others and children, coach their children's sports teams, engage in social justice and other volunteer work, enjoy time on their own and with their significant others, and take care of themselves. Almost all are busy people, and many seem to squeeze more hours out of the day than the rest of us.

Relationships with Students

The twenty-six teachers described in this study consistently choose to develop personal connections to their students. They know their students' names, backgrounds, and personal experiences. They view their students as collaborators and colleagues. They show profound respect to their students and insist that their students respect their teachers, their fellow students, and everyone else in the law school community. They assume the best about their students, attributing good intentions to their behavior. They feel concern about every student, not just a select few, and they see the promise in everyone. They are concerned about their students' futures, aspiring to influence their students to be professional, ethical, caring lawyers who skillfully balance their personal and professional lives. They see teaching as a gift and feel comfortable expressing love for their work and celebrating their students' successes. They become role models and mentors for their students.

Expectations

Because they operate from a strong belief in the capabilities of their students, these teachers set clear, high expectations for their students. They do not curry favor from students by making things easy. Instead, they have reputations as tough teachers who demand careful class preparation and ask hard questions. They challenge their students to move beyond an understanding of doctrine and theory to tasks that require application and synthesis of doctrine, theory, and practice, such as drafting documents to solve clients' problems. They insist that their students live up to their high standards in their classrooms, on exams and papers, and in practice. They also have high expectations in the other sense of that term: they are confident their students can succeed at the difficult tasks they assign. Their students uniformly believe that their teachers have confidence in them. These teachers inspire their students by communicating high expectations for themselves and modeling the work ethic and behavior they expect of their students.

Class Preparation

Because these outstanding teachers have high expectations for their own and their students' class preparation, they devote considerable effort to preparing for class. They reread their reading assignments, reflect on previous efforts to teach the topic, and redo or revise their teaching notes. They conduct additional research to find new cases, news stories that show modern applications of the doctrine, or insights about the parties or the lawyers involved in the cases they teach. They strive to understand their assignments from their students' perspective, to think about the material both as experts and as novices. They focus on specific, articulated learning goals for each class session, and choose teaching strategies tailored to achieving those goals. Most have made efforts to develop their expertise as teachers by studying the teaching and learning literature, but even those not versed in the literature plan their class sessions as if they were expert pedagogues.

Teaching Activities

Student learning is the only salient standard by which these teachers measure their classroom efforts. Students perceive that these teachers will do whatever it takes to help them learn and are eager and able to engage their students. They are great explainers. They use active and varied teaching and learning methods, engaging their students in whole-class discussions, Socratic-style dialogues, small-group learning experiences, simulations, peer feedback, and visual demonstrations. They are comfortable with silence in the classroom and use it well. Although they vary widely in their teaching styles and the methods they use, they are uniformly excellent at whatever methods they choose to use.

They structure their classrooms to be learning communities, in which they actively encourage diverse perspectives and push students to think harder and dig deeper. They model active listening when their students speak and express excitement when their students articulate new insights. Though they have prepared carefully, they are flexible enough to go off script if doing so will help them achieve their learning goals for the class session. They find ways to explicitly link the learning in their courses to real life and law practice, using simulations and news stories to bring authenticity to the doctrine. Creativity abounds in their classrooms; they bring creative ideas, materials, and learning activities to the classroom, and their students think creatively about the materials. And they effectively use the most precious moments in the classroom, the beginning and ending of their courses and individual class sessions.

Assessment

The assessment behaviors of these teachers mirror best practices in the assessment field. Throughout their courses, they are transparent about their expectations for student performance. They provide their students with extensive formative assessment—practice and feedback. To accomplish their formative assessment goals, they use practice exams, lawyering exercises, clickers, small-group exercises, multiple-choice quizzes, and a variety of writing assignments. They provide thorough feedback that balances positive and constructive comments. Their exams and paper assignments are notably congruent with how they have taught their courses: they test what they teach. Their students report that they feel well prepared for exams and paper assignments even though they regard those assessments as being among their hardest in law school.

Lasting Learning

The teachers in the study produce exceptional learning. Their students gain high levels of doctrinal understanding. They learn rules, policy, frameworks, and argument patterns, realizing a level of mastery that leaves many of them feeling able to teach others what they have learned and to contribute to the future development of doctrine. They learn core lawyering skills, including attention to detail, close reading, communication, advocacy, and legal reasoning. Students also learn the problem-solving skills and the judgment needed to draft documents and address client needs.

Students of these extraordinary teachers grow as people. They learn professionalism, including legal ethics, and they learn to value hard work and excellence. They aspire to find balance, between work and family and between self-improvement and excessive self-criticism. They take to heart their teachers' belief that they have talent and can do great things with their lives. Most of all, they strive to emulate, with their lives and careers, the passion, humility, confidence, and respect for others they see in these teachers' classrooms every day.

2

What Is Exceptional Learning
in Law School?

$\mathbf{W}$hile the primary goal of this project was to learn more about the twenty-six law teachers we studied, we had a secondary goal of enriching our conception of what exceptional learning meant in the law-school context. Consequently, we asked the approximately two hundred law professors, deans, students, alumni, and other nominators to articulate their views on what constitutes exceptional learning in law school. We prompted nominators with a working definition of exceptional learning (Box 1). We based this definition on Ken Bain's definition of exceptional learning in *What the Best College Teachers Do.*

We invited nominators to suggest their own definitions. More than 150 nominators offered their perspectives. This chapter

Box 1. Working Definition of Exceptional Learning in Legal Education

Exceptional teachers produce exceptional learning. Exceptional learning, for the purposes of this project, has two main components: exceptional intellectual development and exceptional personal development, although a qualifying law professor need not necessarily produce equally exceptional learning in both categories.

Exceptional intellectual development includes:

- understanding a sizeable body of material;
- developing greater skill in learning within the field and in reflecting on the learning process;
- asking sophisticated questions;
- developing general lawyering skills (e.g., legal analysis and reasoning, case reading, legal research, legal writing, policy analysis and synthesis); and
- developing specific law-practice skills, such as drafting legal documents (e.g., contracts, pleadings, briefs and memoranda) and interactive skills (e.g., negotiations, client counseling, oral advocacy, mediation, trial advocacy, arbitration, fact investigation).

Exceptional personal development includes significant growth in:

- understanding one's self (one's history, emotions, dispositions, abilities, insights, limitations, prejudices, assumptions . . .) and what it means to be human;
- the development of a sense of responsibility to one's self and others (including moral development);
- development or enhancement of the capacity to exercise compassion; and
- enhancement of the ability to understand and use one's emotions.

synthesizes our working definition and the perspectives of law deans, professors, students, and alumni. We offer this different perspective on a question that has emerged as a critical concern for legal educators: What do we hope law-school graduates take away from their legal education experience?

Defining exceptional learning is a challenge. Several nominators wrote eloquently about their difficulty in defining the concept but offered insights and identified elements of the term:

- "Learning is an art, not a science. Like a great painting or symphony, it defies precise measurement. Yet as experienced teachers, we all know it when we see it and experience it" (John Corkery).
- "Exceptional learning is somewhat amorphous, but ... we know there has been exceptional learning when the student comes back for more" (Anonymous).
- "Exceptional learning, much like Potter Stewart's definition of obscenity, is something you know when you see it. The most important characteristic of exceptional learning is that it is motivated from within" (Kyle Woods).
- "Exceptional learning is not a goal to be achieved; it is, rather, an unachievable goal for which to constantly strive, with the success coming not in the reaching, but in the striving itself" (Kerri Sigler).

Most nominators agreed with our two-prong, working definition of exceptional learning. Many offered thoughtful iterations, explanations, and examples of the two categories in our working definition: exceptional intellectual development and personal development.

Exceptional Intellectual Development

The starting point for exceptional intellectual development for us and for the nominators is student mastery of core concepts and skills. Core concepts means understanding the analytical frameworks, important components, and theories for an area of law. Two nominators fleshed out this aspect of exceptional intellectual development.

- "A student who has gained exceptional learning from a course should have:
  - Working knowledge of the basic body of law in the course area, including a useful outline or structure for how the various strands fit together;
  - Understanding of the sources of law in that area so he could find answers to questions he does not know or explore new areas in the field;
  - A sense of the major areas of development or controversy in the field, and some of the arguments and proponents of these arguments on either side; an appreciation for why that subject area is important/useful/interesting" (Carrie Severino).
- "Exceptional learning is the ability to see the large overarching theme, but to also be able to identify the smaller parts of the whole and how they relate to the smaller system as well as the larger system" (Nita Day).

Skills include all of the analytical, practice, and interactive skills addressed in our working definition, and, as several nominators suggested, the development of professional judgment.

- "Exceptional learning in legal education involves active engagement and the exercise of good judgment. Beyond acquiring substantive knowledge, the learner develops skills: asking insightful questions, struggling with ethical dilemmas, analyzing different possibilities, weighing consequences, and recommending courses of action based on informed study and evaluation" (Susan Fortney).

- "Exceptional learning occurs when students are afforded chances to meet with clients, conduct interviews, and write legal briefs. Exceptional learning in law school occurs when students go beyond the casebook" (Lisa Szymanski).

Mastery involves long-term retention of concepts and skills as well as the ability to teach them to others. Thus, mastery includes "development of theoretical and practical aspects of difficult material . . . that can be systematically memorized and recalled at will throughout one's career" (Edwin Wold) and "being able to pass on that learning to others when the situation arises" (Anonymous).

A second aspect of exceptional intellectual development occurs when students acquire deep, nuanced understanding of concepts and skills. Several nominators argued that nuanced, deep understanding is often the product of a passionate engagement with the law and includes facility with the policies underlying doctrine and critical analysis.

- "Exceptional learning [involves] acquisition of a deep body of knowledge that the learner has structured himself or herself and that, in an area as complex and ambiguous as law, has caused the learner to pose and attempt to answer questions of his or her own that do not have obvious answers" (Greg Sergienko).
- "Exceptional intellectual learning is developing a deep understanding and holistic perception of an area of law. It is

understanding how the law works but asking how it should change to become better" (Kimberly Newton).

- "Exceptional intellectual development [includes] the ability to critically analyze a problem, the existing law (and underlying policies), and potential solutions" (Alice Noble-Allgire).
- "[Exceptional learning is when] the student understands both the policies behind the rules that include a historical perspective on the development of the policies, and rules. That . . . greater depth of understanding—the 'why' and 'how'—leads to a greater ability to judge the road ahead and to possibly change it" (Fred Moss).
- "[Exceptional learning is] considering the benefit of change in the law, as well as the necessary elements for change" (Treisa Martin).

Sophisticated learners, according to a number of the nominators, can synthesize concepts from disparate subjects, view problems from various perspectives, and make connections among concepts. They assert that these abilities include the following facets:

- "[Exceptional learning means] a deeper understanding of the material such that the student can see analogies and distinctions between different fields (i.e., tortious fraud and criminal fraud); learning that can be applied in a variety of contexts, not just the specific one in which the information was taught" (Tracy McGaugh).
- "This concept embodies the ability to think about things using various perspectives and approaches" (Nita Day).
- "[Exceptional learning is] sensing a common thread running through a seemingly disparate set of concepts" (Hillary Burgess).

The final piece of exceptional intellectual development is the ability to apply learning in other contexts. Thus, exceptional intellectual development includes applying concepts and skills to future problems, to the practice of law, and to life in general. Nominators captured the concept of application, which educational experts call "transfer," in a variety of ways:

- "developing legal and clinical judgment (apply knowledge and skills in a realistic and constantly changing context with uncontrolled variables and make a strategic and professionally ethical choice based on what you know and what you can't know)" (Mary Lynch);
- "synthesizing the facts and reasoning in a way that allows you to build upon that knowledge when faced with a novel issue" (Eric Robinson);
- "development of a rounded, practical body of knowledge combined with the ability to apply that knowledge in problem-solving situations" (Darrell Ford);
- "taking a vested interest in the subject matter and applying it to everyday life and practical situations, while understanding how to apply what you've learned in the most honest, ethical, and moral way" (Adam Frank);
- "understanding the world we live in, and understanding how law has shaped that world, with the knowledge that, as lawyers, we have the power to reshape the world toward a greater equality" (Susan Goldberg).

Exceptional Personal Development

Personal development begins with self-understanding. Students must gain a deeper awareness of their strengths and weaknesses. They then can develop confidence and see themselves in a new light as both people and professionals. Several nominators explained this process cogently:

- "Students learn about themselves, the manner in which they interact with others, and effective communication and implementation of results" (Susan Fortney).
- "Students become aware of their own cognitive process in a manner that leads to awareness, acceptance, and ultimately confidence in their intellectual strengths" (Joe Bodine).
- "Exceptional law learning is the multifaceted phenomenon of awareness. Most importantly, it is the development of self-awareness in relation to cognitive, ethical and experiential . . . contexts. Such self-awareness should translate into a deeper understanding and appreciation of intellectual, social and institutional nuances in rule creation and application. . . . It should result in empathetic communication skills, superior situational differentiation cognition, and holistic professional responsibility" (Gregory Gordon).

Several of the nominators emphasized that exceptional personal development has a transformational effect on the lives of students, allowing the students to go beyond where they believed they could go:

- "Exceptional learning is learning that changes the learner in a significant way. He or she has new knowledge, new skills, new insights, new thoughts, and/or possibly even a new way of looking at the world" (Anne Enquist).
- "Exceptional learning transcends the subject matter and becomes an experience that impacts you for the better as a person" (Eric Robinson).

- "Learning should be transformational. At the end of the process, students should naturally ask, and be prepared to ask, questions that would not have occurred to them at the onset of their educational experience" (Anonymous).
- "Exceptional learning occurs when the student owns the subject matter. By this, I mean that the student (1) intellectually understands the material, (2) is able to apply the material, and (3) incorporates the material into a larger worldview" (Christopher Robinette).
- "The material is now part of your everyday thought process. The material has infected your life and made you become stronger and more equipped to represent your clients. Exceptional learning is the result of one pushing past the boundary of understanding into a realm of deep, sophisticated knowledge" (Daniel De Pasquale).
- "Exceptional learning is being able to attain academic, professional, and personal goals beyond what a student believes is possible" (Hillary Burgess).

Exceptional personal development is inspiring and self-sustaining. Long after the course has ended, students feel inspired to continue their exploration and development, and they have learned how to learn in the field. In short, exceptional personal development includes both the intrinsic motivation to be life-long learners and the self-regulation skills needed to do so. For a number of the nominators, this aspect of exceptional personal development was critical.

- "Exceptional learning is the process of laying an intellectual framework upon which a student can then build a lifetime of self-direct[ed] learning and exploration. This framework includes the tools for that learning (self-awareness, skepticism, inquisitiveness) as well as the motivation to develop that learning (passion, relevance, determination)" (Craig Max).

- "[Exceptional learning involves a] partnership between teacher and learner that leaves the learner with the tools, the insights, and perhaps most importantly the passion to continue learning after the partnership has been dissolved" (Scott Burnham).

- "[Exceptional learning includes] a sense of accomplishment, a feeling of preparedness, and an unwavering confidence in their abilities. Not only do they understand the law they have carefully studied, with all its subtleties and nuances, but they are secure in their ability to learn new areas of law and to adapt to ever-evolving fields" (Leah Jackson).

- "I . . . would add . . . 'intellectual curiosity,' always wanting to learn more and embrace new ideas; 'intellectual humility,' accepting what you don't know and being willing to learn about it and incorporate into your current body of knowledge; [and] 'intellectual fearlessness,' a willingness to try to put into practice or use what you've just learned and to make and learn from mistakes" (Jennifer Allison).

Finally, the nominators provided expanded understandings of exceptional personal development in the areas of professionalism and professional identity. Students, the nominators explained, must acquire core values of the legal profession, a sense of responsibility, and a purpose beyond personal advancement:

- "Exceptional personal development . . . implicates learning how to conduct oneself with the professionalism required for the practice of law. Professionalism entails being responsible for one's own work, actions, and communications with others, as well as demonstrating respect for others" (Jessica Klein).

- "I would add a third prong for exceptional professional development. This would include 1) understanding the values of the profession, and 2) acquiring a sense of professional identity and purpose based on these values" (Mary Lynch).
- "[Exceptional personal development includes] a greater sense of purpose, the understanding that what we do has vast effects beyond the court room . . . , [and] what it means to be an officer of the court and an advocate for truth and justice" (Bradford Muller).

Other Visions of Exceptional Learning

Several nominators offered other visions of what constitutes exceptional leaning in the context of legal education. Those visions ranged from concise to elaborate to poetic:

- "[Exceptional learning involves] mastery of the three essential aspects of becoming a good lawyer: knowledge, skills, and ethics" (Don LeDuc).
- "I define exceptional learning, in the context of law, to include three dimensions:
  (1) Scholarship, which includes demonstrating an understanding of substantive areas of the law and wrestling with the underlying theoretical structures and assumptions of the law; articulating roles of the law and of legal professionals in a diverse global context; and demonstrating a commitment to graduate-level self-study and learning;
  (2) Professional skills, which include articulating questions that cogently identify client objectives; learning to maximize the value of research tools and materials; demonstrating the

capacity to communicate with and appreciate the diversity of
clients, colleagues, and adversaries; and mastering the ability
to communicate legal concepts in a variety of contexts and
formulates, both formally and informally; and

(3) Professionalism, which includes demonstrating the capacity
for meaningful self-assessment; articulating roles that
lawyers and legal professionals play in promoting justice and
serving community; reflecting on the ethical complexities
associated with vigorous advocacy; developing due regard for
the responsibilities inherent in being a legal professional"
(Falcon Heights).

- "Exceptional learning in the context of law school includes education, transformation, and inspiration. First, it involves an increase in
the student's knowledge—producing an enhanced understanding
and mastery of a subject or skill. Second, it transforms the student,
leading the student to perceive oneself as a professional, shouldering
the professional and ethical responsibilities that come with that
status. Finally, exceptional learning inspires the learner to seek a
higher level of competence, professionalism, and ethical understanding and to continue the process of learning long after the period of
formal education has concluded" (Gil Kujovich).

- "Exceptional learning includes the ability to wade through murky
material clothed in only a big pair of wading boots and a stick.
Although the task seems herculean and at times impossible, an
exceptional teacher . . . can teach a student to cut through the
muck and move quickly with only the pair of waders and the stick.
Exceptional learning is coming to terms with the environment
around you and adapting to unexpected elements armed with
everything that you bring to the table both personally and
professionally. Exceptional learning is synthesizing your own

corpus of learning so that you can fashion additional boots and find additional sticks" (Diana Lin).

Revised Definition of Exceptional Learning

We drafted our working definition of exceptional learning by using our experience as legal educators to adapt Ken Bain's definition. We end this chapter with a revised definition of exceptional learning in legal education. Our revised definition reflects the wisdom and insights of the law deans, teachers, students, and alumni who nominated outstanding law teachers for our study.

Box 2. Revised Definition of Exceptional Learning in Legal Education

Exceptional teachers produce exceptional learning. Exceptional learning has two main components: exceptional intellectual development and exceptional personal development.

Exceptional intellectual development includes:

- gaining deep, nuanced understanding of a sizeable body of legal doctrine, theory, and policy;
- developing general lawyering skills (e.g., legal analysis and reasoning, case and statute reading, legal research, legal writing, policy analysis and synthesis, critical thinking);
- developing specific law-practice skills, such as drafting legal documents (e.g., contracts, pleadings, briefs and memoranda) and interactive skills (e.g., negotiation, client counseling, oral advocacy, mediation, arbitration, trial advocacy, fact investigation); and

- acquiring professional judgment, asking sophisticated questions, and applying concepts and skills to new problems, law practice, and life.

Exceptional personal development includes significant growth in:

- understanding one's self (one's history, emotions, dispositions, abilities, insights, limitations, prejudices, assumptions) and what it means to be human;
- gaining confidence, skill, and intrinsic motivation to grow beyond one's own expectations and to pursue lifelong learning;
- developing a sense of responsibility to one's self and others (including moral development);
- enhancing the ability to understand emotions and exercise compassion; and
- developing professionalism and professional identity (e.g., values of the profession, purpose, and the thirst for justice).

3

WHAT PERSONAL QUALITIES DO THE BEST LAW TEACHERS POSSESS?

Attributes

The outstanding law professors we studied are thoughtful, authentic, and passionate. These attributes resonate throughout this book because who these teachers are shapes what they do. Some qualities, such as enthusiasm and empathy, the teachers intentionally cultivate; others, such as humility, are noticed by students and colleagues.

These teachers also have lives outside the classroom. They coach their kids' sports teams, care for elderly parents, have hobbies, and tackle serious health issues.

These twenty-six teachers also make mistakes, as they freely admit. One told us how he arrived for his first day of class, having prepared the course using a different edition of the casebook than his students were using. Another shared an instance in which she struggled to find her footing when one of her students informed her, right before class started, that the current case she had chosen to discuss in class involved his parents. One of these teachers expressed remorse for instances when he failed to pay attention to his students during office meetings, and another felt bad about being derailed in class one day because she had failed to check she had all her handouts. We also heard stories of failed class sessions because the teacher had designed overly complex and ineffective hypotheticals, and regret for those days when the teacher was unable to engage his students.

One of the striking attributes of the teachers we studied was their shared thoughtfulness about their mistakes and all other aspects of their teaching. Nelson Miller's comments about students embody that thoughtfulness: "Law students get excited about learning and what a precious commodity that is. . . . I love sharing it. I love acknowledging it. I love supporting it and promoting and helping to preserve it. I think the greatest excitement that I see and really share with students is when they begin to place themselves in that practice context to kind of identify themselves as practitioners." This chapter focuses on the thoughtfulness and the other qualities the teachers in our study have in common.

Thoughtful

Examples of thoughtfulness abound. The teachers in our study think extensively about their complex roles as teachers, from the larger philosophical questions of what it means to be a teacher to the smallest logistics. "Teaching is something that is an avocation (if not a philosophy of life) because it is central. I think about teaching in almost everything else I am doing" (Ruthann Robson). "How do I teach to everyone? You know it's my goal; it's my dream, but I know it's not possible.... Simplicity can be boring, complexity can be alienating or difficult" (Patty Alleva).

Steven Homer carefully arranges his office to welcome students: "I've thought a lot about what this office looks like, what the layout is. I put this desk here so there isn't this space between us. I like the lighting ... a little less harsh. The candy dish has been often an excuse for a student to come in, 'I just want candy, but while I'm here can I ask you—' blah, blah, blah. I pay a lot of attention, I don't go for generally cheap candy in there. I'm really trying to think what will bring people in. The art I've chosen is supposed to evoke New Mexico. A lot of our students are New Mexican so I want them to feel comfortable."

As she states in her "Teaching Philosophy," Heather Gerken deliberately calls on students to include diverse perspectives: "The other main reason I use the Socratic method is that it is the best tool for ensuring that women and students of color speak in equal numbers.... If you rely on volunteers only, white men tend to dominate the air space. Even setting aside the racial/gender breakdown, a pure volunteer strategy tends to lead those without a self-editing function to talk a lot, while those who are cursed with self-awareness (and/or have some judgment) don't raise their hands. It's a terrible cycle, especially given that I usually find that the people with a self-editing function—who wonder whether they really have something to say—have a good deal more to say than the people who have balloons attached to their wrists."

As is abundantly clear throughout this book, regardless of subject or class size, all these outstanding teachers care deeply about helping students learn. Bridget Crawford explains how she approaches her required Federal Income Tax course with more than eighty students: "I am trying to reach different types of learners by mixing my teaching methods. I will do just about anything—sing, dance, play-act—to help students learn difficult material."

Tina Stark also thoroughly immerses herself in facilitating student learning, as she illustrates in her "Teaching Philosophy": "I believe that what I teach should be relevant, comprehensible, challenging, and fun. I also believe that my classroom should be a welcoming, comfortable environment where the students (and I) expect excellence from themselves and from me. . . . For material to be relevant to students, it need not be skills, which I teach. Students must feel connected to the material. To do that, I provide context for everything: how new material relates to material learned earlier; why something is important in practice; why a client and her lawyer might differ in their perspectives on an issue."

The outstanding teachers we studied examine and reject false dichotomies between teaching and scholarship, doctrine and skills, and theory and practice. "As a general matter, my goal is to train students to be effective practicing lawyers, including having the skill of learning how to learn new skills and content throughout their professional careers. I see no conflict between theory and practice, and I want them to be reflective about that connection" (Andy Taslitz). "I sometimes hear that 'not every law professor can excel at both teaching and scholarship.' I do not think we should have such low expectations of our profession. I believe scholarship informs teaching. It makes one a better professor, even if one is not doing scholarship on pedagogy. The struggle to understand doctrine and theory, to convey complexities with clarity, and to construct (and deconstruct) an argument are not only important to scholarship but are also skills of teaching" (Ruthann Robson).

These teachers also reflect on how their perspectives on teaching have changed over time. "I am convinced that a good teacher does not hit her stride until the second decade. . . . A new teacher is first struggling to develop a level of mastering of the subject matter and the meticulous attention to detail and the countless hours that that requires does not give a new teacher the luxury of thinking too much about some of the pedagogical [approaches] that could be taken. One is not in a position, I don't think in the first few years, to be a risk taker" (Paula Franzese).

Roberto Corrada echoes this view of teaching as a developmental process: "If you actually think [the class has] gone really well, it probably hasn't. . . . Especially early on in my teaching I'd come away from some classes and go, 'I was brilliant, you know? I answered every question and wasn't that marvelous?' And then in later years, I think more and more that that's an artificial feeling, that, in fact, those probably are not the best classes. . . . Probably the [best] classes [are] where you feel miserable, like some questions were asked and you didn't know the answers, and so you have to puzzle over them, and you thought maybe you handled something inadequately. But understand[ing] the power of the students being able to watch how you handle that kind of a situation is really what's going to help them more in the long run."

Many of the teachers are in awe of their role. "What happens between us is special. . . . Nothing happens in that class that happens anywhere else in the world between these people at this time, at this place. It is unique, it is wondrous, sometimes it's miraculous, sometimes it's scary, but, but, it's special, no matter what happens in it, and I am there solely for my students" (Patty Alleva).

Metaphors

The law teachers in our study reveal their thoughtfulness through their metaphors about teaching. They use words such as "music," "magic," and "journey." They relate teaching to making sense of near-chaos. The teachers convey images of teaching as a significant, dynamic, evolving, and transformative process they engage in with their students. "My teaching philosophy is built around the essential truth that teaching is a sacred trust" (Paula Franzese).

Hiroshi Motomura is one of several teachers who uses music as a metaphor: "I like to think of myself as the conductor. I have the baton, I don't play an instrument.... I'm saying, ... 'I'm just going to be the rhythm section. I just want you to take the solo.' You would never take a music class where you just listen to the teacher play."

Other teachers further elaborate on the metaphor of music. In describing teaching as "an extended and complicated orchestral piece," Patty Alleva articulates her view that "each individual instrument of learning must learn to perfect their own contribution ... so that the whole, hopefully, is a beautiful sound, but at the same time there are very distinct individual contributions, defined and redefined as students grow and learn in making their own sounds. And it's really those individual strands which hold the whole together, just like in an orchestra."

Julie Nice compares playing music to legal analysis: "I think of it as the specific piece of music like reading a specific case ... understanding patterns and seeing patterns within a case ... being able to compare songs, and genres of music and composition." Putting herself in the role of a conductor and the students in the position of musicians, Nice states, "It's magic when it works. And sometimes there is cacophony. Another way that the metaphor really works for me is that we're only as strong as our weakest player and that's why it's important that we raise the floor together." Heather Gerken connects teaching and music in a slightly different way. "It's like playing jazz where the students and I are all playing off each other. I am not conducting. I pick up on where they are, adjust to it. It's great when it works. I do not want to lecture; I provide signals and signals come from the students."

Several teachers link teaching to ideas of powerful movement and near-chaos. Rory Bahadur describes his courses as "intense, thorough, crazy, euphoric, depressing sometimes; they're . . . like life." Tina Stark speaks about teaching as a "roller coaster. Highs and lows and then a thrill at the end." In discussing her teaching philosophy, Susan Kuo writes, "Sometimes I tell them to think of me as the traffic cop at the intersection; my job is to gesture them left or right, to beckon them along faster or exhort them to slow down, but they are the ones driving."

Steven Homer and Paula Lustbader share the view of helping students create meaning in a moving landscape. "[Teaching] is a three-ring circus in a good way. . . . It's consistent with this idea of the big show. Because what I am aspiring to is . . . to hold their attention in my hand and direct it to particular things and to make the experiences of the classroom worthy of their attention" (Steven Homer). Talking about students, Paula Lustbader notes, "Fireworks go off and they've got lots of ideas and lots of thoughts about this stuff. Getting them to cluster them . . . matching and sorting of facts . . . can become challenging because they get overwhelmed with all the stuff that's going on and they're interested in the human stories."

Nancy Levit is one of the teachers in this study who talk about teaching as a journey. "The metaphor was that we're in this adventure together. . . . We're going to have a fun adventure. You're going to teach me quite a few things. I hope I can teach you some things too." Andy Taslitz equates teaching to a vision quest: "It's a journey that you can't make in the life you are in now because the life you are in now is occluding your vision. . . . You can't stop the quest until you've succeeded in finding what you're looking for. And when you come out of the quest, you're a different person, because you've seen things you've never seen before and you can live your life in a different way."

Several teachers compare teaching with coaching and parenting. "I am their 'mental aerobics' instructor . . . who will promote their learning process any way I can, but not do the mental aerobics for them" (Steve Friedland). "You start out with the sense that this kid, this student, can do this. . . . There's that really pushing and pushing to take risks because this kind of teaching requires a boatload of risk taking. So I wanted to push the kid like I pushed my own kid to take risks in sort of a relatively safe environment" (Cary Bricker).

A student expanded on the idea of a teacher as coach, advisor, and counselor, a person who is both demanding and nurturing. "You could see her actually coaching the Tennessee Titans. . . . I mean you could see a 380-pound lineman coming up to her and being respectful, maybe a little bit afraid, because she commands a room when she needs to. But you could also see the same player, when he's having trouble with his family, coming in and talking to her" (student of Beth Enos).

Other metaphors are equally illuminating about the mindsets of the teachers in this study. "I try to plow the field and put the fertilizer out there and put the water out there and then throw the seeds out there and then let them grow the garden" (Larry Krieger). "Museum curator with a practical art lesson afterwards. . . . Study the vases. Now let's all go put our hands in the muck" (Bridget Crawford). "Jigsaw puzzle . . . because you are constantly putting pieces together, and you really don't see the whole thing until the end" (Ingrid Hillinger). "Kindergarten is most like the first semester of law school because they're learning a new language. They've got to be socialized. They have to learn how to think. They have to learn how to talk. . . . So it's like a little kid. You've got to start them out easy. You've got to nurture them. You've got to teach them how to talk, how to behave, how to reason" (Philip Prygoski).

Authentic

Being true to themselves is important to these teachers, as Paula Lustbader's "Teaching Philosophy" reveals. "For me, teaching is an extension of my authentic self. I learn from student[s] and feel very honored that they trust me and are willing to engage and try different ways of learning. I am grateful to them because through them I am able to do my best work."

Susan Kuo and Tina Stark make related points. "It's not about making me look smart or what I look like. . . . You carry whoever you are wherever you are. . . . You're not there on display" (Susan Kuo). "Letting students know that I am personally invested in their learning is central to who I am as a teacher. I want them to know that it matters to me whether they understand what I teach" (Tina Stark).

Patty Alleva points out that authenticity is a way to teach: "Being who I am. To me that's a method . . . I've seen this in the literature, but I now have come to make it my own and understand it. Teaching with the whole person is a method in my view. Another method is teaching to the whole person, which I don't see as much in literature. But it's recognizing that whole people are in [the] exchange and so, the method of teaching and learning has to be tailored to who we are, as wholes."

Larry Krieger connects being authentic with being a good teacher and lawyer. "The more courage I have to be genuine... then my teaching gets better.... That quality of genuineness is so much what people need, and lawyers maybe more than anyone. Because we have to put on so many faces for so many people and so many causes and to try persuade a judge or jury or an adversary and so forth, you really can lose whatever you brought of your self-awareness when you first came to start."

For Julie Nice and Steven Homer, being authentic includes deliberately sharing their personal experiences with their students. "I am literally myself with them. I'm a human being in the classroom. I have life experience. I have a life story. If it's completely on point, I will share some aspect... that I think really adds to their knowledge. I think bringing yourself to the classroom in an appropriate way is key to what I ask of them, which is to bring themselves to the classroom" (Julie Nice). "I share personally with them how shy I am. I have struggled with it for years. I have been in therapy for years to deal with it. I know it's not easy to get over" (Steven Homer).

Steve Friedland and Bridget Crawford observe how they have developed greater authenticity over time. "I have learned over the years to try to be responsive and authentic in my interactions with students. If I do not know an answer, I tell them that. If I am struggling with something, I tell them that as well" (Steve Friedland). "For the first half of the first semester, I was imitating other teachers, and I hadn't found my own voice yet, and finding my own voice did not come naturally to me. I was afraid to be myself; I wanted to be the *law professor.* . . . And then I realized that I didn't need to be sort of some idea of the law professor. I needed to be me, as the law professor" (Bridget Crawford).

Without being asked, students talk enthusiastically about their teachers' authenticity. Paula Franzese's students commented that she is "absolutely genuine," "willing to talk about faith," "vulnerable," and "open to who she is and what she does."

Other students similarly marveled at their teachers' genuineness.

- "She is just substance, substance, substance; she is as real and just everything is out there. She's totally comfortable with herself and . . . that's just who she is, you know?" (student of Ingrid Hillinger).
- "Absolutely was just the most sincere and nicest person that I think I've probably met up here. He has just such a sincere love for his students" (student of Andy Leipold).
- "She gets genuinely excited about your life and your progress and she goes out on a limb to help you" (student of Cary Bricker).

Students reflect that authenticity significantly contributes to teachers' effectiveness. "She was very genuine and it was motivating. I mean it wasn't an act and it wasn't something she had to do. She wanted to be there and that came off to us and it made you care about a subject that clearly none of us really cared all that much about. . . . It wasn't fake or wasn't pompous" (student of Nancy Knauer). "It's not just like, you know, her trying to boost everybody's self esteem. I think she really does expect you to accomplish those things, and she's telling you you can. . . . It's genuine" (student of Nancy Levit).

A final comment illustrates the power of authenticity. "He gave us one of the best experiences I have ever had in my entire life, which was he talked for about three minutes, and he sets up this whole long diatribe about being open and not denying who he is, and he comes out as a square dancer in class and talks about how all of his life he'd been secretly wanting to be a square dancer but was just denying it to himself and everything. And then at the end, he goes, 'Oh, by the way, I'm as gay as a three dollar bill, and if you didn't know that, then you probably shouldn't be in law school.' Just the experience of having a professor being willing to make himself so vulnerable. Personally, I am gay as well, and I have never had a professor do that. And that stuck. To me that was a really big experience" (student of Steven Homer).

Passionate, Enthusiastic, Positive, and Energetic

These teachers are very passionate. "I'm really lucky. I'm so lucky to be able to do this" (Paula Lustbader). "I am having such a fantastic time teaching, and I love it so much that I can't help but laugh and have fun. Teaching is by far the most satisfying professional experience I've ever had" (Steven Homer). Others echo this view. "It's the best job in the world . . . [having] the opportunity to meet with a group of committed, dedicated young people who have the capacity to really change things. It's amazing" (Nancy Knauer).

Many of the teachers convey their deep love of teaching. "I love [teaching] so much I will take the opportunity to teach anybody anything. So I taught my wife how to drive. And I taught her kid sisters how to drive. You know, I just love to teach and so it is something that is always, always, always on my mind" (Andy Taslitz). Rory Bahadur speaks about the joy of teaching: "Personally, classroom time causes me to experience the equivalent of a drug-induced, euphoric high, which I am incapable of hiding."

Ruthann Robson and Julie Nice are among the extraordinary teachers who also are passionate about social justice. "For me it's very particular about doing social justice work. I am contributing to that for some students in a large way and some in a small way. . . . They are going out and doing good work and that's the best" (Ruthann Robson). "She is extremely passionate about the material. She is also passionate about issues of poverty and social justice, which are deeply woven in constitutional issues" (student of Julie Nice).

Many teachers are highly excited about law. "I am not kidding when I say I am a Code geek and one of my teaching objects is to get them to love the Code. . . . I tell them that 'love,' even 'like,' is about the last word they would ever use to describe their feelings about the Code during their first few encounters with it. . . . If they work hard and consistently, I promise them that they too shall see the light dawn. They too shall hear the angels sing. They too shall see the Code as a thing of rare beauty" (Ingrid Hillinger).

Students greatly value their teachers' enthusiasm.

- "She is without a doubt, one of the most passionate professors at the school" (student of Susan Kuo).
- "He seems to appreciate the justice system as a whole so much, and he doesn't have . . . that cynical side that a lot of the professors [have]" (student of Andy Leipold).
- "You could tell he had a passion for what he did without, like, jumping around and cheering about it. I mean admin is very detailed oriented. It could be kind of boring, but you could tell he really enjoyed it and made it his own" (student of Roberto Corrada).
- "She's taught me that it's absolutely okay to be a true believer. She is, and she wears her heart on her sleeve, and she allows me

to continue being passionate about what I do" (student of Cary Bricker).

- "He's passionate about [the law]. He had an interesting solid career as an attorney, and he shares those stories from his time practicing.... At the end of the term he gave this twenty-minute talk about the importance of torts and the relevance today, and I left there feeling really fired up because he was fired up about it.... It's like here's something to get excited about; here's a way to make a difference in the world" (student of Nelson Miller).

The teachers acknowledge the power and importance of conveying passion. "I think a big part of motivation ... is the passion for the subject ... and if they see that you're passionate, and you're jacked up about it, and that you care, they're going to buy into it" (Philip Prygoski). "I motivate them by being excited myself.... If their passion is Chinese lamps, then, by golly, I want to know about Chinese lamps" (Bridget Crawford). "I believe that enthusiasm is essential.... I always encourage my students to 'fake until you make it.... Just fake the enthusiasm right now; you are being called upon, and you're really not too sure, but just smile and say something, say something'" (Paula Franzese). "[I want] everyone in that class to want to learn, and my experience is that there's no substitute for some level of excitement" (Don Hornstein). "The bottom line to excitement, I think, is just are you enthusiastic about it? ... It's the real basic, 'Hey this is great stuff! Are we having fun yet?'" (Steve Friedland).

Students appreciate their teachers' willingness to show their passion. "I'm thirty-two ... and I thought, well, maybe I had to be serious now, you know? ... She really encouraged us to stay excited about things" (student of Beth Enos). "The passion for teaching is . . . definitely palpable with her. . . . Students can tell when professors feel like the class time is important to them" (student of Meredith Duncan).

Students also notice that these highly effective teachers' enthusiasm is enduring and infectious. "For somebody who's been doing this thirty, thirty-five, maybe forty years, for him to still love that process, I've got to find a way to love that process too. Because if it still excites him after that long, I want it to still excite me after that long" (student of Philip Prygoski). "Even with as many years as she has been teaching the same subject matter, over and over again, you would think it was the first day she had discovered the . . . doctrine. And it was contagious" (student of Patty Alleva). "You think about all the memos he is reading on the same stupid problems, all the reiterations of the same argument, and you don't get any of the boredom or 'I'm not here because I've heard it ten times.' He's right there with you, ready to do it again; seems excited to hear it all over again" (student of Steven Homer).

Students perceive their teachers' excitement in their positive outlook, hard work, and energetic approach.

- "She always gives 150 percent to us. . . . She always has more energy than any student in the room. We could be dead tired and she's, like, 'Come on! Let's go!' and she'll be, like, running circles around us to try and get us to have more energy" (student of Cary Bricker).
- "He had to have been in a bad mood at some point in time during the semester, but I mean I really couldn't tell; even from office hours and from class time, I really couldn't tell at all. He always showed this excitement throughout the entire time" (student of Andy Taslitz).

- "I've never seen her have a bad day, ever. It was always amazing. She found the positive, and in the most, you know, bummer of circumstances, she would find the positive" (student of Nancy Levit).
- "He is the most positive professor that I've seen. . . . Just, like, being in his classroom is an uplifting presence, and I think that it's not always something you get [at] law school" (student of Andy Leipold).

Empathetic

Empathy is another quality that distinguishes these outstanding teachers from their colleagues. Patty Alleva explains how important empathy and compassion are to her conception of teaching. "I think I have to demonstrate care . . . that I am not only passionate about it, but I care about them . . . the subject, the process, and my professions, both teaching and practicing."

These teachers want their students to be empathetic and compassionate. "I ask my students to remember where they come from, to remember the humanity and the humanness of our work, and to remember that every case tells a story" (Paula Franzese). Andy Taslitz seeks to have his students develop "character traits, like the strength to stand up to an adversary who is abusive. The willingness to be compassionate with a victim who's been harmed. . . . I hope that they grow in some ways as human beings and not just as little computers."

Philip Prygoski emphasizes the significance of students being empathetic with everyone they encounter: "I think the ability of the student to empathize with the teachers, with the other people in the room, with the people in the cases that we're talking about, [and with] clients, I think that's very, very important." Prygoski stresses the value of modeling empathy for students. "I think they learn by example. I think what the person does in the front of the room does provide a template or a model for the students, especially early on in their law-school careers.... Students will treat their clients the same way they've been treated."

Paula Franzese elaborates on the teachers' role in fostering empathy: "As teachers, we are constantly modeling behaviors for our students. I aim to stay as conscious as possible of this tremendous power and opportunity. I endeavor, both in and out of the classroom, to bear living witness to the precept that wisdom and compassion are indivisible, and that gentleness is to be expected from the strong. Cruelty comes from the weak. On our very first day together, I borrow from Karl Llewellyn and write on the board: 'Compassion without technique is a mess. But technique without compassion is a menace.'"

The teachers' strong empathy skills allow them to place a premium on caring about and recognizing the challenges students are facing. Steven Homer points out that teachers "need to provide context. You need to provide support." He illustrates how, as a new teacher, he learned from his failure to appreciate the obstacles students encounter. "I was talking and asking questions and not getting very much and getting crankier and crankier, and then I realized, 'Oh, they had something due for me this morning that they were all up 'til all hours working on. They're exhausted.' So you have to be cognizant of those things too, I think."

The teachers recognize the power and value of showing empathy for their students. "I think one of the critical first things is to care about them as people, because that will motivate them to want to perform well. They think they're wanting to perform well for me, but they're not. They're wanting to perform well for themselves and that's what I hope that they will ultimately do" (Nancy Levit). Andy Taslitz further elaborates: "There are some students who are going through great tragedies in their lives that they don't really always bring to you. There's often just all kinds of emotional issues too, and if they're not addressed in some way, they're going to interfere with a student learning, and that's a really hard thing to identify what they are, to be able to address them sensitively and to help the student . . . to not let fear interfere with your achieving your goals."

Students greatly appreciate the care and empathy these teachers show. "She really empathizes with students. I mean, she puts herself in our shoes and asks . . . what, as students, are we looking for when we walk into class?" (student of Meredith Duncan). "She doesn't think her class is the only one we're taking. You can e-mail her before class and say, 'Hey, I didn't get a chance to do the reading,' and she understands it and she won't call on you, and you can just show up, participate in class, but you don't have the pressure or the fear of being called on" (student of Nancy Knauer). "She cold-calls a lot, so everyone was always prepared, but unlike some 'tough' professors, she never made students feel stupid" (student of Heather Gerken).

The teachers' caring and empathy motivates students and builds their confidence. "I had just come through a particularly rocky semester when I took Bankruptcy with her, and she had a way of making me feel like the smartest person in the room" (student of Ingrid Hillinger). "Having us reach in and draw out from that well of talent—that was something really special that she was able to do that you only come across once in a decade with mentors in your life. When someone looks at you like that, and you really feel that something special—that she really cares—you listen and you push yourself" (student of Cary Bricker). "Dean Miller is probably one of the most conscientious and personable individuals that you'll ever meet. . . . He has really worked hard to reach into each individual and have them bring out the best of who they are in his classroom" (student of Nelson Miller).

Their teachers' empathy helps students take risks in these teachers' classes. After he had gone "crazy" and negotiated very poorly during a role-play, a student felt safe talking about the experience in front of the whole class. "We talked about it openly, and he's never critical. . . . I mean he was letting me know it was wrong too, but . . . he gave suggestions. . . . He creates a community in the classroom that's really safe for all of us" (student of Andy Taslitz). "She really wants to make sure that we understand it so much so that I don't feel uncomfortable saying I don't understand . . . without feeling like that professor just thinks I'm an idiot or something" (student of Nancy Levit).

Two final comments show how much students appreciate teachers' empathy and caring.

- "My daughter got very ill, and she was able to extend a deadline for me, and she was always asking how my child was doing, and she was just very, very caring and . . . very human, just another mother" (student of Beth Enos).
- "I've never had [a teacher] who cares about you as a student, cares what you're doing in life. . . . I'm just grateful that I was able to have been with him for the period I was with him" (student of Larry Krieger).

Expressive

The teachers of our study are comfortable showing emotions to their students. They use words such as "joy" and "love," as Ingrid

Hillinger demonstrates: "I tell them on the first day, in Article 9 . . . 'By the end of this course, whether you've seen a provision or not, you're going to know how to deal with statutory language. You're going to know where to go in the Code and what to do there, whether you've seen it not. You're going to have a system . . . and you're going to have a sense of what a transactional attorney does. . . . And you're not going to be scared of the Code, and some of you are going to love commercial law.' And I tell them that my greatest joy is the student who, midsemester, comes in and closes the door and in a very hushed tone says, 'I like this stuff.' "

Students have a high regard for teachers' expressing positive emotions, as students of Beth Enos and Patty Alleva relate. "This is an individual who loves what she is doing and totally expresses that. It makes a huge difference in how well we feel about the subject matter" (student of Beth Enos). "She genuinely puts her heart and soul into her teaching, and the way she is so demonstrative in classroom reflects that, in the way she actually cares about students. . . . It's hard to describe how emotionally charged she is by the subject she teaches" (student of Patty Alleva).

Students also recognize the emotional challenges teachers face, as two of Cary Bricker's students noted. "I wonder how she takes care of herself. I'm sure she does, but she does so much for so many people. I wonder what she does to keep her sanity, and how she continues to have a lot of feelings and emotions when she does things, but I can see myself in her position, and I would be overwhelmed and needing to take vacations all the time." "She had breast cancer last year. . . . She had surgery on Friday and she was [in class] on Sunday. I mean it shows a dedication like no other professor I've ever even experienced or mentor or anyone else. She cared enough about her students to be there.... She wanted to be there and she wanted to show us that she was dedicated to this."

Andy Leipold's students are grateful that he conveys warmth for them. "When he sees you and he's taught you, he remembers your name and he greets you, and there's a definite genuine affection." "He's just the most decent guy ... that you know. When you feel free to knock on his door at any time—it's always open—and talk to him about whatever question you have, it just gives you a feeling that he really wants to aid in your learning process. So he's there to help you more as a guide than somebody that's instructing."

Larry Krieger's students explain how his demeanor makes them feel safe in expressing their emotions.

- "I don't know if his office is strategically placed, but I will just pass by, and he invites me in, you know, to see what's going on, and I swear I'm not that emotional, but every time I've gone in there, I end up crying with the man.... He's more than a professor; he's like a friend and even like a psychologist."
- "He was very concerned with our progress and well-being.... He is the epitome of the open-door policy."
- "He treats—which is very uncommon—everybody as an individual. He knows, like, all of his students. He knows their personalities; he knows their personal troubles, their personal successes and triumphs, and he shares those with you.... One day, he's like, 'If you don't mind me eating lunch, you can certainly shut the door and have a cry.'"

Humble

The role of ego in teaching can be complex, as Ruthann Robson articulates. "Teaching in the classroom is not purely performance. I think that one has to have an exceedingly strong ego and simultaneously no ego when one is teaching. It is important to be able to endure the glare of student attention and be center stage, assuming control and not letting particular students derail the class. It is equally important to understand that the class is not 'about' me or about me 'feeling good.' The central project is the students' learning."

Over and over again, the students characterize their law teachers as "humble," "modest," "unpretentious," or lacking ego. "[He's] extremely, extremely humble" (student of Hiroshi Motomura). "It's not about her. It never is about her. And she will never let it be about her if she has her way" (student of Nancy Levit). "He's probably one of the most humble people I think I've ever met, honestly. . . . He has no airs about himself at all" (student of Andy Leipold).

Students perceive that their teachers' humility is a powerful tool in their learning process. "She's very modest and soft-spoken despite her many accomplishments, and that also makes her less intimidating and, again, facilitates discussion" (student of Meredith Duncan). "Humility is important because it helps you to ask a question in class. Because you know that, especially in a big class, where, you know, I'm sometimes reluctant to say something . . . I didn't really feel it as much in that class, because you knew that . . . he was going to treat your question if it was intelligent. He was going to give you an intelligent answer" (student of Roberto Corrada).

Students contrast the humility and modesty of these teachers with their other teachers. "If there's an understanding problem, I feel like he assumes that it's him, and I don't think that I've had that with any other law professor" (student of Hiroshi Motomura). "One of the reasons why we take the feedback so well is because of her humility. She teaches by saying, 'I've done this before and it didn't work for me and let me tell you how bad I messed up in court and how that made me feel.' And then she would explain to us why doing something different might work better. And so she teaches without that air of arrogance that is so common among law professors" (student of Cary Bricker). "I've never had a professor who was as good as Hornstein, who also didn't try to beat me over the head with how good he was. . . . Prestigious professors here—they try to beat you over the head with how great they are and how intelligent they are" (student of Don Hornstein).

Students also observe humility in how their teachers treat their accomplishments or expertise. "He never gets pretentious about having been a clerk. He'll bring that up often to help illustrate points, but I've had lots of professors who I think are being pretentious when they talk about their experience, like, 'Oh I worked on this case because I was a big shot lawyer.' You never feel that from him. You just feel that he's doing this because he thinks it will help us learn. It's never to brag" (student of Andy Leipold). Other students echo this point.

- "He has such a spirit of humility and that was communicated in the classroom in such a way that I never felt as if he portrayed himself as having all the answers" (student of Nelson Miller).
- "She admits when she doesn't know material: 'I never thought about that before, but I would think . . .' She acknowledges her

lack of knowledge: 'I haven't read that article. I don't want to say things that I don't know. I do that in my writing'" (student of Heather Gerken).

- "I find that she's very humble. And that you can imagine if you caught a professor in a mistake, they would break into a cold sweat, and that appearing wrong in front of the class would be righteous and the kiss of death. But with Paula she's, like, oh well, 'I don't know. I'll have to check. I'll have to get back to you'" (student of Paula Lustbader).
- "Professor Levit also has the honor of being the smartest person I have ever known. What I love . . . is she is very humble about it. Rather than showing you how smart she is, she always makes it a point to let you know how smart you are" (student of Nancy Levit).

Teachers reveal their humility in many of their comments. Many expressed surprise and delight after learning that they would be included in this study. "I'm actually astonished that I was nominated for this . . . I just work really hard to make sure that I know my stuff because it's my job to be able to answer their questions. That's what they're paying for. That's what they are here for" (Susan Kuo). Teachers were similarly humble about many other aspects of teaching.

- After a course was not going well, Bridget Crawford told her students, "I'm really sorry. You deserve better. Let me try."
- "The more confused they are at the end of class, the more I figure that I haven't taught the class well" (Meredith Duncan).
- "I will concede a matter that I don't know, that I need to look up. I will talk about my successes as a lawyer but also my failures. I'll talk about my best day in law teaching and then a lackluster day" (Paula Franzese).

- "We are all fallible and your job isn't to win; your job is just do the best you can and really try and get some love into what you are doing. Either it is love for the world, or love for the people, love for yourself, and love for the cause. But that requires that willingness to be fallible, because that is how we are" (Larry Krieger).

- "My bottom line for teaching: know your audience and always remember why you are there. It's not about you. It's about them" (Nancy Knauer).

- "Ultimately it's inevitable that classes are centered on the teacher. But I really don't like the class to be more about me than it needs to be. It ought to be about them and about their development, and so I try not to tell stories . . . about me . . . unless it really, really, really illustrates the point, and, as best I can, I try to make the story, 'Here's how I screwed up one time in practice, as many of us do'" (Andy Leipold).

Responsible

The teachers we studied believe they owe a significant duty to their students. "Why do I teach the way I teach? Because, for me, teaching is not about the teacher; it is about the students. The test is not whether I have delivered the information successfully but whether my students have learned it" (Susan Kuo).

They feel responsible at multiple levels, as Larry Krieger puts it in his "Teaching Philosophy." "First, I recognize that the learner is to be the central focus of teaching; and second, I believe that total respect is due each student, in recognition of his/her intrinsic, immense capability for learning." He adds that the teacher "should focus on creating conditions that catalyze the learning process within her students. . . . The material and methods of teaching should involve the student in a holistic, engaged level of learning."

These teachers hold themselves accountable for the way they conduct class. "I'm very aware of the clock. . . . I don't want to waste their preparation and study time, and I know that, if I have assigned them thirty pages, and I only get to two of them, they don't appreciate that, and I don't blame them" (Meredith Duncan). In her "Teaching Philosophy," Tina Stark expresses her duty to teach students the skills necessary for transactional practice: "They need to learn how to be neither unduly formal nor overly familiar." Even though many students find it awkward initially, "I have all my students call me by my first name." As she explains, lawyers project confidence when they address their seniors by their first names.

Many of the teachers express their obligation to prepare students for the future. "The stakes are high. This matters. What we're doing matters. And so maybe they ought to get a little nervous, and maybe I ought to get a little nervous" (Andy Leipold). "I have a fiduciary responsibility to enable my students to pass the bar exam and hit the ground running when they enter practice" (Nancy Knauer). "I'm their last link to the academy before the profession totally takes over. . . . If they hadn't been excited before about ideas, this is our chance" (Don Hornstein).

Ingrid Hillinger is delighted when she sees students applying their learning in their jobs. "[A] student will e-mail me and say, 'You really prepared me for practice. . . . I may not know the answer . . . but I know where to look' . . . That's what I really want, because that's all I can give them."

Students are grateful for teachers' commitment to their learning.

- "She wants everyone to get it. She's willing to do whatever necessary to help" (student of Bridget Crawford).
- "If you, maybe, say something in class that's not correct, he doesn't think, 'Oh, you've failed because you're not paying attention.' He thinks he's failed you because you don't understand. . . . That's something you don't get from a lot of other professors" (student of Steve Friedland).
- "He definitely cared about whether or not students were learning. . . . If it didn't work the first time—people were still confused—he'd spend extra time with it" (student of Roberto Corrada).
- "She never says, 'It's all the students' fault.' . . . She always thinks, 'What can I do better?' first" (student of Patty Alleva).

Attentive

Many students in this study observe how well their teachers listen. "When you're in her office, when you're on an e-mail or [the] phone, she makes you feel like you are the only person that has her undivided attention. . . . You do. You have her undivided attention" (student of Meredith Duncan).

Students distinguish these exceptional teachers from their other professors, based specifically on their extraordinary listening skills.

- "There are a lot of professors who like to hear themselves talk. And he is an excellent listener. . . . He goes back to comments that people have said, you know, like, 'As Max said, he raised this point a couple days ago,' and so he's, like, always referencing what students say" (student of Hiroshi Motomura).
- "You often feel like professors are on to their next question before you've answered, because they already know what you're going to

say. . . . They just sort of lead you by your nose and then tell you that's where you should have gone. . . . But . . . she's really listening" (student of Beth Enos).

- "In her letter of recommendation for my clerkship she [noted] 'He made a connection between these two sections of the bankruptcy code that I thought showed some promise and insight for a second-year law student.' And it was, like, wow, I can't believe that she remembered that. . . . She listens to what you say" (student of Ingrid Hillinger).

- "She is such a careful listener, and so quick on her feet, that she can almost invariably hear something constructive in even a relatively squishy or errant student question or comment, and she can prod the student to develop that something, whatever it is, into a comment that moves the discussion forward in some illuminating or incisive way. Perhaps because she has this skill, [she] is able to give students the sense that she takes us seriously and thinks we have something to say. This tends to inspire students to try to live up to those expectations" (student of Heather Gerken).

The teachers we studied recognize the importance of listening to students and are thoughtful about their role as listeners. "I think I sort of help them by being cognizant of who they are, what their skill set is, what their confidence level is, and then sort of work off that. And that's just doing this a lot of years and sort of working both with intuition and actually really listening to them" (Cary Bricker).

Steven Homer also deliberately makes every effort to listen to his students: "I try to think about my body language and posture. . . . I try to be in the moment, present to what the expression is on my face and how am I sitting here. . . . I'll do a lot of 'Tell me more about that' to get them to open up. When they get upset, as they very often will . . . I try to not to freak out about it. I'll try to ac-knowledge, 'I can tell this is frustrating.'"

And Julie Nice eloquently describes her efforts to attend to what her students say. "I feel strongly you listen with your eyes. You listen with your ears, but you're only listening to one student at a time with your ears. But you have to listen with your eyes. Con-stant roaming eye contact with all of them to try to track. They tell you so much nonverbally when they're confused, when they're just bored, when they're just out of it, when they're doing something else, when they're distracted."

Creative

The teachers are creative in the ways they help students learn. As is described in more detail in Chapter 7, the teachers we studied take students on field trips, conduct outside research by calling attor-neys on cases they assign, bring in guest lecturers, and use a variety of creative approaches to help students learn. Paula Lustbader ex-plains how and why she uses the creative process. "Theories sug-gest that when students engage in making visual art, writing lyrics, acting out a skit, or dancing to express a concept, they deepen their cognition and exercise their creative thought process. My hope in introducing these exercises is to keep students engaged, to help students persist when the studying gets difficult, and to encourage them to keep a flow of creative ideas so they can be creative prob-lem solvers" (Paula Lustbader).

Two of Paula Lustbader's students offer examples of her creative methods. "She includes a broad spectrum of different principles and techniques of teaching criminal law. Art was mentioned. An-other thing that we did was meditate. We also did a lot of poem reading, which was inspirational." "She used a unique range of different learning methods to convey one idea. An example would be utilizing an outline that's very linear for some people who think that way, as well as getting us to create that same outline in an art-piece format where we would create a drawing."

Knowledgeable

Students generally find all these outstanding law teachers to be knowledgeable. Students articulate the additional value teachers bring with their expertise about substance, skills, or teaching. "She really knows the material back and forth. . . . Most professors do, but she knows what she wants to say and how she's going to say it so there's really no fumbling" (student of Meredith Duncan).

Students are grateful when teachers use their expertise to help them connect the classroom experience to practice. "It's also great to have her in the classroom, because it's kind of like taking a master class from someone who has had so much courtroom experience. . . . Somebody that has had over 100 trials, is giving us one-on-one feedback, is something you can't put a money or dollar value on" (student of Cary Bricker). "He really helped me get a feel for what it's like to practice and gave me a sense of how the law applies to real clients" (student of Nelson Miller). "[She] approaches the cases like an actual lawyer before the Supreme Court (or the clerk that she was). So rather than grand constitutional theory, you get strategy and close reading of arguments" (student of Heather Gerken).

Having extensive knowledge is also valued by students. "Her vast knowledge makes her ability to teach effectively and comfortably, leading us students to really look behind what a contract means" (student of Beth Enos). "Clearly knows a lot about the course and, because of that, makes me want to learn more about the subject" (student of Susan Kuo). "He has amazing breadth and depth. I would have rated him a 10 on this scale (scale of 1–7)" (student of Rory Bahadur). "I can honestly say that he was far more well informed on his subject than any of the professors I have had so far in any subject" (student of Don Hornstein).

Students have additional praise for teachers' expertise.

- "She brought to the classes amazing intellectual expertise and knowledge of the subjects. I know, to some extent, this is to be expected of a law professor, but [she] definitely goes above and beyond" (student of Julie Nice).
- "I think part of what makes him so successful is just the knowledge he has. . . . So he's constantly not just making us think and keeping us in tune with everything, but he does it for himself. . . . I don't think he'll ever reach the point to where he thinks he's been doing this for so long that he can't learn something or that he can't keep up with things. He's always learning" (student of Philip Prygoski).
- "[She] has an amazing encyclopedic knowledge base. In Sexuality & Law, she is an expert. [She] has an amazing working knowledge of material. [She] knows cases, policies" (student of Ruthann Robson).

Committed to Continuous Improvement

Part of the reason these teachers are so effective is that they are committed to continually improving. They actively seek new information and use existing data to learn how they can improve. "I have a lot more to learn as a teacher. . . . I don't want stasis. I want to find other ways of reaching them. . . . I just want to keep figuring it out" (Cary Bricker).

Meredith Duncan and Roberto Corrada show how they view teaching as an evolving process, an attitude all outstanding teachers share. "I always do try to do something new and fresh each course" (Meredith Duncan). "I'm just always playing around with is there a better way to teach this? Is there a better way to, you know, get my students to be engaged and passionate about this stuff. Is there a better way to get them to become better lawyers down the road or better people? And so I'm always fiddling with things. I'm always tinkering" (Roberto Corrada).

Students commend their teachers' investment in continuing to grow. "He works very hard at the art of teaching and understands it very well. I think that sets him apart from other law-school teachers I had. . . . I'm also sure that for many of them, the teaching is significantly less important than their research. I never had that sense from Hiroshi. It would be easy to say that he is a born teacher, but I know how hard he thinks about teaching and works at making it work" (student of Hiroshi Motomura). "She tries whatever approach works; used clickers to gauge every class and give and get feedback during the class. She is open to anything" (student of Bridget Crawford).

Excellent teachers rely on a variety of methods to improve their teaching. None solely depends on students' final course evaluations. Instead, they solicit informal feedback from their students during the course. They conduct midterm course evaluations. They scrutinize exams, assignments, and course evaluations. They regularly reflect on their teaching. They go to conferences, read about teaching, talk to colleagues, and learn from practitioners. And extraordinary teachers pay attention to the material they collect. "The everyday tutors in the project of teaching myself to teach have been my students. I constantly encourage them to tell me what works and what doesn't and to be candid, specific, and critical in giving me feedback. Because I experiment each time I teach a course, I genuinely desire feedback from each set of students. And I take their feedback seriously" (Julie Nice).

Many of the teachers gather informal feedback, as Philip Prygoski and Ruthann Robson describe. "I will see them walking around; I'll see them downstairs. 'How'd it go?' 'Are you getting this?' 'Do you like the stuff?' 'Is there anything that you don't get?' 'Is there anything that I can do to help?'" (Philip Prygoski). Ruthann Robson points out the value of collecting feedback during class: "In observing students or conversing, I gain incredible feedback on teaching and their learning. In other words, when I am giving feedback, I am also getting feedback. I have found the process of assigning small projects during class to be invaluable as a way of adjusting my teaching."

Midway through their courses, many teachers administer their own midterm evaluations. Larry Krieger illustrates a method many use: "I just take five minutes at the beginning, and I ask them, 'Okay, three questions. It's going to be anonymous. Tear off a piece of paper. What's good about the course? . . . What's not good about the course? And what would you change if you could?'" Based on their students' feedback, the teachers modify what happens in the classroom. "What works for one class doesn't work for another class. So oftentimes I change up what I do based on the feedback that they give me. . . . I think there is value in acknowledging that there's a problem or concern that they all have, talking about it, even if I don't do anything about it" (Meredith Duncan).

They also regularly reflect on their classes. "If something didn't go well, I will write myself a note in that folder and say this didn't work, think about maybe doing this first or explaining that.... [What] I always try to think about is how do I redo this so that they get the vocabulary, they get the basic stuff, but they also get the stuff that, you know, is sort of new and what they need to" (Ingrid Hillinger). "When I see explanations aren't working, like yesterday . . . I made a little note: I need to figure out a better explanation of this" (Don Hornstein). "The little sticky notes? Those are my notes to myself after every class. I don't believe you can get better without constant self-assessment" (Nancy Levit).

To gather helpful feedback, the teachers study end-of-term student evaluations very closely. Some teachers add their own course-specific questions. They take detailed notes on students' responses and follow up on suggestions. As a new teacher, Tina Stark learned that students found she spoke too fast: "Now, for a New Yorker, I didn't speak too fast. But for an American, I spoke too fast. So I went to a speech therapist and learned to slow down.... I did some research on it, you know, about how it affects learning, and discovered that slower speech is actually processed better and—you know—so I thought that was a legitimate goal."

Teachers also engage in a cyclical process of reviewing students' evaluation responses, revising their teaching to better meet their students' needs, and soliciting input again. In her "Teaching Philosophy," Heather Gerken explains how she applies this feedback cycle: "I give students a detailed survey about what worked and what doesn't work, as I find that law-school surveys don't get you enough information on the specifics.... I ban laptops in the class . . . because students have a bad tendency to act like transcribers, writing down everything that is said rather than thinking about what's going on. In my end-of-the-year survey, students always say it was a good idea (by a significant majority)."

Students deeply respect teachers' willingness to gather and learn from honest feedback.

- "She is always trying to improve herself and her classroom effectiveness and her knowledge of the law and asking for our feedback on that and how she's doing" (student of Nancy Knauer).
- "He didn't want me to, you know, praise him and tell him how awesome he was and how much I learned. It was more like, 'talk to me about my experience'" (student of Philip Prygoski).
- "She takes responsibility for things that don't go so well. When different teams approached a problem differently, she asked, 'How can I improve the directions?'" (student of Tina Stark).
- "She is open to suggestions from students on how to improve. She demonstrated a genuine desire for students to learn" (student of Susan Kuo).

Inspiring

Teachers are inspiring in many ways. "[She] provides an excellent role model for those of us interested in pursuing both a high-powered career and a life as a parent. She gave birth to her first child during the middle of the spring semester in my 1L year, and I remember being incredibly impressed that she organized her class schedule so that she taught intensively up until the baby was born, took some time off, and then returned to finish the semester in an intensive teaching spurt, continuing all the while to work on her research. This creative scheduling, and the confidence with which she did it, made it seem as if everything was possible" (student of Heather Gerken).

Another student appreciated that a teacher "didn't push me to take the highest-paying job at the most prestigious firm in town. I had two offers. One was from a big, high-paying firm. The other was from a smaller, modest-paying firm. I chose the one for less pay, but the one that I loved. I am grateful every single day for that decision" (student of Nancy Levit).

Students are inspired by teachers' passion, energy, and excitement.

- "He loves doing this, like coming in every day, being here early, and answering all the questions. . . . If I can be that happy with what I'm doing five years from now, I will be having a very good life" (student of Andy Leipold).
- "She was so curious and so energized. . . . She's always looking for the next thing and always wanting to learn more herself, which makes us want to learn more" (student of Beth Enos).
- This class . . . help[ed] me remember why I wanted to come to law school. This class is/has been the only time . . . that I have felt inspired to be a lawyer" (student of Bridget Crawford).
- "You are a great role model. I hope to be half of the person you are someday" (student of Nelson Miller).

The teachers' success in helping them develop confidence also inspires students. "More than any other professor he gave me the confidence that I could be an attorney. . . . Doing a jury trial or picking a jury or opening and closing seemed, like, just so far off and impossible, but after that class, you really build your confidence. . . . He's good at making you feel like you can do it" (student of Larry Krieger). "No other class has given me this type of confidence to be able to practice the subject matter that the course is in" (student of Tina Stark).

In addition, teachers' knowledge and caring greatly inspire students. "He knows so much and his knowledge is so thorough you just can't help but want to get to that point, and I'm not there yet, naturally, but you know it's just very inspiring" (student of Philip Prygoski). "It is the great law professor who can turn that knowledge from intimidating to inspiring. . . . So what was it that made Professor Nice's vast amount of knowledge inspiring rather than intimidating? First and foremost, she cared. She cared about the subject matter, and she cared about whether her students were grasping the subject matter" (student of Julie Nice). "Don has an uncanny ability to reach all students . . . inspiring each of them to care deeply about themselves and their relationship with the law" (colleague of Don Hornstein).

Many teachers inspired students to love a doctrinal subject. "I think he really develops interest in the subject to everything he teaches" (student of Steve Friedland). "Thanks to him I love constitutional law like I didn't think I ever would. . . . I'm pursuing an LLM that's constitutional-law based. It started in his class" (student of Philip Prygoski). Similarly, many of Bridget Crawford's students pursue LLMs in Tax Law and practice in that area.

Some of these teachers inspire their students to be excellent and authentic future law professors, as two of Heather Gerken's students note. "She brought out the best but also suggested that students not replicate herself when they became teachers. . . . [She] did not want to make Heather Gerken look-alikes." "There are so many things that make Heather Gerken a fabulous teacher: she's a whip-smart, dynamic scholar and a master of her subject matter, not to mention a superhumanly energetic person with a wicked sense of humor. But most of us can only dream of emulating those qualities."

Other students similarly aspire to rise to the level of their excellent teachers. "If I had the grades, you know, I could be a law professor. I would want to be just like him. I mean not just like him in a freaky kind of way but just remembering how he treated his students, remembering how he prepared for us and so that made us want to prepare for him and [if you do not] you feel guilty like you were letting him down, not that you were going to get yelled at and humiliated. . . . I would want to give back because of what was given to me" (student of Andy Leipold). "Because everybody knows he's an expert; you kind of want to be like him, so you want to emulate those types of behaviors that he exhibits to the students. . . . I'm a dean's fellow, and so when I'm talking to my students, I try to emulate some of the things that Professor Taslitz has done" (student of Andy Tazlitz).

Teachers pay attention to the qualities students find inspiring, as Steven Homer and Bridget Crawford describe. "I have gay students, so modeling for those students and gay friendly students. A gay man who has done it, gotten through law school successfully, has been a lawyer . . . I hope, anyways, makes it a safer place for students. . . . And for nongay students, who hadn't considered that gay men could be the tough one, well, guess what? We can be" (Steven Homer).

"More subjectively, I can claim to be an effective teacher when someone from the very first class I ever taught contacted me to thank me, five years later, for getting him interested in tax. Or when I ran into a graduate from two years ago who said, 'What you said at graduation meant a lot to me. You told me I was going to be a great lawyer, and I'm working to live up to that.' Or the student who told me she was going to drop out of law school, but somehow my class hooked her back in to the excitement of learning. Or the student who told me that she liked studying Tax because it made her feel 'smart' when the rest of law school made her feel 'stupid.' Or the student who said she is considering a career in teaching after completing an independent study with me. I measure my success as a teacher in these stories, and the ones I will never know" (Bridget Crawford).

Conclusion

A few final comments illustrate exceptional law teachers' humility, responsibility, commitment to improvement, and passion. "I've always been critical of myself because I think you can always do better. You're never doing well enough. You can always do better" (Andy Taslitz). "I strive to be the teacher I wanted to have and that I want to have. I want a teacher who is respectful, professional, punctual, fair, funny, knowledgeable, humble, accessible, encouraging, forgiving (but not lax), hard-working and rigorous" (Bridget Crawford). "I wish that all my professors had just half of the passion that [he] has shown in this class" (student of Rory Bahadur).

4

How Do the Best Law Teachers Relate to Their Students?

Day One

All teachers begin to establish a relationship with their students on the first day of class. The teachers we studied are particularly thoughtful and intentional about the messages they send at the very beginning of a course.

Nancy Levit explains how she prepares to build a positive relationship from day one: "The most important cornerstone of how I teach begins with establishing a relationship with each of my students. This begins before the first day they are in my class. When I get the class lists, I look up how to pronounce each student's name and make it a point to know who each student is immediately. The first week of class, I send each a personal e-mail with just a few brief questions about themselves. I invite all the students to stop by my office and introduce themselves within the first two weeks of class. Usually over half of the students accept this invitation. The personal meeting allays fears about the Socratic dialogue and allows me to assist individuals with any adjustment issues."

Steven Homer also aims to strip away his students' anonymity by knowing each student's name on the first day of class: "I want to communicate that you're not a number to me in this room, I know who you are. I tell them a joke, 'I expect you to know my name, so for the money you pay, it's not too much for me to know your name.' But it also puts them on notice. I am paying attention to what is happening in this room, who is here, who is not here, who is participating, who is not participating." Likewise, Paula Lusbader asks students to tell her about themselves and their aspirations. "So the first day of class they fill out a little information sheet, something a little bit about who they are, something that they're proud of, and what did they come here to do?"

These first-day connections have powerful positive effects on students.

- "I remember getting an e-mail from her before my first class with her asking to introduce myself and why I was taking her class and that was—wow—it made me feel important to her" (student of Beth Enos).
- "I'll never forget the first day of class. There were probably thirty of us in a section, and he comes in and rattles off everyone's name. He learned our faces and names from photographs, and he's the only professor that ever did that. . . . And as the semester evolved, it turned out much more that he showed us that 'I know who you are. No one is going to fall . . . through the cracks, [and] there is no back benching here'" (student of Steven Homer).

- "We walked into that classroom, sat down, and he immediately started asking us questions by first name. I mean the interest he takes in his students is apparent and was apparent, I think, to all of us on that first day of class. And he really has created, quite purposefully, an environment that caters to a strong relationship between students and professors" (student of Steve Friedland).

- "On the first day of my Torts II class, Dean Miller waited quietly as each student found a seat. Then he came over to each individual and introduced himself. Perhaps even more amazingly, Dean Miller remembered every student's name for the entire term from those brief how-do-you-dos. In a law student's world of class rankings and anonymous grading, this simple gesture immediately created an environment of trust" (student of Nelson Miller).

Know Students' Names, Backgrounds, Interests, and Aspirations

Teachers in our study who are unable to know all of their students' names on the first day of class still find important reasons to learn those names during the course. Learning students' names is the first step in a larger effort to connect with students.

Susan Kuo articulates the role student names play in her teaching philosophy: "I cannot reach my students unless I know who they are as individual people. Of course, that means that I need to learn their names as soon as possible. However, to better understand them, I also ask students to fill out note cards listing where they are from, where they went to college, and why they chose to attend law school." Hiroshi Motomura expands on this theme. "I'm trying to reduce the anonymity factor in the classroom. . . . I'm trying to meet each student where he or she happens to be, psychologically, with respect to the whole experience. And that starts with knowing their names." Bridgett Crawford concurs: "Even in a large class, I try to interact with each student personally (in addition to calling on him or her) over the semester. On the most basic level, that means learning every student's name. If I need to make myself flash cards, I will. Subway rides are especially good times for learning student names. I want all students to feel noticed, that they are more than a number or name on a seating chart, that my classroom is a community of learners, and that they belong to it."

Because the teachers learn about their students' experience and backgrounds, they can use that information effectively during the course. Paula Lustbader notes how she uses student experience to motivate them: "I know who they are; I know what they came here for, and then when I'm meeting with them, and they're, like, 'I don't think I can do this,' I'm, like, 'Dude, you're the guy who ran with the bulls. I mean come on! You know you can do that; this is nothing.'" A student recognized how Hiroshi Motomura drew on student expertise in the classroom: "Hiroshi did an excellent job of first of all understanding and really getting a baseline understanding of what our levels of expertise were and then really blending it into the class in a very natural way. And so that when we are in class and when we are talking about education, you know, he immediately called on me as a teacher, or as a classmate, as a social worker, and wove that into Immigration in a way that was so profound that I think other classes just completely failed in comparison into really utilizing the expertise that already existed in their students."

Many students notice and report favorably on their teachers' interest in their lives in and out of law school.

- "Despite her busy schedule, Professor Gerken takes the time to get to know each of her students. She not only learns the name of each student in her class, but also makes you feel like she cares about you and what's going on in the rest of your life" (student of Heather Gerken).
- "Levit is outstanding. She is interested in her students' lives in both law school and outside of school" (student of Nancy Levit).
- "It feels like he really makes an effort to get to know his students on a personal level so that connects you to him so much more. For example, one time I had to miss a class, go take my cat to the vet because she got hurt, and every time he sees me, he's, like, 'Oh, how's your cat?'" (student of Don Hornstein).
- "He takes a particular and sincere interest in his students. His door is always open, and he takes great care to get to know students' background, aspirations, and challenges" (student of Nelson Miller).

Students recognize the link between their teachers' interest in them and the students' motivation and willingness to engage in the course. "He seems to care about your life outside the school. . . . And I think that really helps because then, maybe, you feel like you want to invest a little bit more of your time in that class too, and you really want to give it a little bit extra because you feel like that professor is doing that for you too" (student of Roberto Corrada). "She sent out an e-mail. She wanted all of us in her class to write just a paragraph about who we are outside of law school. She's like, 'I know you're in law school, but what do you do outside of that?' . . . And she wrote back in fifteen minutes, like, a four-paragraph answer. And was, like, 'Oh, you like this? Well you should go here and here and here and do this.' . . . It just made it feel, like, oh, well, if she wants to be here, then I should definitely want to be here" (student of Nancy Levit).

Mutual Respect between Teachers and Students

The teachers also identify mutual respect between themselves and their students as a fundamental aspect of their teaching philosophies.

Julie Nice uses a metaphor to describe the power of mutual respect for students and teachers: "Mutual respect is where it begins and ends. I treat my students with an incredible amount of respect. I tell them in each class, I believe you're here because you actually want to be here in law school and in this course, and that you want to develop your knowledge and skills, and you want to expand your own repertoire. I believe you are really bright and interesting people. And I am going to treat you with that kind of respect, and I know you'll treat one another with that kind of respect. . . . I think it's our job to set the tone of mutual respect. I think it's really important to their motivation, sense of encouragement when they feel seen as human beings. . . . It's like watering the flower. They respond so powerfully to those little drops of water."

Nancy Knauer ties the notion of mutual respect to the expectations she has for students: "The key to my teaching philosophy is mutuality of responsibility and respect. I have high standards, but then my students are professionals. I am accessible and will answer as many questions as they can pose, but they have to meet me halfway. They must engage the material and sometimes struggle with it."

Paula Franzese links mutual respect and the expectations she has for herself: "So I tend to encourage my students to feel that this is an atmosphere of mutual respect and of mutual trust, and I hope to inspire their preparedness by telling them that I will bring it to each and every class; I will be as prepared as I can possibly be out of respect for them, and that I would hope that there would be a mutuality of that respect."

Patti Alleva expands the concept of respect to include respect for the learning process and the profession: "At the heart of this educational dynamic is respect: Respect for students, respect for the teaching and [the] learning process itself, and, ultimately, respect for the ideals of the legal profession that we, as teacher-scholars, seek to advance." Alleva then describes the transition from having respect to demonstrating it: "But *having* respect for these things is merely the starting point. *Modeling it,* with principled consistency, is vital to the teacher's credibility, and hence, the impact of the potential learning. In this way, teaching is living out learning. What we ask of our students, we must ask of ourselves. Whatever those traits or tasks that I require of them or request they aspire to (e.g., preparation, punctuality, thoughtfulness, open-mindedness, uprightness, and respect for others, for self, for the law, and for the act of learning), I must also strive to possess and demonstrate to the best of my ability. Authenticity is perhaps one of the greatest teachers."

Two of the teachers describe hard lessons they learned about mutual respect. The first applies to a relationship with an entire class. "Early in my teaching, when I was not much older than my students, I developed a mutual dislike with the students in one of my courses. I perceived a disconnect and disregard from the outset of the semester. They seemed to me to be constantly whining, one of my least favorite behaviors. Unfortunately, rather than focusing on interrupting and redirecting this dynamic, I simply groused that they didn't like me and I didn't like them. In other words, I turned on them. This was an enormous mistake. It simply perpetuated the negative cycle. It was the most demoralizing teaching experience I've ever had. Since then I've tried never to group the students all as one, and I've actively looked for common ground to connect with each class of students as a whole."

The second teacher describes lack of respect for an individual student.

One of the things you always worry about when . . . you're young, you're untenured, you're female, you're a person of color, whatever, is that one of your students will decide to challenge you. Virtually every young female professor I've known has had someone do that to her in her class: question her authority, get in her face, etc. . . . The lore passed from female professor to female professor is that if you didn't shut it down immediately, it would spiral, and you'd lose the respect of your students.

So here's the mistake I made. There was a guy in one of my early first-year classes who looked like the stereotypical challenger. His hand was always up, and he was always a little obnoxious when he spoke. One day he got riled up about something I said and gave a long speech, and I took it for a challenge to my authority. So I dropped him, eviscerated him. I turned every bit of intellectual firepower I have on him and left him (figuratively speaking) bloody and beat. I departed from every rule I have about students—treat them with respect, treat them with kindness, see the best in them—and treated him like he was a sexist jerk challenging me because I was a woman.

Want to know the awful thing? As I got to know him better, I realized he wasn't a sexist jerk. He was just a nerd. An unschooled, uncouth, rough-around-the-edges nerd, whose enthusiasm sometimes made him seem arrogant or obnoxious but was really just a sign of a nerd unable to contain his excitement. Luckily, he forgave me. Luckily, there was enough good will and trust in the classroom that the rest of the class forgave me. Because they shouldn't have forgiven me. I certainly haven't forgiven myself.

Nancy Levit articulates several concrete methods she uses to show respect: "The respect teachers demonstrate for students comes in many ways: finding fair methods to call on students (I shuffle a deck of cards); looking for the good in their answers to give them the comfort to think more deeply; encouraging collaboration (I associate cocounsel, another student in the class, if someone gets stuck); demonstrating sensitivity to the other matters on their docket (by adjusting the assignment load according to large memos or writing projects they have due in other classes); and giving immediate turnaround on papers, midterms, writing projects, and grades. I always arrive early so that we can begin class promptly each day; I end class equally promptly to respect their time."

Students identify other actions, big and small, that establish respect in their relationships with these teachers.

- "I felt like he respected our time while he started class on time, he ended class on time. A lot of the professors don't. It's a little thing, but it matters. . . . He gave us a manageable load, and I think that's respectful. Some teachers forget, I think, that we have other classes. . . . If we went and talked to him after class or e-mailed, he was just respectful in his demeanor" (student of Roberto Corrada).

- "Professor Krieger, to me, really always seemed respectful to students, but that's because he always looks you directly in the eye. He knew your name. He smiled at you. He knew who you were as a person" (student of Larry Krieger).

- "When he answers a question, his response totally indicates that he understands what you're trying to ask. And he shows understanding but also a lot of respect as a student. Like you don't feel like you're asking a silly question, ever" (student of Hiroshi Motomura).

- "Some heavy issues are dealt with in Criminal Law, particularly when we were studying rape. . . . She made all of those classes completely voluntary in terms of who felt comfortable participating. . . . You know, you look at the statistics, and you know what one in four, one in five women have dealt with rape or molestation in the course of their lives. . . . I think that's one concrete example of how she showed respect for students" (student of Meredith Duncan).

Students contrast these efforts with the behaviors of many of their other law teachers, whom the students perceive as hindering the development of an environment of mutual respect. One of Paula Lustbader's students compares Lustbader's teaching with the "intellectual warfare" that takes place in other classes: "Some professors wanted you to be sure that they are the smartest in the room. And they will do whatever they could to show that . . . whereas Paula respected our intellect and didn't try to belittle us in a way that would somehow embarrass us. It was a mutual respect and an intellectual respect as opposed to an intellectual warfare." And another of Paula Lustbader's students recalled a particularly "demeaning" and "unprofessional" incident: "[Another teacher] treated students like babies. I can remember she handed out pacifiers to the entire class because people dared to complain about particular . . . ways she was handling things. I question why that person was teaching."

A student appreciates Andy Taslitz's respect for students' time in contrast to professors who treated students' time as unimportant: "The professors can be late. They can skip things. They can do whatever they want, and you just can't say anything, because your time is simply unimportant." Similarly, a student of Hiroshi Motomura noted the absence of mocking and humiliation in his classes, in contrast to some other courses: "Hiroshi didn't harass any students who hadn't done the reading; nor did he mock the students [who] perhaps didn't understand the relevant points as well as they could have. . . . For that reason, you didn't have the sense of dread that accompanied certain other classes, where you could feel humiliated if you weren't exactly on the professor's wavelength."

Concern for Every Student

The teachers create a connection with every student in their courses. They want no students to fall through the cracks.

Patti Alleva believes that she has a fiduciary duty to protect the interests of her students and to treat them even-handedly: "I feel very much that their educational care is entrusted to me, and that I must be protective of their interests presumptively, that they deserve the best from me. They deserve the benefit of the doubt from me. This is how I would define fiduciary in the educational context. . . . I feel very strongly about treating all students as equally as I can and maybe a better word is *even-handedly*. . . . It's very important to me to avoid the appearance of favoritism. To make all students feel that they have access to me."

Ingrid Hillinger describes her concern for every student and a special attraction to those who are struggling: "Every student at this school is special. Every single student has a story.... I am particularly drawn to students who are struggling for one reason or another—anything from disappointment with their law-school performance and lack of confidence in their ability to be a good lawyer to serious medical problems, family problems, depression, loneliness, being older and feeling like a duck out of water, etc., etc. I am drawn to these students because I admire and find inspiration in their courage and determination to see the struggle through. Law school is hard enough on its own terms. How these people summon the inner strength to cope with law school *and* their other problems always amazes me. They have my utmost respect, and I try to do anything I can to help them."

Ruthann Robson is particularly concerned about the "average" students, who tend to get less attention at many law schools: "I think at most places there is a lot of emphasis on the best students and the students who are not doing well.... Who are the average students? Who's in the middle, and what are we doing about those students? How are we bringing the B student to a B+? How are we supporting that person?... They need something, or they don't feel as entitled, or they have just decided that they are going to be a B student, or that you have no interest in them."

One of the teachers describes the negative effects of failing to connect with a student due to the teacher's misconceptions:

I had an older male student who always sat in the back of the
room with his chair tipped back and arms folded across his chest.
He often had a grimace or a sour expression, and he never did the
group work. I thought he was not engaged and was hostile

towards me. Every day I came to class I dreaded having to see him, as I read his body language and facial expressions as dismissive of me. Years later, I had a dinner party and a friend had just started dating this guy. She asked if she could bring him. I said sure, but she might want to check with him, because I didn't think he had a positive experience in my class. Long story short: When he arrived at my house, he gave me the biggest hug and said he learned so much from my class and that my class was a wonderful experience for him. During the time he was in my class, he was going through an awful and contentious divorce and at the same time was suffering from severe back pain and was often on pain medication. My class offered him a bit of distraction from his otherwise difficult time in his life.

Students appreciate these teachers' attempts to help each and every student.

- "Professor Friedland kind of finds out where our class is and where each individual is and makes sure that everyone gets it . . . and [even] in a class . . . like Evidence [where] we had, like, a hundred people" (student of Steve Friedland).
- "Unlike other professors, he cares about each and every student. He doesn't play favorites. . . . He likes to take the time to value everything everyone else has to say and also understand what they're going through" (student of Andy Taslitz).
- "She always goes deeper and makes sure that everybody in the class either understands it or has the opportunity to ask her a question inside or outside of class. So they are on the same page and everyone gets what's going on; no one gets left behind. . . . I think that shows how much she cares. It's almost like every one of us is almost one of her children" (student of Patti Alleva).

- "She has this vision for you; you can take it or leave it. You don't have to take it; it's just an idea. But she'll have the same . . . for the next person and the same . . . for the next person. Not the same vision, but she'll have a vision for every person. I just love that about her" (student of Paula Lustbader).

Focus on Student Learning and Success

The teachers focus on their students' learning and success. Nelson Miller makes a cogent distinction between his teaching performance and his students' learning: "If I have the capability of speaking in an articulate or even inspiring manner but do not exhibit a suitable willingness to adapt my activities to your needs and interests, then I am only making hollow noises. My teaching is not for show but to help you equip yourself with meaningful skills and purpose. If I exercise unusual foresight and insight and show extraordinary persistence with regard to both but do not bend my capabilities to your service, then my teaching means nothing. It is you who should be enlarged in your heart, skills, compassion, and understanding, not me in my claims of teaching expertise. If I give everything I have to teaching—even sacrificing my own well-being—but do so for my own pride and satisfaction rather than for your deliberate benefit, then I have really done nothing."

Susan Kuo asks students for feedback about her teaching so that she can maximize their learning: "I ask students to help me teach them more effectively. I administer my own evaluations midsemester, asking general questions about course pace and student comprehension as well as questions about the effectiveness of specific teaching methods or course materials. I then dedicate a portion of a subsequent class to discussing the results, summarizing responses, and addressing specific issues raised by the students. I tell them that I not only care about their feedback, but I care about their learning in the course."

Tina Stark and Cary Bricker identify student success and learning as the bottom line for them. "I believe that my high availability to students outside the classroom sends a strong message to those who take advantage of the opportunity to meet with me and to those who know the opportunity is there. Bottom line: I want my students to know that I like them, that it is my pleasure to teach them and to get to know them, and that what I want most is for them to succeed" (Tina Stark). "It's are they getting it? . . . I have some classes I try that don't work as well, other classes where damn! That worked! But it's not about me. It's did they get it?" (Cary Bricker).

Susan Kuo and Tina Stark express the joy they feel as their students develop. "I love watching them learn and get it, getting to know them as people, helping them. I like them as people. I want them to succeed, get jobs, feel good about themselves" (Tina Stark). "In class, I love watching them put things together" (Susan Kuo).

Students comment again and again on their perception that their teachers are deeply invested in their learning and success.

- "The professor genuinely seems to care about the success of her students." "She's so excited about learning, about the students, about students after law school, what they're doing, where they're going, staying involved. I have never seen a professor with such enthusiasm for just learning" (students of Nancy Levit).
- "Prof. obviously invested himself in this course and his students. Felt that he genuinely cared about the students, that we learned the material" (student of Andy Leipold).

- "Incredibly caring for students and genuinely wants to see them succeed" (student of Steven Homer).
- "She just sets everybody up to succeed. She wants you to succeed and she does everything she can, you know, in her class, in life" (student of Ingrid Hillinger).

Promise, Potential, and Confidence

Exceptional law teachers like these see the potential and promise in their students and help students see those qualities in themselves. "You realize that who you are has value, you know, not just what you learn but who you are as a person, your experiences, what you bring to the table that distinguish you and make you of value as a clerk, as an attorney, as a student. And I think she finds those things in you" (student of Ingrid Hillinger). "He always saw the potential in everybody and made you feel like you had a lot to contribute, because we all do, and you know I think it's fair to say that anyone who would go see him would walk out with a feeling of optimism. I do have something to contribute; there is a place for me; I can find it. I can be happy. . . . I can be successful" (student of Larry Krieger).

Students of Meredith Duncan feel transformed by her ability to see their potential. "I think she makes the students feel like we have potential so that depending on who you are and what situation, you feel like you have a right to demand respect or you feel like you have an opinion that's worth voicing and sharing. You feel like you have the potential to take on this project or to try and write an opinion or paper, and you feel, like, not necessarily that you're going to succeed but that you're someone who has the tools, that you're someone who could succeed. . . . I think that encourages a lot of people to try to succeed in ways they might not otherwise try." "I almost quit law school . . . after my first semester, after I received my legal research and writing grade, because I didn't know how to write. . . . I felt like a failure that day, you know, the day that I walked in [her office]. And, when I walked out, I thought, you know, I'm not the biggest goof on the face of the earth. You know, if Meredith Duncan sees something promising in me, then there must be something there."

Student interaction with these teachers in and out of the classroom builds their confidence in law school and beyond. "She can present all this information, and you can sort of reason through it yourself and understand it, [which] gives you this confidence to move forward into, I guess, whatever field you want to go into" (student of Nancy Knauer). "I think that she makes students feel as though they have something to offer, something important to share with the class, and even, I mean at times, with the larger community. I think that's probably one of her greatest strengths as a teacher and probably as a person too" (student of Ingrid Hillinger). "When I walked out of that office, I was like, wow! Not only did she answer my question, she asked me about my career, and to top it off, I came out of there feeling like Superman. And that's something that I think Professor Levit really does a good job of—is instilling confidence in students" (student of Nancy Levit).

Teachers build students' confidence in themselves through encouragement and positive reinforcement when students perform at a high level. One of Julie Nice's students notes how Professor Nice's confessions of her own struggles with some of the difficult concepts in the course help build students' self-confidence: "More than merely confessing her own difficulties, she continually encouraged us and reassured us that we were all capable of understanding the concepts. By both exposing her own difficulties with the subject matter and encouraging us to overcome ours, Prof. Nice . . . fostered our learning." One of Heather Gerken's students emphasizes the value of positive reinforcement, which can be rare in law school: "And when we came up with an original idea, Professor Gerken made sure we knew it; she was generous in her support and encouraged us to develop our own opinions. In law school, an environment where criticism typically far exceeds praise, Professor Gerken made us realize that we sometimes had excellent ideas. For me in particular, Professor Gerken's class gave me a new confidence. It helped me realize that I was, at times, capable of first-rate legal thought, a point which had not been clear to me during my first three semesters at law school."

Caring about Students' Lives and Learning, in and out of the Classroom

These outstanding law teachers care about their students' learning and lives. Ingrid Hillinger puts it succinctly: "I think it comes down to caring. I mean they know that they can come here and I will care. And I'll try to help. I will listen."

Julie Nice is supportive when "life happens" to her students: "I try to be very accessible to my students, and I also try very much to recognize that life happens. One of my family members was very ill while I was in law school. There are times in your life when you deal with these things, and we all know life happens for law students as well. I try to really pay attention to that, let them know it's okay that life happens, just basically exhibit caring about what happens to them and how they're doing, and how they're managing, and how they're coping. It's very genuine because I respect them and I like them and I am grateful to them."

Steve Friedland wants his students "to see I care about their learning as much as I care about them as people." For many of his students, Professor Friedland's attitude of care comes through:

- "I think he just cares about every one of his students as a person, and he's really engaged in making sure that you're getting it in the classroom, but also that you as a person are okay."
- "We're dealing with classes of seventy-five or a hundred people, and he's charismatic enough to realize when one person is having an off-day and e-mail them and say, you know, 'If you have any problems come talk to me. Is everything going alright in class?'"
- "But even outside, in passing in the hall, or passing by his office, a lot of times it's, you know, 'How are things going?' 'How was that interview you had last week?' I mean he just knows what's going on in your life and genuinely cares about it."

Students deeply appreciate that the teachers help them when they are facing academic or life challenges.

Patti Alleva's concern mattered for a student who was experiencing the shock of receiving less-than-optimal law-school grades in the first year: "I recall a time in my first year, where it was after exams and you were getting grades back, and you, you meet with her to go over your exam and see how you can improve your exam, and what not. And I had e-mailed her and said, 'I want to talk to you about it.' She sensed that something was wrong, and she called me and talked to me over the phone to make sure everything was okay. . . . And I think that's above and beyond what a teacher has to do. I've never received a phone call from a teacher before, out of worry for me."

Nancy Levit provided refuge for a student who experienced a death in the family: "When my grandmother passed away my first semester, I contacted my five professors regarding my loss. I received no response from one; two e-mails [including] one [that read]: 'well, then, I guess I just won't call on you.' Then I went to Professor Levit's office. When I sat down and tears began to well up, she neither looked impatient nor confused about why I was sitting in her office. Instead, she simply handed me tissues, listened, and then told me stories that made me smile without diminishing my loss."

Love, Celebration, and the Privilege of Teaching

Given the care these teachers demonstrate for their students' learning and lives, it is no surprise that they describe their relationship with students in terms of love. They feel privileged to teach their students. They celebrate with students in class.

Julie Nice describes the privilege and honor of teaching her students: "Honestly, in the broadest collective sense, I love my students. I feel like it's a privilege to teach; it's an honor to teach. These very bright people pay a lot of money, and they sit there, and they trust me, and they commit, and I just really feel like I don't take this gig for granted. And it's because of them. All together that is something I still feel, like, is really magical and really special, and I do not take it for granted. I treasure it. I learn so much from my students. The questions they ask in office hours, the questions they ask in class, but also the things they ask in e-mail or in office hours are often very astute. They are often really on to fine-tune points that could merit a very well placed law-review article. I'm in awe."

The teachers we studied enthusiastically describe the characteristics they love and admire in their students. "They are a very dear, kind-hearted, very compassionate group. They work so very hard, and I appreciate that. I really—truth be told, I love my students; I truly do. I value their contributions; I value their thought processes; I value their energy" (Paula Franzese). "I really admire them, especially because so many students now are coming to law school with some experience under their belts; many of them have families, you know, so they're juggling a lot of things. I just think it's a tremendous challenge for them to be here, and I really respect that and what they're going through" (Beth Enos). "They're the greatest thing about this whole job.... I love their willingness to take risks. I love the epiphanies they have when it clicks and they say, 'Oh yeah, I can do this!' I love their enthusiasm" (Cary Bricker).

Paula Franzese builds a close, positive relationship with students by celebrating, often with the entire class. Near Valentine's Day, she conducts a Loving the Law Day in class: "It's magical. It's based on something Justice Cardozo said to the first graduating class of NYU. He counseled the lawyers to love the law and treat it as if you love it. That is what loving the law is. It is the opportunity to be governed by what we admire instead of what disappoints us in the practice of the craft.... We have all sorts of alumni who come back to proclaim why it is that they have been inspired by the law, why it is that it is such a precious and powerful weapon. We also have family members come in to experience a little bit of law school. We have musicians, invariably we have magicians.... It's our celebration of the connections to each other and a celebration of the promise ... of our craft and how we want to contribute to make that promise real."

Available and Accessible to Students

The law teachers we studied are available and accessible to their students outside class. They welcome student interaction at any time through any means—answering questions after class, meeting in the office, talking on the phone, exchanging e-mail messages, and joining their students for meals.

It is striking that their students describe the availability and accessibility of these teachers in terms of absolutes: they "never" put up barriers to meeting with students; they were "always" available.

- "He always manages to make time for his students. 'Walk with me' is one of his most effective tactics, where, if he cannot sit with you, he asks you to walk with him from point A to point B in order for you to hash out your issue or ask your question" (student of Don Hornstein).
- "Professor Enos provided encouragement and was always available for conversations or questions" (student of Beth Enos).
- "From my perspective, the most appreciated and enduring quality about Professor Levit was (and is) her accessibility. From my first week in law school until I graduated, she was always available and accessible." "She always was available to answer my many questions, to edit my many drafts, and to simply talk about my thesis. She was available to me during office hours, after office hours, at home, and via e-mail." "I never once heard her say, 'I don't have time.' . . . She always made the time for what the students' needs were, whether it was a question about torts or a question about this [—that] happened in my family" (students of Nancy Levit).
- "She is very approachable. And in law school, I think that in this environment you feel like doors are shutting on you in a variety of

ways, and with Paula I feel like she always has her door open to you" (student of Paula Lustbader).

- "I have never seen her door closed to her office. If she's there, it's open, and she is there more often than I" (student of Julie Nice).
- "Prof. was very helpful and always available to her students" (student of Patti Alleva).
- "She responds to every e-mail, every call. She is always willing to meet with you on weekends, on evenings. Anytime you need to meet with her to discuss things, she'll do that" (student of Cary Bricker).
- "Professor was so approachable and always made time for students." "He's never said, 'No, I don't have time to meet' or 'These are the only office hours'" (students of Andy Taslitz).
- "Hiroshi also stands out as being the most accessible professor to his students. When he joined the UCLA faculty, he filled a tremendous void for students wanting to study immigration law. He was undoubtedly a very busy and sought-after professor, and he juggled many new commitments among a community that was hungry for an immigration expert. Despite his busy schedule, Hiroshi remained ever present with his students" (student of Hiroshi Motomura).

One way that these teachers signal to students that they are available is to remain after class to answer questions. A student of Beth Enos comments that she was willing to teach "outside of the class" and notes that "she was the last person to leave the room after every single class, also." Similarly, one of Roberto Corrada's students notes that "he always stayed after class to answer any questions or if there was another class coming and he'd say let's go

up to my office, and he was very approachable and very accessible."
One of Hiroshi Motomura's students explains the message students took from his availability: "I was always surprised when he would stay after class to address the line of students with questions. Sometimes, he would even return the next day after having looked up some material to better answer a question from the previous day. It was these little gestures that signaled to his students that he is truly invested in our experience in the classroom." A student of Susan Kuo recalls this incident: "She also may be the only professor I have had that is willing to keep answering questions and work out concepts after class for as long as she has. I have stayed after in the hall and discussed ideas for more than an hour."

Office hours present another opportunity for the teachers to be available and accessible to their students. Although most law professors schedule office hours, some nevertheless remain inaccessible. As one student put it, "Some professors . . . have office hours, and they won't even be in their office during office hours or you have to make an appointment. They make it really difficult to meet with them."

The teachers also make it clear, through their words and actions, that they welcome interaction with students in their offices. One of Steven Homer's students notes that he "is very receptive to office visits and reminded us each class when he would be available." A student describes Andy Taslitz's "never ending" office hours. "He would invite people to his office hours and tell other people to come in. It was like an endless chair. 'Oh, just come in and sit down and be a part of the discussion, and when you're done, you can leave.' . . . It was just kind of this continual learning environment in his office." And one of Hiroshi Motomura's students appreciates the counseling he received during office hours: "He was the one professor I had in law school who was utterly generous with his time during office hours.... The time he spent with me during office hours did more than help me understand individual concepts. His willingness to help me 'get it' helped me cope with the whole law-school experience at a time when I felt distinctly unhappy [with] the whole law-school enterprise.... I've come to learn that Hiroshi has provided this kind of personal assistance and mentorship to a great many of his current and former students."

The teachers extend their availability to students beyond the school by phone and e-mail. Many students note that, as exams approached, these teachers gave students their home phone numbers and encouraged them to call with questions, even in the evenings and on weekends. For example, one of Andy Leipold's students comments that "before finals he gives you his phone number and tells you to call him at home. He doesn't care if it's on the weekend; call him. He wants to be able to answer your questions." Students also comment on teachers' prompt and detailed responses via e-mail. One of Steven Homer's students says, "Open door policy and turn-around on e-mail responses was excellent. He really cared about everyone." A student of Don Hornstein feels that his "e-mail responses also show that he really cares about what we're learning.... He'll give you detailed answer[s]."

Sharing a meal with students is an especially personal way the teachers make themselves available to their students. Tina Stark invites students and their significant others to her home: "I make my mac-and-cheese and wings, offer beer and soda, chocolate brownies and ice cream, have baggies so students can take extra food with them. I have fun with them." Bridget Crawford uses lunch invitations to send an important message to her students: "Every semester, I include in my syllabus an invitation (okay, plea) for groups of students to organize buy-or-bring-your-own lunches and invite me along. Even if students don't take me up on the offer, I think the invitation sends an important message: students are my focus." Paula Franzese uses lunch meetings to learn her students' stories: "We will do small lunch sessions and that helps as well, meeting with maybe twelve students at a time, and I want to hear their stories. Everyone has a story. Why are you here? What are you hoping to do with your degree? What has inspired you so far about being here? What are your passions?"

Students articulate the benefits they get from sharing a meal with their teachers. One of Andy Taslitz's students puts it succinctly: "Eat with your students. . . . There's something about breaking bread with somebody that makes you get to know them and makes you feel comfortable. . . ." A student of Heather Gerken notes that she "took all of her students out to lunch in groups. This generous extension of her time encouraged shyer students to take advantage of the opportunity to meet with her." A student of Don Hornstein describes the dramatic effect of accepting his invitation to meet students at a local restaurant: "He actually invited anyone in the class who wanted to go out to just meet at this place, and we went, and it was a really good opportunity just to get to know him. . . . We all sat in a circle, and he was very interested in getting to know us, getting to know what we wanted to do. . . . I've never had a professor that really cared that much to actually spend time outside the classroom or office hours to really get to know students and want to know what he can do more to help us."

Going Beyond the Call of Duty—Extra Sessions, Student Organizations, and Service

The teaching efforts of the outstanding law professors extend well beyond the classroom. They conduct extra sessions for students, work with student organizations, and participate with students in a range of service projects, including pro bono. These teachers go to great lengths to help their students learn and succeed.

A student of Patti Alleva describes her midsemester conferences: "For her upper-level courses, she has midsemester conferences where everybody gets twenty, thirty minutes to meet with her and . . . to discuss whatever you want to discuss. . . . Then everybody has a chance to meet her personally, their own time. You can talk to her about anything in the course, anything in your career, what you're interested in. She has a genuine interest. I think it's really, really great."

Two of Cary Bricker's clinical students appreciated her willingness to work with them on the weekend to help them prepare for a couple of upcoming trials: "[We] work at the federal defender's clinic with Cary, and we've had two trials together, a bench trial and a jury trial. In preparation for both of those trials, we needed her to come in on the weekend to the office and help us prepare and help us do our closing arguments and cross-examinations. She found baby sitters, came downtown, and spent three hours with us on separate occasions just to help us prepare."

Ruthann Robson goes to the student lounge to make herself available to answer questions as final exams approach: "I do a question-and-answer session the day before the exam. I go to the student lounge. I set up a time, and I will stay there as long as there are questions. I say, 'You are welcome to come whether you have a question or not; you are totally free not to come if this is the kind of thing that freaks you out, but I will answer every question.'"

Some teachers conduct sessions to help first-year students adapt to law school. These sessions are open to all students, not just the students in these teachers' classes. For example, Heather Gerken holds optional sessions for first years, such as "How to navigate law school," "How to take an exam," and "How to choose additional classes." Meredith Duncan presents a workshop on outlining. And Roberto Corrada has created a multimedia presentation for the student bar association on test preparation and performance. "He gave about an hour and a half talk with video on strategies, key ideas, keeping in mind ways of attack and approach exam problems, when it comes to finals, and how to prepare for that. . . . And so that was pretty helpful and showed that he had the interest in kind of giving folks the idea on how to succeed when it comes to the law-school experience as a whole" (student of Roberto Corrada).

Many students mention that their law teachers get involved with student organizations: Nelson Miller helped students found an animal law society; Steve Friedland attended the public interest group's tennis tournament; Nancy Knauer advises the women's law caucus; Andy Leipold led a trip to a major-league baseball game; Don Hornstein has coached moot court for more than twenty years; and Ruthann Robson, Andy Taslitz, and Nancy Levit have advised student-edited law reviews.

A colleague of Don Hornstein summarizes his commitment to his moot-court teams: "Don was the advisor for our Holderness Moot Court teams for twenty years. At the same time, he was the coach for our two environmental-law teams and the national team. He is not an advisor in name only but, rather, energetically moots students, recruits colleagues to moot students, and frequently travels with students to their competitions."

Nancy Levit explains the extent of her efforts with the law review: "This entails teaching an extra course that meets once a week, each semester of every year; direction of sixty students in writing notes or comments (student articles); personally editing four or five student articles each semester; supervision of the production process to publish four issues of the 250-page journal each year; selection of new student members in a write-on competition; [and] appointment of a new editorial board."

Students value the opportunities these law teachers create for them to experience law making, advocacy, and pro bono work in real life, outside the classroom. A student of Hiroshi Motomura describes one such project: "He's even helped with a group of students who picked a case in the community. It was a terrorism prosecution that people were really interested in and wanted to work on, and he helped us find an attorney for the family."

Don Hornstein's students describe a multitude of opportunities that he makes available to his students: "He took a couple students with him to the state legislature last year in our insurance-law class when he was working really closely with some of the state representatives on a hurricane-insurance issue. . . . He took the time to, like, meet with us afterwards and explain what had happened and kind of go through if we had any questions and just really wanting us to participate, wanting us to learn." "He actually sent S___ to one of the public hearings that was being held by the EPA up in DC. He's created working groups outside of the classroom for students to actually get involved in policy work . . . and even helped me go to some conferences as well."

One of Nelson Miller's students concisely articulates a critical lesson the student learned by engaging in pro bono work with Miller: "I would frequently see Dean Miller heading to a local shelter to volunteer or provide pro bono services. Often, he would invite students along, and, through him, we learned to care about the community and to give back to those who need help."

Viewing Students as Collaborators, Colleagues, and Peers

Most of these exceptional law teachers and their students view their relationship as collaborative rather than hierarchical. The teachers see their students as colleagues and peers and treat students as adults and professionals. These collaborative relationships take place in and out of the classroom.

Hiroshi Motomura's teaching philosophy centers on collaboration: "Teaching is a collaboration between teacher and student. This is true for each individual student, and it is true for each group of students in a class. Teachers and students are not equals, but they are colleagues in very important ways. It is important for them to treat each other with respect, and for them to work together."

How do teachers establish collaborative relationships with their students? In a variety of ways, large and small, in and out of the classroom:

- "He treats people like you're an attorney already, and you're a young professional" (student of Steven Homer).
- "She feels like a peer. She doesn't feel like someone who's standing in front of me preaching to me, and her attitude is more of let's

work together to arrive at the best solution for you" (student of Cary Bricker).

- "Professor Bahadur treated me like an adult. . . . He told us that 'you guys are going to be attorneys; we'll be colleagues'" (student of Rory Bahadur).
- "[She] treats students like junior colleagues . . . like they are part of the firm she is in" (student of Tina Stark).
- "He honestly, genuinely treats you like a peer" (student of Hiroshi Motomura).
- "He treats you as an adult if you're prepared and willing to try. . . . And that's nice. It makes you comfortable. It makes you willing to speak" (student of Philip Prygoski).
- "It was from day one we were colleagues and we were going to do this together" (student of Andy Taslitz).

Nancy Knauer explains how her service on the admissions committee allows her to see her students as colleagues: "I volunteer for the admissions committee each year because it gives me a unique insight to the composition of our student body. When I look out at my Property class, I don't see a bunch of scared, first-year law students, but rather a group of very accomplished young people. I also see the faces of my future colleagues, and I make a point of reminding my students that they will go on to do a wide range of things. They will be judges, professors, tax lawyers, policy makers, and entrepreneurs."

Students explain how interactions with the teachers outside class helped them feel like peers: "I think his ability to connect and just to make you feel like you are a peer as opposed to just his student. . . . I remember discussing with him movies that brought issues about criminal law, and he was just always more than happy to discuss it and talk. He asked you about your other classes and things like that, like actually wanted to get to know you and actually wanted for you to feel comfortable and feel on his level and not as if he's on some pedestal and you're just a lowly student" (student of Andy Leipold). "Paula makes the time to get to know you, to see how you're doing, and, as a result of it, when I see her, I don't see her as a professor, I see her as a friend, as a colleague, as one of us. . . . That level of attention that she gives to students, which I don't think I've ever got from any other professor at any level of my education" (student of Paula Lustbader). "She sends out those e-mails that say 'Dear Colleagues,' and she just signs her first name so it's not like I'm on top of you, and I'm the professor, and I'm somebody big and important" (student of Nancy Levit).

The teachers share with students some of their personal and professional experiences, which shortens the distance between the students and their professor. "He has a willingness to share things about his life, like his family. . . . I think that expresses a certain amount of caring about students just because he's willing to share personal things about himself and relate them to you. . . . He trusts us to tell us certain things" (student of Andy Taslitz). "I tell a story about an absolutely horrible interview I had with Justice O'Conner. . . . Who knows, maybe when they have a bad interview sometime, you know, maybe that'll be okay. I tell the story because it's funny and because it gives them a chance to laugh at me properly" (Andy Leipold).

Other students describe how these teachers create a collaborative environment in the classroom. "For me, knowing the names was huge, and more than that, knowing who you are as a person, speaking on our terms, and making a place for us within the law. But I think all of that for me comes down to Julie Nice is engaged in a dialogue with us, a process with us. She's a coparticipant in this engaging dialogic process with us. That's what class is. I don't see it as her class; I don't see it as my class; it's ours together, and we do that. And that's whether it's seminar or it's a hundred people. We're in this together and we're going to break down the concepts together; we're going to hatch it out together; we're going to argue; we're going to love each other together. It felt like a family to me every time I'm in class with her" (student of Julie Nice). "He does make these self-deprecating remarks, which . . . allows us to kind of see the humanity. Professors are often, 'I got straight A's; I went to Harvard (Stanford, Yale . . .),' all these kinds of things. Hiroshi says, 'Look, I didn't go to Harvard, Stanford, Yale; I didn't get the best grades.' . . . By humanizing himself and simultaneously asking his students to act as professionals, there's a camaraderie that opens up" (student of Hiroshi Motomura).

Paula Franzese describes how she uses a microphone to turn her students into teachers: "I would be getting to the nuances of the opinion, and I needed to be sure that they were heard, and I also needed to give them an added source of authority. The microphone is a really wonderful prop/tool to enhance that capability, so it's almost as if they were the teacher in regard to those two cases. . . . The microphone becomes the portable podium, and, when the student is commanding that lectern, by virtue of the mic, they have the voice of authority."

Mentors and Role Models

The teachers in our study become mentors and positive role models for their students. They offer advice to help students face challenges, including dealing with law-school grades and finding an appropriate life/work balance.

Many students express gratitude to the teachers we studied for their excellence as mentors:

- "A great professor and a great mentor. He'll have a lasting impression on my career" (student of Steven Homer).
- "Professor Gerken's engagement inside the class turned into encouragement outside of it, and she became a mentor to me and to many of my classmates. In that role too, she excelled, using the same combination of rigor, intellectual excitement, and fun to inspire her students down different paths" (student of Heather Gerken).
- "She's always Professor Alleva, the mentor, regardless if it's in the classroom, outside, if it's at the Union—you know—getting coffee, she's always that same mentor, inside class and outside" (student of Patti Alleva).
- "There is a real sense of personal investment that comes with Professor Hornstein's mentorship. I began the early application stages for the Rhodes Scholarship this past year, and, when one of my faculty recommenders fell through on submitting a letter of support, Professor Hornstein literally dropped what he was doing to submit a letter for me on time so I would not lose my eligibility" (student of Don Hornstein).
- "And I've heard other students who have had issues with finding jobs or with the personal things in law school. If they had made a connection with her in class, even a big lecture, she was a wonderful personal mentor to a bunch of people for a whole wide range of reasons" (student of Nancy Knauer).
- "I primarily represented persons in deportation proceedings, mainly in asylum cases. . . . Hiroshi has been a friend, mentor, and great supporter of my work. Asylum work is exhausting and

emotionally draining. It was very important to me to have someone to talk with who understood the legal as well as the personal nature of the work" (student of Hiroshi Motomura).

In their role as mentors, these teachers offer advice for students facing difficult issues in their personal and professional lives. One of Philip Prygoski's students credits his advice for a successful summer position: "Over the summer I worked for a public defender's office, but I had a huge dilemma because I wanted to go to the prosecution side. That's always what I've always wanted to do, and I actually went up and spoke to Professor Prygoski, and he sat down, and he started discussing the constitution and how . . . you have two clients. You have a defendant, and you have the US Constitution. You are defending the US Constitution. So, because of what he told me, and how we sat down, and how we discussed the whole issue, I decided to . . . do public defense rather than the prosecution, and . . . thanks to him, it was a rewarding experience." A student of Andy Taslitz emphasized the professor's listening and advising skills: "I can't tell you how many times I've sought advice from him about how to be a working mom. He's not a working mom, okay? But he has such good advice to give. I mean he really listens. . . . And he really wants to help you find a solution to your problem."

The teachers we studied willingly help any students regardless of the particular need. Paula Lustbader described to us how she helped two particular students survive personal crises: "I've actually taken two students to the hospital to prevent suicides. I'm not saying if I wasn't there, they would have committed suicide, but I do feel really grateful that I was there, and that I did represent a place that they could come in that moment of need."

One challenge for many students is to put their law-school grades in perspective. A student of Beth Enos recalls Enos's advice about grades: "[She said], 'Twenty years from now, if the best thing you can say about your life is that you got top grades in law school, that's pathetic. If the worst thing you can say about your life is that you did not get top grades in law school you will be blessed.'" Similarly, one of Larry Krieger's students reports that he internalized Krieger's perspective on grades: "Your grades are not going to be what makes you into a good human being for the rest of your life. . . . It's like you're not going to go into a courthouse and get an A, B, C or D. . . . Once you're out of school, exams are over, grades are over, and it's just about doing your job and doing it well, and feeling confident in what you've produced at the end of the day."

Perhaps the greatest challenge for law students, law teachers, and lawyers, is to maintain a healthy balance between life and work. Meredith Duncan says, "I want them to learn that they can be successful lawyers and be healthy and happy, well-balanced lives." Her message gets through to her students: "She honestly cares about students' and attorneys' mental health and thinks it's very important in our future career to recognize the dangers that can be posed by substance abuse and other things. And I think of the stresses of first-year law students; she recognizes them and wants you to face them right away, knowing that that stress you face is not going to die when you graduate. It's going to get worse. So that's recognizing it and trying to help you through that is one of the things that separates her from most of my other professors."

Two of Larry Krieger's students summarize the messages he sends students about balance, happiness, and fulfillment: "Krieger's overarching themes come through over and over again: while it is important for lawyers to do the best they can, all lawyers make mistakes sometimes; don't sacrifice your health or family to your job; you can do your job well and still not win, so focusing on results can be unhealthy; acting with integrity can help you remain happy and sane; most significantly, grades do not matter at all once you are in your job." "People who have the great job but who are miserable and whose personal lives suffer because of the hours they work just to acquire the status symbols. And I just think he's kind of a lone voice in the legal community saying . . . 'You can be a happy lawyer. You can make a real contribution. You can have a career you're proud about and make a real difference in people's lives without being law-review, moot-court . . . silk-stocking firm.'"

Paula Lustbader describes an activity she employs to emphasize the importance of purpose, friends, and family during law school: "On the first day of class in the summer and in the first general orientation workshop, I ask students to write down their purpose for coming to law school. I suggest they share their purpose with each other and loved ones so they can be reminded of their purpose. I also have them write down the names of three people who are most important to them and make a commitment to see them regularly during the semester."

Law teachers can be influential role models for students seeking balance in their lives. "[She's a] great role model for women and for professionalism, and she has had a great career. She clerked for Judge Jones in the circuit. She obviously is a great professor, but yet she still comes to class, and she'll tell stories about her two boys and the family time she spends. . . . I know that looking out into my career future, that's one thing that's very important to me is how to be respectful and professional and have a great career and balance all of these things while still having a family life" (student of Meredith Duncan). "He basically stresses the need for balancing professional and personal life because he did always set aside time for family" (student of Rory Bahadur). A student of Beth Enos recalls her saying, "I'm going to be out there at lunchtime with my dog, trying Creek State Park, right behind our law school, and you should really close your books and come take a walk and remember to breathe a little bit and know that grades aren't the most important thing."

Two of Nelson Miller's students see him as a model of commitment to social justice: "I would look out the window and watch him walking down to the soup kitchen, where he would take off his suit jacket and put on his apron and serve the homeless." "Working with him and seeing what type of lawyer he had become helped me realize my love for engaging in the community and modeling that for students. He also helped me understand what it means to be a socially responsible leader in the community."

Students of Nancy Levit and Ingrid Hillinger view them each as role models for being a successful lawyer: "She's emulating what a fabulous managing partner would do from the get-go. She shows up to class, dressed professional. She shows up to class prepared. Sometimes I'll find myself sitting in a meeting and . . . thinking, well, how would Nancy Levit do it? [She taught] us how to be good lawyers without saying, 'Good lawyers show up prepared. Good lawyers show up looking professional. Good lawyers know their subject matter'" (student of Nancy Levit). "We're going to function as lawyers out in the legal community, and this is how you can be forceful and be professional but also be totally collegial and respectful" (student of Ingrid Hillinger).

Andy Leipold explains a choice he makes in the classroom to model for students: "I want students to have intellectual integrity, so if I am wrong on a point or careless in my analysis, I admit it to the class. If I make a typo in the syllabus, I fix it and repost it. If I don't know the answer to a question, I admit that I don't know, but I try never to say, 'I'll get back to you.' We don't let students give that as an answer; a judge won't let a lawyer give that as an answer, so I don't get to do it either. Instead, I try to model what I want the students to do: reason from what I do know to figure out what I don't. Even if I do this awkwardly, I think there is value to the exercise."

Professionalism, Clients, and Ethics

Most of the teachers we studied focus a significant part of their teaching, mentoring, and modeling on professionalism. How do their students begin to develop their professional identities, their view of attorney-client relationships, and their professional ethics? By listening to what their teachers say in and out of the classroom; through the relationships they develop with their teachers; and, perhaps most importantly, by observing how their teachers act.

Nancy Knauer teaches professionalism through her words and deeds: "If you treat them like professionals and remind them that this is a professional school and that their reputation starts the minute they walk in that door, right, and the folks that they are with are their professional cohorts for the rest of their career for better or worse, if you treat them that way, they will get to believe it." Professor Knauer directly challenges her students to explore their professional identities: "I ask them to imagine a time after law school and consider the basic ethical questions: What kind of lawyer will you be? What are your core professional values? How will you integrate the law in your life?"

Beth Enos has explicit professionalism goals for her students: "I want my students to be competent lawyers, but beyond that, and perhaps even more importantly, I want them to be lawyers (and people) with integrity and compassion. I want them to understand that the parties in cases are real people, and that the choices that the lawyers and judges make have real consequences. I want them to be humbled and sobered by the responsibility they have not only to their clients but to the profession and to the wider community."

Students of Nelson Miller and Nancy Levit learned how to be civil within the adversary system. "I think he recognizes clearly [that] this is an adversarial system, but you don't have to be mean-spirited. . . . You're not out there to beat up the other lawyer. You're not out there to beat up the other side. Yes, you want to protect your clients' interests. Yes, you want to be passionate about it. Yes, you want to use everything that you know and can acquire to do that. But there's still an appropriate way to conduct yourself in that process. . . . He's trying to, I think through example, teach you the appropriate way to conduct yourself" (student of Nelson Miller). "So I need to do my very best and particularly in a profession that is driven in large part by adversarial dynamics. . . . You have to litigate your case, but you don't have to litigate your opponent. . . . We're going to do our best, but we're not going to do that at the expense of another person" (student of Nancy Levit).

A student of Andy Leipold describes how he learned nuanced lessons about the complex nature of the attorney-client relationship: "I felt like he did a tremendous job in Advanced Crim. Pro. of giving you a sense of being someone's advocate. I mean he talked about some pretty unsavory people that he represented, and he talked about it honestly, you know? And some of the real emotions you go through in representing . . . certain defendants. . . . He just projects such a strong sense of what your duties [are] as a lawyer—how your duties as a lawyer trump whatever those feelings might be. But he also doesn't just ignore those feelings."

One of Nelson Miller's students recalled a specific incident when the student was inspired by Miller's ability to connect with every client: "I went with him once. He was doing counseling sessions, basically free legal advice, and I saw some of the worst examples of poverty walking in the door. I mean, I'm talking about folks who have fluids running from every orifice and not smelling real good, and their stories aren't the most savory stories in the world, and he can sit back and be absolutely nonjudgmental . . . and make these people feel at ease with him across the economic, racial spectrums. . . . I'd like to be able to emulate [that]."

One of Nancy Knauer's students reports that the student discovered the satisfaction of both intellectual challenges and client service in Knauer's classroom: "I'll remember her excitement about both finding the right legal solution to somebody's problems—that intellectual satisfaction—but then also the kind of satisfaction of helping people or getting the right thing done, sort of the equity issues that we talk about. So there's these two parts to what makes practicing satisfying: the kind of puzzle part, and then the helping people part."

One of Meredith Duncan's students describes powerful lessons about clients, law, and the role of a lawyer. "In our professional responsibility class, Meredith brought in . . . an African American lawyer out of Galveston who defended the Ku Klux Klan. . . . But for me that was pretty profound for her to bring in somebody who was an obvious red flag, and for her to be able to stand up and say, 'No, this is important. This is an important issue because it's not just about what the color of your skin is, or who your client is, but the underlying principles of constitutional law and the right to counsel and right to due process.'"

Many exceptional teachers prioritize the development of students' professional ethics:

- "As I have developed as an educator, my primary goal has been to inculcate students with the importance of developing powerful legal skills, ethics, and a sense of professional responsibility that will result in their becoming responsive and responsible lawyers" (Cary Bricker).
- "I want them to learn to be professionals. Regardless of the course I'm teaching, I'm always trying to throw in . . . professional responsibility issues" (Meredith Duncan).
- "I can show that habits of intellectual honesty and rigor and caring about the ethics of a situation rather than just a rule of law [are necessary]. . . . My experience with ethical issues and practices is they never come to you on a silver platter. . . . They always sneak up, and all of the sudden you find yourself in a situation where you're not sure. . . . I give them time in a safe setting to work through and think about ways that ethical problems might present themselves" (Andy Leipold).
- "The last thing I ever tell them is to go out and always take the high road and do the right thing. . . . Never compromise on . . . your ethics" (Beth Enos).

Career Counseling, Connections, and Community

Nearly all of these exceptional law teachers take an active role in their students' career choices and opportunities. They assist students in every aspect of their job searches, from alerting students to potential opportunities, to writing reference letters, to connecting students with employers. These teachers create a community among their current students and alumni, which helps students find jobs and thrive after graduation.

A student of Meredith Duncan notes how she helped students expand their career visions: "[She] actively encourages us to think about our careers. . . . We had a panel of people whose careers had changed over time. . . . There was kind of a younger attorney and a female attorney (a mother) and the older gentleman who had gone through different jobs, and I think that was her way of getting us to kind of imagine our own careers." Likewise, a student of Hiroshi Motomura appreciated his efforts to help the student sort through summer job options: "He sat down with me and said, 'These are the pros and cons of each one.' He really took the time to help flush that out to make a decision that was best for you based on him getting to know you in class and what you'd express your interest to be, which I really appreciated."

Other teachers create internship and clerkship opportunities for students. "He's actually created internships for people in the class because he was worried about us because there aren't many internships now because the economy is so bad. So he just creates these things for us to do to help us for our resumes and our future careers" (student of Don Hornstein). "I want to place as many students as possible in bankruptcy court clerkships. A clerkship opens doors students don't even know exist. Bankruptcy judges are less concerned about grades than a student's passion for the area and a capacity for hard work. Those are qualities my students have in abundance. This year, eight graduating students will go on to bankruptcy court clerkships" (Ingrid Hillinger).

Many of these teachers provide students with a full range of services to prepare them for the hiring process. They review students' cover letters and resumes, and conduct mock interviews with students. Like most law professors, they serve as references for their students, but they take their reference role to another level:

- "Her impact on her students is summed up by the fact that virtually every person I know in my eighty-person section listed her as a reference for jobs two years later. It is not that she was an easy grader—and they all got A's. Quite the contrary. Rather, she was the professor that most students felt got to know them best both intellectually and professionally" (student of Heather Gerken).

- A student of Andy Taslitz marveled at a recommendation letter he wrote for her: "It was so detailed and so long and so uniquely written just for me. . . . He had funny antidotes and analogies of this is how _____ was as a student. And it was great, and it was clear that he had really taken time to put together this product."

- "I requested that she write a letter of recommendation for me in my third year of law school. That evolved, because she never does anything just a little bit, and I mean that in the warmest possible way, with a full-blown review of my cover letters to my resume. . . . So she taught me what I needed to know to present myself to employers to obtain employment" (student of Patti Alleva).

Teachers can use their personal and professional relationships with lawyers to help their students get jobs. Students of Bridget Crawford, Meredith Duncan, Paula Franzese, Heather Gerken, Ingrid Hillinger, Andy Leipold, Hiroshi Motomura, Tina Stark, and Andy Taslitz emphasized that these teachers jump-started their job searches by connecting them with potential employers.

Some teachers strive to create a community among their current and former students, which helps students find employment and mentors in the profession. A student explains that Paula Franzese sets up a web that connects students and alumni working in similar areas. Similarly, a student notes that Andy Taslitz "has that investment in seeing the students do well, succeed, and connecting us with other alumni that may be able to help us out in the future."

Hiroshi Motomura sees his current students as part of his future community: "I can tell in the first week that these are people I'm going to know for the rest of my life in some sense. I mean, I'll see them at some bar function; I'll be referring my students to them so that they can hire my next group of students." One of Professor Motomura's current students describes Professor Motomura's immigration-law community: "He knows people who are doing this work, and a lot of them, because they were his students. So he can help us get jobs and do this if it's what we're passionate about.... There's just a lot of Hiroshi fans in the area. I went to a conference and people kept coming up, and he'd be, like, that was my student from, you know, however many years ago, and they're doing this work, and they're passionate, and they all tie it back to him. So you feel like you're part of a big community.... It makes it a lot easier to then go out and actually do this work if it's what you're passionate about, because he's got a foot in the door."

Paula Lustbader's students describe the effects of the sense of community she creates among students and alumni: "The way that I think that it helps students learn is that, in creating a community, there are mentors that are now a part of these current students' lives. And a lot of students, I think, had the same experience as me, as not having any ... relatives in law or knowing anything about the practice of law. But now that this community is being developed, the folks who have gone through this program are now mentors to those that are going through it. And so it definitely helps them with their educational experience and professional experience." "I work in [a building] downtown. She sends me an e-mail and cc's three other folks who are working that same building. . . . All of a sudden folks that are from different years, that I may not have even gone to law school with, [are] having coffee and lunch."

Outstanding law teachers maintain their contact with, and commitment to, their former students after graduation. Steve Friedland developed a postgraduate program to help students pass the bar. Nancy Levit helped a student publish a law review article after graduation. Ingrid Hillinger made herself available evenings and weekends to talk through problems an alum was facing in practice. Nelson Miller refers clients to former students. One of Patti Alleva's students summarizes this type of lifelong commitment to students: "She is involved in your whole career, not just your law-school education, but everything before and after it, and is willing, and very, very willing, to help with that at any time." Finally, one of Paula Lustbader's alums has this humorous and flattering comment: "Paula is sort of a CLE, a lifelong CLE. I wish we could get the credits. . . . She remains approachable. . . . She keeps the door open, metaphorically speaking. You can contact her at home. You can contact her at the office."

Conclusion

Three comments provide a helpful framing of the relationships the teachers we studied have with their students.

First, the teachers struggled with only one of the twenty-five questions we asked in our interviews: "What do you like least about your students?" Although most were able to eventually come up with something in response—students' failure to engage, consumerism, multitasking in the classroom—most had difficulty responding. For example, Andy Taslitz said, "Dislike? It's hard to answer the what I don't like because I sort of like everything about my students. You know? There's the occasional student who . . . no matter what you do, seems to check out or not connect, . . . but that doesn't usually make me dislike them. I usually experience that as a failure on my part. There's something missing. I'm not seeing something."

Second, a student of Nancy Levit offers this wisdom for us all: "What I would hope professors and, quite honestly, lawyers would learn from Professor Levit is that we're supposed to follow our heart. We're supposed to have a passion. We're supposed to remember why we became law professors, or lawyers, or parents, or spouses, or whatever. . . . And you can tell from Professor Levit that, hey, she knows why she is a professor. She knows why she's wanted to do it, and she's pursuing that with all the excitement and vigor of a first-year student. . . . But she still remembers that professors are about students, and you're not doing anything for students with your door locked."

Third, Heather Gerken captures the power of caring and respect in our relationships with students: "Nothing can substitute for caring for and respecting one's students. What matters most to students are the invisible things—not the showy teaching style, but a willingness to learn every one of their names by the first day of class, give them feedback, take them out to lunch, help them think through career choices."

5

What Do the Best Law Teachers Expect from Their Students?

Expectations matter. Students respond positively to the teachers we studied, who have high expectations, demand much of them, and challenge them. These expectations include mastery of complex doctrine, critical thinking, and acting like a professional. Those same teachers respect their students, care about them, and have confidence in them. They also model their expectations through their own hard work. Their students are inspired to excel—they do not want to let down the teacher, their peers, or themselves. Ultimately, these high expectations include deep levels of student preparation, fully engaged class participation, and conscious, reflective thinking as well as the development of student responsibility, professionalism, and identity.

High, Achievable Expectations Balanced with Care and Respect

The teachers begin with high expectations for their students. "I pushed students to prepare and perform to the limits of their abilities, then pushed them some more" (Cary Bricker). "My classes are a lot of work, and students must be ready to work. Classes are pitched really high. They have to get called on and must be prepared" (Heather Gerken).

Students recognize the dramatic effect of high expectations on their preparation and performance. "He sets really high standards. He has very high expectations of his students, but he doesn't do this in a way that is imposing or demeaning or, you know, even intimidating in a sort of scary way. You can just feel that if you are not prepared for class, you know, you probably shouldn't be there that day. . . . He is not going to be satisfied with your mediocrity" (student of Andy Taslitz).

Paula Lustbader begins her course with an assumption that students want to excel: "On this first day of class, I tell students how they have unique gifts to bring to the law school and to the legal profession; I tell them that their clients are waiting for them; and I tell them that my job is to push them to excellence. If they only want to get by, they need to tell me, and I won't push so hard. Otherwise, I will assume that they want to achieve excellence." At the end of her course, one of Professor Lustbader's students wrote on the course evaluation form, "Thank you. I'll make you proud." Likewise, one of Steven Homer's students wrote: "I really felt challenged and had a sense of accomplishment after finishing this course. Thanks!"

But high expectations alone are not enough. These teachers' success is more complex than that. Part of the reason their students feel motivated to excel is because the students' perceive that the teachers' expectations are both high and achievable:

> He, without a doubt, has high expectations, but he also conveys that you, as a student in his class, are absolutely able to achieve and meet those expectations. And I think one of the things that he does right off the bat is with his syllabus. And I mean his syllabus essentially says this is a contract between you and me, and you know you're expected to come to class and be prepared and contribute meaningfully. And even in those discussions, I think one of the great things about him is that it is a high level of discussion. It's not a very, kind of, cursory "Here are the basic elements of whatever it is you're learning," but in addition to that, he's actually going to require some high-level thinking and high-level analysis, applying the law to different factual scenarios that may not be something that you would see immediately. And so I think, in all of those ways, that he has high expectations, forces a high level of thinking and analysis and then conveys to you that you can meet those expectations.
>
> —STUDENT OF ANDY TASLITZ

Neither the students nor the teachers confuse a safe learning environment with low expectations. As Tina Starks puts it, "I believe a classroom should be a safe, comfortable environment, one in which questions are welcomed and students not embarrassed. . . . But this does not mean that I dumb down what I teach. Students quickly learn that I expect them to think analytically at a sophisticated level. They also learn that I expect their best work and that my critiques of their work will be thorough and detailed." Professor Stark's students understand the distinction: "She is remarkably good at keeping balance—really tough, but she is empathetic. Love and challenge."

Many students agree that the balance of high, achievable expectations with care for students is motivating: "He challenges you but at the same time cares about you" (student of Steve Friedland):

- "There's that high expectation of professionalism, but it's coupled with a recognition of the emotional needs that students have" (student of Nancy Levit).
- "She is an amazing teacher and really cares about her students. The class requires a lot of preparation, and she has very high expectations, but it is definitely worth it to put in the work" (student of Heather Gerken).

These teachers' combination of high expectations and respect describes the ideal motivator for many students:

- "I think that a huge component of effective teaching and effective learning is fostering a mutual respect between teacher and student. . . . I think it is evidence of how effective Professor Duncan is. . . . 'I respect you by not tearing into you if you miss some point and you respect me by giving me your undivided attention.' I really think that that relationship is key to effective teaching and effective learning" (student of Meredith Duncan).
- "He does a wonderful job of challenging us and respecting us" (student of Andy Leipold).
- "She has very high expectations of the students and . . . she's respectful at the same time with students and understands that other things happen in life and is interested in what's going on in

life. . . . They don't need to be impossible, and there are some professors that I think make it—take joy in making it—too difficult. That's not her goal. Her goal is making the students learn and getting a good experience in the process, and with her high expectations, I think the majority of the students do better and want to do better because of her" (student of Nancy Levit).

- "He expected students to be well prepared as a matter of respect for the students, him, and the profession's responsibilities" (student of Rory Bahadur).

Clear Expectations for Preparation, Participation, Exams, and Beyond

The teachers' clear expectations help students prepare for class, perform in class, succeed on exams, and become effective professionals.

Many of the teachers we studied convey their expectations and teaching philosophies to students very early in the course: "I start all of my courses by explaining what my expectations are, that I take my teaching very seriously, that I expect them to be prepared, that I expect them to be on time, that I expect them to be respectful and professional. And that they can expect the same for me. . . . I'm not going to hold them over. And I'm not going to be late. I'm not going to cancel classes" (Meredith Duncan). One of Julie Nice's students explains the value of hearing about the teacher's expectations during the first class session. "One thing that I really appreciate is that at the beginning of class, the beginning of the semester, she tells you what she expects from you. She has, I think, really high expectations of us. And she says this is what you're going to get out of my class; this is what I am going to bring to the table.

And you should be able to analyze critically by the end of the class these specific situations, specific scenarios. And that just gets you excited as a student, excited that this is what you're going to be learning, and it makes you actually help her reach her goal and, in turn, you become a better student."

Paula Lustbader explains that part of her responsibility, as a teacher, is to help new law students understand what law school demands in terms of preparation and performance:

> I help them learn by putting the burden of learning on them.
> Right? I will build you a bridge, but I won't carry you across it.
> You've got to do your part in this. . . . I expect them to be prepared.
> I expect them to have tried. I expect them to do their best in
> everything. And if they come in not prepared to do that, I let them
> know . . . because they may have had prior learning experiences
> where they could just get by. . . . So I understand that part of my
> job is to also be explicit about what [preparation] means. But I
> expect them to do well. I expect them to do well, kind of knowing
> how to be a good student and be a respectful student and being
> prepared. But also that I expect them to be able to master the
> material and write killer exams and learn this stuff and think
> about it and make a difference in it. And the only way they get to
> make a difference in it is if they've mastered all this.

The teachers' clear expectations allow students to prepare for class effectively. "She makes her expectations very clear. She's says she's not going to assign a lot of reading, but the reading she does assign she wants you to know, and when you approach it that way, I mean, you're spending the same amount of reading as you would for, you know, forty pages or whatever, but you're focusing on what she wants you to take out of it, which is very helpful in class" (student of Nancy Knauer). Two of Steven Homer's students comment on the clarity of his assignments: "There was never a time that he did not have a set agenda of what we would be covering for the day. . . . You knew exactly what you would be covering that particular day." "I really like how clear his expectations are. I think that's really important to help gauge your progress, and it helps with your preparation for class, because you are really clear [about] what's expected." Likewise, one of Roberto Corrada's students emphasizes the value of clear expectations for student preparation: "He set very clear goals for what he wanted from students and how he would want us to analyze a problem . . . what areas we should know for an exam, or just more generally, and setting those guidelines up front would help a student to know what's expected of them and how they should prepare. Whereas, [with] a lot of other professors, it's kind of [a] guessing game."

As the course progresses, these clear expectations help students stay on track. "If Professor Enos says you're not meeting her expectations, you're doing something wrong, because her expectations are reasonable and fair, and she tells you all along what they are. There is no hiding the ball" (student of Beth Enos). In many of Stephen Homer's classes, he calls on each student multiple times during the class. His students appreciate the certainty this system provides. "You know you are going to have cold calling, so there is no opportunity to slack off on the materials, because everyone is going to get questioned. I think that kind of structure . . . is how it should be done. He breaks it all down very clearly." A student of Andy Leipold notes how he continually clarifies expectations for performance during class: "He tells you this is how you say things. This is how you make this argument. . . . Constantly, every time you say something, he's, like, 'Wait! We've got to be careful about what we're saying.'"

The teachers use positive reinforcement to help clarify their expectations and to motivate their students. Students appreciate knowing what performance meets high expectations. Ruthann Robson notes that one way to motivate students is to set out clear, high standards and then to acknowledge and reinforce excellent student performance throughout the course. Heather Gerken puts it succinctly: "I am clear when they are doing a great job. . . . I emphasize that we are all in this together."

Students emphasize how clear expectations allow them to prepare for exams effectively. "There was no mystery what she wanted going into the final exam. There was none whatsoever. I knew exactly what she wanted" (student of Meredith Duncan). "Her exam is by no means easy, but it's very tuned to what she wants you to learn from the class, and if you hear the themes throughout the class and . . . the examples she uses in the class, then it's very easy to prepare for the exam" (student of Nancy Knauer).

Not only do the teachers' clear expectations help students prepare for class and exams, but also they foster effective student participation in class and shape students' professional behavior. Paula Franzese demonstrates her expectations for professional performance in law school: "If the student the first week of class . . . says 'the plaintiff's case sucks,' I will say, 'Well, no, that's not really what one would say. Put that in a more elegant frame. Give that to us as a good counselor making a court appearance might give it to us.' That quickly makes plain what the expectations are. I ask my students to liken their classroom appearance to court appearances to be as prepared as they can be, to be as professional as they can be, and to be as gracious as they can be, and they rise to that level of expectation." Susan Kuo's explanation of her expectations is designed to improve student learning during law school and their professional demeanor in practice. "I am as clear as I can be about my expectations and how I will evaluate their performance. Often, I will explain why I am assigning particular material—how it fits within the design of the course. When students understand what is expected of them and believe that they are colleagues in a collaborative process, I find that they are willing to work harder and that they learn more quickly. Also, by maintaining an equitable classroom environment, I hope to model professional behavior that they can adopt in the future when they interact with other lawyers and with clients."

Confidence that Every Student Can Excel

Students notice that these teachers have high expectations that apply to every student in the course. "She expects a lot from each and every student. Yes, she does have a really caring and fostering and way about her, but she expects a lot, and she's hard on you. I think anyone that has had Trial Ad, or Advanced Trial Ad, or Defender's Clinic with her will tell you that in mock situations with her, she expects a lot and she's tough on you, but she's tough on you because it makes you learn more" (student of Cary Bricker). "He wants us all to succeed. So in order to succeed we all have to work hard. He knows that; he's not going to work for us, but he's going to give us as many tools as he possibly can for us to do the work right" (student of Steven Homer). "He never uses the words . . . 'I have high expectations for you,' or 'This is going to be difficult.' To him it's just . . . 'We're going to learn criminal procedure and everyone's going to learn it'" (student of Andy Taslitz).

Steven Homer's students note several positive effects of his uniform, high expectations:

- "He expects an equal amount of work out of each of us and holds us all to a high standard. I wish we had the choice to take him again next semester."
- "Professor Homer has that rare and gifted ability to push us all to do our best by instilling the importance of the task at hand."
- "He expects the best from everybody. And I think it's sort of reciprocal because I think he gives us the best too. It's very clear in his class that you're expected to work very hard and you're expected to turn in a good product. And I love that because you cannot slack off."
- "I think he really wants everybody to rise. It's quite remarkable that he does that and pushes the way he does without it becoming threatening."

While these outstanding law teachers convey high expectations for every student, they also find ways to individualize their expectations. They assume that each student brings her own strengths and weaknesses, that every student starts from a unique place and faces different challenges. "She can be really tough on you, which is good because she knows how to push you and what to say to make you better. But it is very individualized. . . . She has a sense of her students, of which students she can say certain things to, because I've never seen her ever upset anyone. Everyone walks out of her class feeling like, 'Wow! That was amazing! I feel like I've grown a lot'" (student of Cary Bricker). "I think for me he really challenged me to become better. He has a knack for knowing what certain students need, and I think he will challenge certain students in different way[s]" (student of Steven Homer). Steve Friedland explains how he tries to motivate each student: "I have learned that students tend to learn best when challenged, so my goal is to challenge them in a positive manner as they climb the mountain—to go at their pace, but to extend themselves and maximize their course learning experience. This means I reach out to students, sometimes on an individual basis, and create exercises in and outside of class for the specific purpose of challenging them."

The teachers we studied feel confident their students can excel. "I begin with the premise that each possesses innate talents that will serve him or her well in the legal community. To succeed in my classes students must check their egos at the door, become facile integrating the Federal Rules of Evidence and Model Rules of Professional Conduct into their trial practice, perform simulations over and over again, subject themselves to constructive (and sometimes harsh) critiques, then get up and try again" (Cary Bricker). "He believes that law students can change the world if they learn the right skills, have the right experiences, and have appropriate confidence in themselves" (colleague of Don Hornstein). "My job is to raise the floor. By the time everybody is ready to take my exam, I think students should all have mastery of the content. . . . I hope we're all teaching ourselves, and we're raising the floor together. That keeps their motivation high" (Julie Nice).

Students respond to the confidence their teachers have in their potential to achieve great things. "I love teachers who are demanding. . . . I really like the fact that he pushes all of his students, and he sees, like, our potential, and he kind of just draws us into himself" (student of Andy Taslitz). "She also makes it clear that she expects you to rise up to her expectations, not in a mean or demeaning way, but 'I'm treating you like a professional because I know you can deliver like a professional' and that makes you want to" (student of Meredith Duncan). "I think the best thing that she does is she is very supportive of us. You can tell she truly believes that we can do better and we can do well. . . . I think that helps, when you believe someone believes in you, to go ahead and achieve" (student of Cary Bricker).

The positive effects of these teachers' expectations and confidence in students extends beyond the course to success throughout law school. "It challenged me to prepare for class and to study and to think like I hadn't before . . . I think being in his class made me a better law student. . . . I started applying that level of study and preparation to all my classes, and I'd like to think it made me better for having been subjected to what I felt his expectations of me were" (student of Philip Prygoski). "You can tell that she doesn't just want you to be successful in her class. She wants you to be successful throughout law school. So I remember the very first semester we had her she talked about—around—Thanksgiving break time. 'This is the time you need to start going back through from the beginning of class and really crunching in for your exams'" (student of Meredith Duncan). And what teacher would not want to read a comment on student evaluation like this one from a student of Nelson Miller: "You have instilled confidence in the majority of the class, confidence not limited to comprehension of torts, but confidence that success in law school is not only feasible but actually achievable."

Inspire Preparation, Engagement, Excellence

Students of the law teachers we studied strive to excel, not out of fear or intimidation, but because their teachers inspired them. "Heather Gerken taught her classes using the Socratic method, but unlike some other professors who used the method to intimidate or even embarrass students, Heather used it to engage and inspire students. I was prepared for every class, not because I was afraid but because I wanted to impress her" (student of Heather Gerken). Several of Andy Taslitz's students echoed this theme:

- "He has this ability to really get everybody involved and to inspire students who maybe have had trouble with other classes for some reason. There's a spark when you go into his class that you want to be a part of it. You don't just want to sit there."
- "He has extremely high expectations and it's clear from the beginning that . . . expectations are so high . . . but people reach them because you want to do well for him. You want . . . to be able to say something in class and have him smile or nod his head."
- "The fact that Taz gets personally invested in his students I think is a big reason why I did so well in his courses. . . . I wanted him to be proud of me. I know that sounds, like, ridiculous but . . . I did. I wanted him to be proud of me because his opinion meant a lot. So while I definitely read for all my courses, I always studied for all my courses; I did extra for him."

Students want to impress these teachers. "It makes you want to work harder, and it makes you . . . want to impress him because he's a person who you want acceptance from" (student of Philip Prygoski). "You don't want him to think that you didn't do the reading. You don't want him to think that you didn't care about his class. . . . When I was on call, I was shaking uncontrollably. I love Professor Corrada; I knew exactly what I was talking about, but I wanted so badly to do a good job because I respected him that much that I wanted him to be impressed with my presentation of the case" (student of Roberto Corrada). "She makes you feel special. She wants you there. You are special to her, and you want to make her proud. I want to come, and I want to do well for myself, but also because I want to make her proud. She obviously expects a lot of me and holds me to a high standard, and I want to continue to be at that standard" (student of Cary Bricker).

These teachers' passion and energy also inspires their students to prepare and engage. "Because she cared so much, it made me want to care so much more than, maybe, I normally would have cared and made me want to be more engaged with the material just so I had something to contribute" (student of Nancy Knauer). "I feel like what she brings to the table that's different is her excitement, her enthusiasm, about the subject itself. . . . So, you know she's excited about it, so you want to do the reading and you want to have the base-line knowledge so you're prepared, because in class we go beyond . . . the assigned reading" (student of Julie Nice).

The teachers' enthusiasm and passion influences the students' feelings and outlook; they come to share their teachers' excitement and love for their courses and students' learning. "When you see the amount of time and effort you have to appreciate and respect him. . . . It wasn't that I was scared of him; that's not why I prepared. I prepared every day because I respect him as a person and . . . you can just tell how bad he wants you to get it. . . . Because he is just so into it, and I haven't found or studied from another teacher that's like that, and no other teacher has ever been able to make me want to learn as much as he has" (student of Rory Bahadur). "He'll say, 'I love what I do. I love teaching. I love my students and I love this subject' . . . And it gets you really pumped up. . . . Because you do want to make him proud. Because he's proud in what he does so you want to be proud in what you do. And just kind of raises you to another level, I think" (student of Andy Taslitz).

Desire to Not Disappoint Teacher, Students, Self

Current and former students of Bridget Crawford note that they wanted to prepare and perform well because they did not want to let her down. Their desire to not disappoint their teachers is a common source of motivation for students of these highly effective law teachers.

- "She has so obviously put so many hours into every lecture, discussion plan, and hypothetical, that students are simply unwilling to disappoint her class by giving anything less than their all" (student of Nancy Levit).
- "You know that he sees something in you and he expects you to live up to your potential, and then you don't want to disappoint him by doing that. He did lay out what he wasn't going to tolerate, like late work and missing classes, because that's not tolerated in the real world so why would it be tolerated here" (student of Larry Krieger).
- "It was one of those classes that you actually wanted to do the reading for her because you didn't want to let her down on some level" (student of Beth Enos).
- "You see him a lot at the outside functions. We had Barrister's Ball the other night; we saw him there. The Women's Law Association had a 5K run and he was there. When you see a professor actively engaged in the social stuff as well and supporting you, it kind of goes back to the you don't want to let him down, you want to do a good job because he's invested in you and you want to give back" (student of Steve Friedland).

Students' desire to "be there" for their teachers extends to attending class in challenging circumstances. "If she has to be away from class for a conference or something she always makes it up, and she makes it up at 7:30 in the morning. And that class is full. There is nobody who is not there at 7:30 in the morning, and she's got the coffee and the muffins. And I said to her once, 'You have no idea. Most people don't even go to their regular classes' ... Of course, you would get up and go because, first of all, you would miss something. You would actually miss something, and you just wouldn't want to disappoint her" (student of Ingrid Hillinger). "Who he is comes out in every lecture and that makes him very accessible, and that's why I think you have 3Ls who, the day before spring break, are there at 8:45 in the morning because there's a personal connection. I feel like I like this guy and I don't want to let him down" (student of Don Hornstein).

Beyond not wanting to disappoint their teachers, students feel a responsibility to their classmates and themselves. "I feel like he really made us accountable or at least feel like we were accountable to the class and to ourselves that we really wanted to excel and put the time in because there was just more of an incentive of doing other than just taking an exam at the end of the semester that every class I wanted to walk in, feeling prepared to talk" (student of Roberto Corrada). "I wanted to be prepared for her class.... Like, I would always read for her class my first year.... Her class was the first class I read for, because going in when you don't know what you're talking about and she can tell. She doesn't yell at you and make you feel belittled. She makes you disappointed in yourself in this very uncanny, like, professional way, and you just feel like you've let her down, and that inspired me to want to always be prepared. So I think that's one way that she fosters that professionalism is that it makes me want to come in and be professional" (student of Meredith Duncan). "Because every day you could see how much effort he put into preparing for the class, and on those days when I had put forth any effort to prepare, if I got called on and just derailed [in] class, I felt, you know, that's my fault; that's all my fault. That's why I would feel bad" (student of Andy Leipold).

The primary motivation for students of these teachers is not grades. Instead, students want to perform at a high level because of the relationships they have with their teachers. "Even though the class is like a pass/fail class, so initially you would think, 'Oh, I don't have to worry about that as much,' but actually makes me put in more hours weekly for that than for some of the other graded classes, because I feel more loyalty to him, because I realize he's working harder at it. He is paying attention to what I'm doing" (student of Larry Krieger). Students flock to these teachers even though they are tough graders. "Each student who's on the Howard Law Journal has to write a note or a comment, and you can pick a faculty advisor, and then you get graded from your faculty advisor. So everyone knows there are some professors that you can go, and they won't read it; you'll get a 99. It's easy. People know that he's hard and he still has the most . . . advisees" (student of Andy Taslitz).

Even when their students do not earn high grades, they want their teacher to know that they worked hard and feel bad that they did not perform well for the teacher. "Half the people who get bad grades in my class, who come to talk about their exam, they don't want to talk about the exam. They simply want me to realize that they didn't blow it off, that they didn't, you know, shortchange the class, that they really were interested. They really did try hard" (Andy Leipold). "I received my worst grade in law school from Professor Enos and the only thing that came out of that for me was feeling like I let her down, not that I was mad at her or that I thought that she was unfair, and it made me work that much harder" (student of Beth Enos).

Model Expectations and Work Ethic

These exceptional teachers consciously model their expectations for students. They walk the talk of high expectations. "Modeling what I expect, being prepared, being on time, you know, starting class exactly at 9:05, closing the door to signal that we are now beginning, and the students know that. Open-mindedness on my part, being able to criticize myself and say, 'Well that question maybe wasn't good. Your answer suggested to me something else.' Being able to model what I expect from them, is I think motivating, being a learner with them, saying, 'Oh, I never thought of that; that's a great point; what a nice way to say that; I didn't think of that.' Telling them my own need to struggle with the material. I think that's motivating to students" (Patti Alleva). "I want my students to learn first and foremost the importance of hard work, because I think, as a lawyer, as a law student, hard work and self-motivation is what determines success more than IQ. And so I go into class incredibly prepared, knowing every fact, having anticipated every question, and I want them to see that level of preparation that I am coming into class with. When they misstate a fact slightly, I want to be able to say, 'That's not what the case said. This is what the case said, isn't it?' . . . So the one thing I want them to learn is the importance of preparation and, rather than say that, I model it" (Rory Bahadur).

Students understand that these teachers are demonstrating their expectations. Students view these teachers as role models. "She set an example of utter exactness, forcing me to strive continually for greater alacrity of thought and clarity of expression. And also, she was always engaged, excited, ready, and willing to help. She served sort of as an ideal upon which one could attempt to model oneself, an archetype. And she makes you want to be a better lawyer, and you want to learn, not just to learn but to please her, to become a better advocate for your future clients by learning the intricacies of the law" (student of Patti Alleva). "Her expectations of us are her expectations of herself. I mean, she really pushes herself to do as hard of work as we do. She's there for every class. She's there when she's sick. She expects us to be there, and she's on time, and she brings energy every single class, and she's prepared. I feel like, to that extent, we're looking up at her as a role model, and she realizes she is, so how she acts also encourages us to be meeting the expectations that she has" (student of Cary Bricker).

Many students note that the high expectations were mutual—teachers expected as much of themselves as they did of their students. "Professor Levit sets high expectations for herself and conveyed similarly high expectations for her students" (student of Nancy Levit). "I could tell that [he] was working as hard as the students were working. Because it's very difficult for first-year law students in particular to grasp new concepts, and it is definitely a struggle. But I could tell that he was working just as hard in providing as many comments as he did. . . . His ability to inspire you to work as hard as you could was in part based on how much work you could see him doing" (student of Steven Homer). "What I take away from her is—and what she has taught me the most is work ethic, in that she works so hard in preparing her lesson plans, and she works so hard in really telling you what she wants and individualizing it and also bringing it to a group. You want to prepare as much as she does or even more" (student of Cary Bricker).

Several students phrased their reaction to mutual high expectations in terms of respect. "You could see how much effort he was putting in, and you wanted to put in that much effort because it was really showing that he was respecting your work and you really wanted to respect his as well by doing as well as you could" (student of Steven Homer). "It's like you get what you receive, so he always comes 110 percent. You better show your respect and give 100. . . . I don't owe you that respect, you know? You have to earn my respect and trust, right? He earns it . . . and so that's why I think people are a little bit different in the way they approach his class" (student of Andy Taslitz). "When a professor tries, the students notice that they're trying, and at least I know I feel like I so much more want to respect them and show them that I'm giving them my full attention because I know how hard they're trying" (student of Roberto Corrada).

Depth of Preparation, Class Participation, and Analysis

The teachers we studied explicitly communicate their expectations that students prepare deeply. "I also assign the students with the task of reading deeply and struggling with the material; that's part of my assignment to them. I ask them to read deeply. I ask them to go deep. I ask them to struggle. That's what you must do as part of this assignment, in my view" (Patti Alleva). "One of the things I tell the students is that I'm rereading the cases. If they're only reading the cases once, I can't imagine how difficult that must be for them, because how would they possibly going to be able to master the cases and understand the cases? . . . So I say to students, 'If you've read a case once, . . . that would be like you sit down with a sheet of music and you played it once, and then you go into a performance, and you're going to be called on in the performance to play the music, maybe explain the music, explain how it relates to all the other music you've had, but you've only sight-read the music once.' . . . I refer to reading a case once as moving your eyes across the lines once. You haven't prepared for class because you've moved your eyes across the pages I've assigned" (Julie Nice).

To allow students to prepare deeply, the teachers keep the amount of reading manageable for each class. "She really focused on depth and not breadth. . . . She's got a really good balance between reading and thinking. Because with more manageable reading assignments came the opportunity to synthesize it and put it together" (student of Patti Alleva). "He expected you to know in depth one or two cases, to really know in and out of what's going on . . . rather than 'I'm going to make you read six cases and then maybe we'll get a rule of law out of each of them'" (student of Roberto Corrada).

Two of Roberto Corrada's students note that his use of the Socratic method in class influenced their level of preparation: "I would say that he uses Socratic method, which really forced me to do the readings every night, really know what I was looking at, review it before class and then go into class. You would talk about it. So you kind of had three different steps where he's really making you learn it at three different times. The first time you read it; second time you review it; and then when you're in class. So you definitely want to be prepared for every class because he might call on you." "I briefed cases at the beginning of law school. Then I completely stopped, and I restarted for that class, and since then I only do it in some classes, but it's the same classes where I think I'll be on call for extended periods."

Students of these teachers tailor their preparation to match the extraordinary depth of questions that they will encounter in class. "You could think that you are very prepared for class and you are not. There were many cases in which he would say, 'And what did Thomas's Plurality say? And then, what did . . . Scalia say?' . . . He wants you to break down every single opinion. He's not looking for the rote, 'Okay, here's what the majority held and maybe here's what the dissent held.' . . . He wants every single justice's opinion, and why that's consequential to an outcome, and which one do you agree with and why" (student of Andy Taslitz). "He didn't ask dumb questions. He asked very, very hard questions; questions that you couldn't just look down and read from the book. You had to look up and think, and it was kind of nerve-racking, but it actually made you kind of synthesize what you'd learned" (student of Roberto Corrada).

The discussion and analysis in these teachers' classes go beneath the surface, beyond the elements of the law, to underlying policy, and to growth and change in the law:

- "In my mind he goes beyond the elements. I mean, I think there's a tendency in law school to break everything down and to factor in some elements and itty bitty components and almost make it into a trivia or, you know, that it's just black and white law. He's willing to go into the gray areas, and he expects you to go into the gray areas on his exams. He wants you to take a bigger picture instead of just focusing on this element is met, yes or no. . . . And so he challenges you to think outside of those rigid parameters" (student of Nelson Miller).
- "It seemed like every single case we would read, she would touch on the policy behind that law or that particular ruling, what the

judge is trying to get, and what alternatives there are. And so, when you're thinking about a particular . . . issue, I guess, [you need] to always be asking, 'Well, why is the law this way?'" (student of Meredith Duncan).

- "Not only does he want us to think about the past law . . . the things that have already been decided, he wants us to think of how things are going to be going in the future. . . . What's the new law that would be constructed from this opinion? What's the new law that might be constructed, based on these facts and this case? He makes you really, like, kind of think ahead and not just rely so heavily on the books and the rules." "He wants you to question things. He wants you to really go deep into the analysis, and he keeps the discussion very open" (students of Andy Taslitz).

- "The eye of inquiry is a little device I use. I draw an eye on the board, with a question mark in the middle of the eyeball. But I want my students to reach the eye of inquiry; I want them to constantly question and inquire. . . . The Civ Pro submarine. Get into your Civ Pro submarines. Let's go beneath the words of the rule. The words are the starting points. Let's go below the surface, and let's look at the intent of the rule, the application of the rule; let's get beyond the surfaces. So using the Civ Pro submarine, particularly in Civ Pro, when students are just beginning to understand that what the rule says is not necessarily what the rule means. To get below the surfaces" (Patti Alleva).

Responsibility, Professionalism, and Identity

Perhaps the highest expectations these teachers have for their students concern the students' development as professionals. That development begins with an expectation that students take responsibility for their learning while in law school. "Students learn to teach themselves only if they understand that the ultimate responsibility is theirs. A teacher needs to inspire and persuade students to prepare diligently for class, participate actively in class, and take the course material seriously. At the same time, the teacher should make sure that the students have enough guidance to do this hard work productively and efficiently" (Hiroshi Motomura). "I try to have the students take responsibility for the class. I discuss with students my goals for the class as well as my content selection and my assessment methods. We talk about all of these things in the context of appropriate goals. For example, we talk about the value of content versus process knowledge. I change and modify my approach to each class based on the thoughtful input of my students. TWEN and Blackboard are invaluable tools for surveying student thinking. My hope—and I have seen this happen—is that students will understand more about how to be proactive both in learning the substantive knowledge of a law course and in taking responsibility for their own learning" (Roberto Corrada). "I require class attendance. I say [that] not because I think that I have something so brilliant to say every second of the day but because this is a professional responsibility. It's a professional appointment that we have with each other. I have to be here because I have an obligation to you. You have to be here, not because you have an obligation to me but because you have an obligation to your classmates to be here and share your ideas, and you have an obligation to the people who are going to be depending on you to know how to do this stuff. So I try to motivate them through having a sense of responsibility" (Beth Enos).

One common strategy used by these teachers is to communicate that the students are already members of the legal profession who will soon be serving real clients; the teachers strive to train their students to focus on their clients' perspectives and needs. Paula Franzese begins class by greeting her students, "Good morning, property lawyers!" During class, she repeatedly asks, "Okay, property lawyers, how will you advise your client?" Likewise, Tina Stark explains her expectation that students learn to think transactionally: "They don't know what transactional lawyers do. They have to learn how to think from the client's perspective, learn how to explain so the client understands the deal." Steven Homer ties his high expectations to the needs of his students' future clients. "I'm not having high expectations because I want to see you squirm. I have high expectations because, at the end of the day, you are going to have a client and they need the best you can give within life-work balance issues. But they need the best that you can give."

Students learn professionalism, in part, through their teachers' expectations about classroom conduct. "She engaged the students in a way that you would expect to engage in a professional setting. I think that gave a lot of us an introduction to how we should behave, how we should comport ourselves, how we should expect to be treated, and those kinds of things" (student of Meredith Duncan). "I have a high expectation of professionalism in my classes. I tell students that class is a professional appointment, involving professional responsibilities. However, I do recognize that they are juggling many things. For example, if a student is unprepared, the student can simply tell me before class, and I will not call on that student" (Beth Enos).

Patti Alleva explains her efforts to help students develop their professional identities.

> I think perhaps one of the most important things is not subject
> but . . . that students learn more about themselves and their place

147

in the world. By that I mean a deeper self-awareness, a deeper other-awareness that leads to new ideas, new understandings . . . that what they learn is transformative, and they grow. . . . In any course, regardless of its position in the curriculum, these are . . . things I really . . . want my students to learn. Number one is the importance of what I call struggling with the material that I really want students to understand and experience. That learning is a) lifelong, and b) requires [a] process that they have to work at, that going deep requires working out your nonunderstanding, that it's something you have to grapple with. So I tell my Civ Pro students, "Guys, if you are not struggling, I'm wondering whether you are learning."

Second is I like them to learn the importance of questioning and challenging what appears to be. I like them to go below surfaces; I like them to test constantly. I like them to also next monitor and rethink their assumptions, which is part of questioning and challenging; want them to not be comfortable with the status quo either in themselves or in society. They may decide they like the status quo, but at least I want them to filter that through some type of system of questioning. And I would like them to learn the importance of open-mindedness. I think that is so critical to a) learning, and b) lawyering.

To me that also leads to humility. So I have this phrase called the "humility of open-mindedness," that if you are open to diverse viewpoints, and people, and ideas, you tend to realize, "Wow! I'm not the only thing in this world. There are a lot of good people, a lot of good ideas." So I think open-mindedness leads to humility, which to me is a critical feature of a lawyer, good lawyer.

In Professional Visions, I think students find very challenging, in terms of their learning, going inward, because the course pushes them inside themselves. It asks them to really confront who they are and who they want to be. It asks them to think and feel, hard, about where they are in their lives, why they want to be lawyers, and what does it mean to be a good lawyer, and a responsible lawyer.

Conclusion

A foundation for these teachers' educational excellence are the clear, high expectations that these teachers and their students have for themselves and for one another. Three final examples help illustrate this principle.

Some of the reading materials Ruthann Robson assigns are articles written by former students; this creates a powerful motivation for her current students. If they perform at a high level, their papers could be assigned in the future.

A student notes that Steven Homer's high expectations extend to his interactions with students outside class: "You don't go to him with lazy questions. You do your work beforehand. . . . He feels you out to see how much effort you put in yourself, and he matches that effort. That's what pushes you to strive to exceed his expectations with your own expectations, because you know you'll get the same quality out of him if you rise to that level."

Patti Alleva summarizes her expectations for her own teaching:

And so, in the end, teaching is about integrity, the integrity of teaching *intentionally,* and being self-conscious about setting and satisfying learning goals; and of teaching with *transparency,* and making known, when appropriate, what I am trying to achieve, and why; and of teaching with *consistency,* myself adhering to the standards I ask my students to meet; and of teaching with *high but reasonable expectations* for my students, believing in their potential, making it my responsibility (at least in the first instance) to motivate them, and encouraging them, again and again if necessary, to face the cognitive and emotional struggles often necessary to learn deeply; and, of course, teaching with *humanity,* treating students with fairness and respect, ever mindful of the power differentials and the multifaceted challenges of learning how to lawyer effectively and responsibly.

6

How Do the Best Law Teachers Prepare to Teach?

Preparation

The teachers we studied prepare themselves for every class as if they were doing so for the first time. They reimagine themselves as novices in their fields and consider the student perspective. They prioritize their most important learning goals, and they plan teaching strategies to achieve those goals. They reflect on their role as teachers and role models as they prepare. Andy Liepold describes his thinking about class preparation in a way that epitomizes the teachers we studied: "Taking teaching seriously means working very hard to prepare for class. . . . The hard part is to do the scud work. . . . There's an endless number of small details that . . . I need to be ready for."

Time on Task

Overwhelmingly, these teachers spend significant time preparing for class. On the days they teach, Rory Bahadur and Ingrid Hillinger arrive at their respective law schools long before the sun rises. Even if she is teaching a class that starts at 1:00 p.m., Hillinger, who has been teaching law for nearly twenty-five years, reports that, before she goes to sleep the night before, she reviews "some notes or a case or an article or something so that my brain will be working while I sleep," and she will "typically start to actually work on [her] class at 4:00 a.m." on the day of class. Similarly, Bahadur gets to school at 4:00 a.m. "for an eight o'clock that I have taught probably ten times in the last seven years."

Susan Kuo prepared diligently for each class session from the beginning of her teaching career: "When I first started teaching, I spent seventeen or eighteen hours per hour of class just prepping." Paula Franzese reports that she spends "two to three hours per class [session], and these are classes that I have taught many, many times before."

These teachers recognize that the small details matter and spend hours on them. "I read all the materials again, sometimes more than once. . . . I have my little Post-its and my little tags that I [use to] flag places in the casebook that I want to make sure that I direct their attention to" (Meredith Duncan). "I just think there is no substitute for fully preparing your material and mastering your material. You just have to do that. You have to put in the time until you get to that place. . . . It's a constant process. If you don't want to be stale, you have to be fresh with the material" (Julie Nice). While Nice acknowledges that her attention to detail is "stressful," she nevertheless tracks "what's happening in a real-time basis in constitutional law issues as they are developing . . . trying to figure out immediately how to incorporate those." "I reread very often. I go through the federal rules of evidence over and over again" (Cary Bricker). Paula Franzese even plans how she will use the white board during class: "I know what it is I'm going to write on the board. I know when it is that I won't need to write on the board simply because I want the students to listen and react. But I do know ahead of time precisely what it is that's going to be the visual. It's funny. I think about something as small as what am I abbreviating, when is it that I will state something orally to allow the students to jot it down, but actually what I am transcribing on the board is different from what I am saying to allow the student to enter the information by looking at what they just wrote down, by hearing what I said, and then looking at the board. Now three different things, three different ways of getting to the same point."

Ruthann Robson approaches the reading in three ways:

I prepare quite extensively for every class, even if it is material I have taught many times before, perhaps especially then. I read every assignment several times:

I first read as a student. I do think about particular students in the class at times, but mostly as a generic student. I try to think only about what we have covered so far in class. I look for new concepts or aspects of the readings that might be difficult, unfamiliar, or dissonant. I try to read the material as if I have never read it before.

I then read as a lawyer. I think about the parties' arguments, about how this case could relate to new situations, how the noncase material could be relevant in litigation. I look for any lawyering aspects of the material, including procedural matters.

Finally, I read as a law professor. I think about how the material fits into the overall learning goals for the semester and how the material could be tested. I evaluate it for how it relates to the previous classes and how it relates to future classes. I think carefully about how the material should be taught to this class at this time. I review my notes from previous semesters (if it is material I have taught before), including the notes I have made after previous classes assessing a teaching strategy used then. I then decide how the material should be taught in class.

Andy Taslitz repreparares from scratch every class session, even though he usually teaches out of casebooks he wrote: "I never use the same notes again. I always do new notes. It's very time-consuming, but I do that for every class. And I find it forces me to rethink what worked, what didn't work, what can I experiment with?"

Tina Stark also repreparares: "Every semester I redo the materials. . . . Each time I teach, I look for another way to explain the process. [For example], this year I completely rewrote the 'end game' materials—and 80 percent of the students got it. . . . I add new stuff every class, like using [party noisemakers] to make a point. I keep changing what I cover in each class and try to keep notes on what I covered and didn't cover. Often I am reordering the material." Philip Prygoski reads the cases he assigns and all the lower court cases that have applied the constitutional law cases he teaches. "Go to a case, find out what lower courts have done with it, and I think that's really a valuable exercise. . . . Most of the stuff happens just quantitatively in the lower courts. . . . I figure out how they extrapolated from it, how they interpreted it, and . . . relatively frequently, I'm rereading this stuff and say, 'Geez, that's new,' or 'I missed that.'"

Beth Enos rereads the materials and rewrites her teaching notes by hand: "I find that sometimes I read something, maybe a case I've been reading for years, and I'll read it again, and I'll think, 'Ah, I never thought about that.' I'll see it in a new way. So I always try to read what they've read for class. And get a fresh perspective on it. I use handwritten notes . . . because just the process of writing it out by hand helps me focus on things."

Rory Bahadur offers some rationales for this hard work: "I owe it to the students to be that prepared. Because if I'm not prepared, I can't be an effective teacher. . . . [Students] should never come to my class and say, 'Well, I'm just as prepared as you are,' which is not really prepared. I want to be able to say, openly, 'I spent three hours preparing this one case, and I've done it eleven times. How many hours did you spend?'"

Students recognize and appreciate their professors' hard work. For example, Nelson Miller's students laud his preparation as the best they have ever seen: "If you ever saw him prepare for a class, Dean Miller goes over and above anything that anybody has ever done." "He's working as hard as we are."

Students of other outstanding teachers we studied say similar things:

- "She's so obviously well-prepared and you know where the class is going, so you never really get lost, even if there's some sort of concept that's really out there" (student of Ingrid Hillinger).
- "She was the best prepared teacher I've had at any level of education" (student of Heather Gerken).
- "He puts more time into preparing and organizing each class than any professor I've had" (student of Stephen Homer).

- "It is obvious that she puts a lot of thought and preparation into each class" (student of Susan Kuo).
- "Degree of preparation and resulting mastery of subject material was outstanding, beneficial not only because of potential for 'learning' facts, rules, techniques, etc., but also because of effect on classroom environment" (student of Nancy Levit).

At least some of these teachers consciously chose to make preparation a priority after having a bad experience because they were once less than optimally prepared. For example, one teacher told us a story she entitled, "The Revenge of the Accountants":

> I was twenty-nine when I started teaching, but looked twelve. My second semester, I was assigned to teach the large evening introductory tax course of about eighty students. . . . I had not thought about some of the issues that I covered in my syllabus since I had taken tax in law school. . . . When we got to the section on depreciation and cost recovery, [my] tenuous hold unraveled. I knew walking into the classroom that evening that . . . things were still a little fuzzy in my own head. . . . I thought that we would run through the basics and then move on to the next (much less boring) subject. For many of my students, however, we were finally getting to a point in the course where they had some real life experience.
>
> I knew that I was in trouble within the first fifteen minutes. The student questions were much more detailed than I had anticipated. Given that I didn't have any clear answers, some of the accountants in the classroom intervened and offered their own answers, leading to a heated a discussion about company cars that I knew was off topic, but I couldn't seem to redirect. Toward the end of the class, all I could keep repeating was, "Really

good question. I'll look into it and get back to you next class." By the time class was over, I was defeated. I knew that they had lost confidence in me as a teacher, as well as my command over the subject matter. I felt like a fraud. It was terrible.

I spent the next several days learning everything that I could about cost recovery, its history and current uses. I determined that the company car conversation really was off topic, except now I could explain why. I was also able to explain which details we needed to know, and, most importantly, which details we did not need to know. I went back to the classroom full of enthusiasm, information, and examples. I worked very hard to stay in good cheer about the events of the prior class and even made a couple jokes about Temple students being a tough crowd. I could tell that the students appreciated my efforts, and it was a turning point for that class.

I think that things could have gone terribly wrong if I had reacted differently or let my frustration show. It was tempting to be angry with the students and dismiss their actions as unprofessional. After all, who were they to challenge me? I could have plowed right through to the next topic and shut down discussion by becoming more dictatorial in class. However, those knee-jerk reactions would have been a mistake because the problem had nothing to do with the students; the problem was my own lack of preparation.

Another teacher we studied reported a similar experience:

I was doing hypotheticals with students in a Civ Pro II class and neglected to change the numbering in my lecture notes, which contained the answers to the hypotheticals I was asking the class. A student came up with the correct answer, and I agreed with him that the answer was correct. I asked the obvious follow-up question, which required the student to justify his answer choice by pointing out specific language in a specific section of the rule. . . . However, the section of the rule, which the student correctly used to support his answer, was now numbered slightly differently than what my notes said. I . . . challenged the student to find the correct section of the rule. The student and I went back and forth and the student was adamant that he was correct. When I realized that the entire class was looking at me as if I had . . . gone completely nuts, I actually checked the rule book, and the student turned out to be correct. I immediately realized my mistake and told the student he was correct . . . I simply wanted to fall into a hole and never return because I had not practiced what I preached . . . The next class I used the opportunity to demonstrate in a humorous, self-effacing manner how, in rule and statutory-based litigation, checking and incorporating amendments is an essential part of professionalism. The admission was cathartic, and, thankfully, I survived . . . [but] when I think of the class, I still get a hint of that sickening feeling in my stomach.

Goal Driven

The teachers we studied focus their preparation on articulating and then planning how they will achieve their learning goals. Paula Franzese offered a global perspective on setting goals: "I take time at the start of each semester to ask myself, 'What do I want this term?' I want a classroom environment that inspires challenging, fruitful, and rigorous exchange, predicated on mutual respect and caring for each individual. I want the classroom dynamic to produce conversation in its original and most hopeful form—*conversare*—from the Latin meaning 'conversion.' I aim to direct that exchange, but not to control it with too tight a grasp. I hold on loosely (with apologies to 98 Special), and welcome the moments of recognition, of enlightenment, of connection, and of self-correction, my own and my students."

Bridget Crawford designs class sessions with goals in a way that is typical of these exceptional teachers: "First and foremost I ask, 'What do I want them to get out of the class session, both specific substance, then skills?' Then I also ask 'What do I want to convey to them? What's the message either about the field, the subject, the profession?' So I try to be as clear as I can about what I am trying to accomplish. . . . I include in my course materials a clear statement of 'Learning Objectives,' i.e., a list of what each student should be able to do (or distinguish, analyze, explain, name, calculate, etc.) after each unit. At the end of the semester, a student who meets each Learning Objective will be able to answer successfully any final examination question."

Nelson Miller believes that identifying goals benefits both him and his students: "I am explicit in stating for my benefit and the benefit of instructional design and students' benefit what . . . each course's general goals are and then also specific class objectives. I am as transparent about those goals and objectives as I can be. . . . And I display them before every class, at the beginning of every class so we're just all on the same page." Julie Nice and Hiroshi Motomura similarly note the importance of having goals. "Every class session and every course I have different goals over all and specifics. And those are never out of my mind. My primary question going into any class session or any course is, 'What knowledge and what skills and what values do I want to emerge from the practices of my classroom?'" (Julie Nice). Hiroshi Motomura reports that, in preparing for class, "I write down three things that I want to get out of the class. I mean, they're typically very specific things about the material, you know, that I want them to understand—that—the relationship between the specificity rule in pleading and who has the burden of pleading, that would be the main thing. [Another] thing that I do preparing to teach any given hour is I think about coverage and, sort of, what's the minimum I want to do and what do I feel comfortable not getting to?"

Susan Kuo prioritizes her goals: "In the back of my mind (which is also in my scripted-out notes), this is what I need to get through to make my point for today. There are always some parts that I don't get to, but it's not important."

Don Hornstein focuses on what he calls the four or five "emotional and intellectual high points." "I have that as a subscript for every one of my classes. . . . I sit there for a half an hour before the class, and I remind myself what that is, and that's really my outline for the class—is those four or five things."

Specific Goals

While all of the teachers we studied teach with multiple learning goals in mind, they vary in terms of their specific goals. For example, Nancy Levit's goals are broad ranging: "I want them to learn how to learn. I want them to learn how to learn the material on their own. I want them to think about the ways in which they learn material differently depending on, say, a substantive area. . . . The other thing [I want my students to learn] is to learn how to treat people from day one." Bridget Crawford and Julie Nice also want their students to grow as learners. "Mostly I want them to learn to be self-sufficient learners. What more could one want?" (Bridget

Crawford). Nice attributes her increased emphasis on learning to her development as a teacher: "Trying to impart knowledge to my students used to be my primary focus. Increasingly I think having my students develop the skills of acquiring knowledge and a way to understand what values are being reflected are increasingly more important to me."

Ruthann Robson aspires to multiple goals including teaching each student to be "a good social justice lawyer; how to do good work; what are the kinds of things you can do? . . . I really do think of law school as 'training to be a lawyer,' but . . . it's not just about lawyering skills; it's critical thinking skills; it's how to make a good argument, how to make a precedent." Robson also wants her students to understand and use theory in practice: "Theory is a kind of skill. . . . You can talk about originalism as a theory, but how does it drive the cases? . . . How do you use it when appealing to someone who agrees with it? How do you use [theory] when you are making an originalist argument, when you're countering an originalist argument?"

Andy Leipold has a core goal of teaching his students to exercise judgment: "This most important thing I can do for students is to teach them a way of thinking about legal issues that is independent of the subject matter. . . . Legal reasoning is not about finding the right answers, but about exercising mature judgment after considering the competing interests. Or, as I frequently tell students, a legal education is not about what you think but how you think. A big part of my job is to lead them through this process, then ask them to articulate their analysis in ways that advance the process of solving legal problems."

Rory Bahadur has practice-focused goals: "I want my students to learn first and foremost that lawyers don't ever have answers.

They have arguments. . . . I want them to learn to think like a law-yer in terms of a concrete task that they will be doing as lawyers, and so I introduce into my classroom a lot of practice documents." Paula Franzese also has law-practice goals: "I provide reminders as well of what the imperative is, of what the goal is. The point is to do good as a lawyer. . . . I like to set up moral presets as well, 'What does it mean to be a good person, to be a good lawyer?' 'Can we perceive the struggles of our clients?' 'What does it mean to recon-struct the case so we are thinking about the people behind the tragedy?' "

Roberto Corrada's goals include disrupting the normal teacher-student hierarchy: "[I pay a lot of attention] to hierarchy and . . . try not to go in and pretend, you know, I know it all, and they don't know anything. . . . And of course everything in the classroom is playing against you there because you're at a podium, the lights are shining on you, and it's very clear who the one important person is in here, and that's before you even say word one. So I consciously think about what I can do to sort of get away from that as much as possible." Corrada's major second goal is producing analytical thinking. "I try to get beyond the doctrine, like . . . 'Is there another rule that could be better?' 'Can we talk about policy here?' 'How can we sort of deconstruct this doctrine?' "

Hiroshi Motomura's and Patti Alleva's goals are evident to their students. "I think that he makes it a point to—at least in Immigra-tion class—to do policy, to do doctrine, and to do statutory inter-pretation" (student of Hiroshi Motomura). "In her course syllabus she doesn't just list the pages to read; she also has overarching learning goals. And I think that's primarily what you take from her course; it's not just the law. . . . You also need to think of policy, social justice concerns, thinking critically, communication and interpersonal relationships, and ethics and professionalism, along with your readings" (student of Patti Alleva).

Larry Krieger is particularly ambitious; he not only wants to help his students become effective lawyers; he also aspires to help students maximize their lives: "What I do to prepare to teach each class is I keep working on myself as a human being. That—you know, the evolution of my teaching from being, I would say, [a] really fairly stressed teacher . . . too much ego, too much talking. . . . I keep working on myself to try to get what I'm trying to impart with the students, which is how to live a good life as a human being within this work context. . . . That's what I'm trying to teach."

Taking the Student Perspective

In preparing for class, the teachers also strive to be empathic and understand their students' perspective. Tina Stark asserts that taking the student perspective is a necessary part of class preparation: "To teach a complex subject, a professor must first look at the material from the students' perspective." Nancy Levit explains a very similar approach: "I try to empathetically imagine if I were learning this for the first time, what would this forest look like to me?"

Roberto Corrada articulates his approach to sensitizing himself to the students' perspective:

> I try to remember what I was like as a student. What tripped me up? What was going to be hard in that class? What was going to be counterintuitive versus what was going to be intuitive? And then when I'm setting up the syllabus for a class, I think about that and I remember, here's this counterintuitive doctrine. I'm going to spend an extra class on this or maybe an exercise related

to this. . . . I found that over the years as I get farther and farther from my law-school experience as a student, and the more I'm a professor in class teaching subjects that I'm already very familiar with, it's tougher and tougher to be empathetic, and so now I rely on research assistants or former students. . . . I may bring them in and ask them some things about, you know, what was hard here and what was easy, especially with new courses that I'm teaching.

Andy Taslitz and Beth Enos similarly focus on the student experience. "I say, okay, I'm the student. Will I understand what he's saying? What does he want me to get out of this? How am I supposed to not only know what he wants me to know, but how am I supposed to get there? What tools are there? What were the points of the class? . . . One of my criticisms of many teachers is that they adopt casebooks for themselves and not for the students. . . . They're not necessarily the best tools for the student to learn" (Andy Taslitz). "I try to see the material the way I think they're going to see the material. What's going to catch their attention in this material? What's going to confuse them? Where might they get off track here, especially with cases sometimes? The court went off on this tangent, that's just—that's wrong. Don't go there" (Beth Enos).

Nelson Miller makes a similar point about being sensitive to students' experience of his course materials: "Law has a vast knowledge base, and I don't ever want to underestimate a student's challenge in acquiring it, because I think the moment I do make assumptions about their capacity to quickly acquire some of those what seem like very basic frameworks and how they're used . . . is probably the minute that I've missed where they are in their learning and failed to support it."

Paula Lustbader changes her class as she comes to better understand her students' needs: "I have a series of materials; I have a series of hypotheticals; I have a series of my assignment sheets from last year that I keep working on, but they always change because I'm now depending on where I see the classes and what I think that they need to be doing."

Students appreciate that their teachers consider their perspectives:

- "He's also really respectful of our time. There's no hundred-page assignments, read twenty pages that are just unimportant to anything you'll ever do. Everything is very calculated and, for a reason, thought out ahead of time to make sure that we use our time in the best way we can" (student of Steve Friedland).
- "She assigned relatively small amounts of reading but it was very clear about what you were supposed to get out it. It was very well-designed. . . . It wasn't read sixty pages to get two points out of it. It was, you know, ten, twelve, twenty pages at most, and . . . it was easy to keep up with the class and therefore be prepared to speak intelligently in class" (student of Ingrid Hillinger).
- "She doesn't write her syllabus for the whole course. . . . She sort of maps out the first couple of weeks, the things she knows she wants to get to, and then, based on what people's interests are . . . will tailor the class to what people are most interested in, in the class" (student of Julie Nice).

Detailed Teaching Plans

The teachers we studied strive to plan their classes so that the students learn what the teachers want them to learn. Many teachers carefully script their questions before class, anticipate student questions, familiarize themselves with the teaching methods literature, strive to maximize each moment in the classroom, make conscious choices about how they start and end class sessions, find ways to motivate students, ensure their class sessions are well-organized, and think about students as individuals as they plan for each upcoming class.

Scripting Questions

Nearly all the teachers plan their questions. "I think through some specific questions that I want to ask in class. It may only be the one question that matters, that I start with, or maybe the second question, but it'll be the question that in some sense, you know, aligns the class into where I want them to go. Often it's a tactical question about 'What is the point of doing this?'" (Hiroshi Motomura). "I do a really detailed outline. It's really kind of [a] script. When I have questions that I want to ask them, just like you would do for direct examination, I write out the answer that I think I'm looking for. (I also write out the questions.) And I think of the sequence in which they come, and, like, what I want to ask first, where I want to start, because having the right answer written down helps me to listen to what they're saying" (Steven Homer). "I think about important questions. I write the questions and the answers in my notes for class" (Heather Gerken). Cary Bricker plans her questions to ensure an active learning atmosphere: "I do a whole outline for myself of questions I'm going to ask them, because I like to keep it really, really active, and I want them to do all the talking."

Anticipate Student Questions

The teachers we studied also anticipate their students' questions. "I imagine every single question I think a student could ask," says Rory Bahadur, going on to explain that he then reads an article or case "that provides the answer for that, so I could be thinking eight or nine steps ahead of them. I have to go into class comfortable in my gut [with] what I'm teaching. I can't go into class with any doctrinal gaps. If there are doctrinal gaps in what I'm going to teach the class, I'm uneasy, and I'm off my game, and it's obvious to me, so I never let that happen."

Meredith Duncan anticipates her students' questions so well that they believe she can answer any question: "She never comes to class and she hasn't quite you know fully anticipated questions or read through the case in a way that allows her to answer questions" (student of Meredith Duncan).

Teaching and Learning Expertise

Many of the teachers in our study educate themselves about teaching and learning and use their learning in preparing for class. "I really do believe in instructional design. I am truly committed to it, to discerning and stating course objectives, outcomes, and then aligning instruction and assessment to those objectives and in making the old-fashioned Maher-style measureable objectives and doing it responsibly and having criteria for when those objectives are achieved" (Nelson Miller).

Paula Lustbader illustrates her expertise regarding teaching and learning in explaining her approach to course design:

People learn and develop cognitive skills progressively. They work from a foundation of acquired knowledge and skills, and, as they learn new information and skills, they build upon this foundation. My pedagogy is modeled in large part after Jerome Bruner's spiral curriculum. I begin by teaching students the necessary foundation of information and basic skills and then build progressively with more complex and sophisticated concepts and skills. My courses are designed to help students move through the developmental progression. I take the time to teach each stage, model it, and then give the students exercises so they can master each stage. Each class builds upon the learning skills, developmental stages, and substantive law that we covered in the previous week. I use practice exams and writing exercises that become progressively more sophisticated. As the class progresses, I provide less explicit instruction and place greater responsibility on the students; thus, my role shifts from being a sage on the stage to a guide on the side.

Roberto Corrada uses his expertise in planning ways to recapture his students' attention: "[Studies] suggest that nobody can really pay attention for more than twenty minutes at a time. . . . If you're continuing for an hour and fifteen minutes on a line, you can lose a lot of people. . . . I try to plan moments every twenty minutes or so in the classroom to stop, make a joke, or just pause and collect everybody back."

Bridget Crawford keeps up with the literature on teaching and learning, looking through "about every book the library gets on teaching techniques. . . . Sometimes I get great ideas; sometimes I don't, but I'm always on the lookout." Beth Enos similarly uses her understanding of teaching and learning to design her class sessions:

"We've got an hour-and-a-half class. That's a long time to pay attention. . . . One topic might be more case dense. So we have more cases to read on a particular topic. Another topic—I think we don't need to read a lot of cases on that. We're going to read one case on that and do some problems on this. So I think about what techniques I'm going to use, based on what topic we're covering, and then also to make sure I'm doing a variety of things throughout the class."

In preparing to teach, the teachers we studied intentionally connect explicit student-learning goals, understanding of students, and their knowledge of teaching methods. Steve Friedland ties his planning process in with his learning goals, his sense of the limits of his time with students, and his goal of using a wide variety of teaching methods: "I think of it as a meal. I don't want to have all entree; I need appetizer; I want to have some dessert, which is why I now show more video and things like that just for a couple of minutes. . . . I also ask what do I want the students to be doing, and how they're doing it, and where do I want them to be at the end of class?" Andy Taslitz similarly believes in having a carefully constructed plan for his courses that includes goals, reading assignments, and how, when, and why he will use specific teaching methods. To accomplish his goals, Taslitz says, "I start preparing for class when I do my syllabi. [I want] to have a very clear idea of where I'm going for each class and what it's going to lead to and why I'm doing that. So I spend a lot of time preparing my syllabi down to not just the pages but, you know, what goals do I have for each class, what methods am I going to use for each class? And so I try to do that way, way in advance." Tina Stark also prepares by focusing on achieving her teaching goals: "I will use whatever technique of teaching works best: lecture, collaborative exercises, role-play,

Socratic method, videos, demonstration, or, more often, some combination of techniques."

Maximize Value of Classroom Time

Many of the teachers strive to maximize their classroom time with their students. "My sense of how he prepares for class is he thinks about what he wants to cover in those fifty minutes, and [the] other one of his virtues is how intentional he is about wanting to get through these thirty-six things in fifty minutes. It's, like, boom! The starting gun fires, and he works through it. . . . One of the things I love about him is the pedagogical focus, you know. He is completely self-conscious each day about what he wants to get through" (student of Hiroshi Motomura). "You feel like everything she does, there's a rationale behind it. Like, you feel pretty confident that you're not wasting your time in anything that she gives you" (student of Meredith Duncan).

"I didn't like [it]—as a student—when I didn't feel confident that the professor knew where we were headed and had a plan on how we'd get there. It drove me crazy. So I want to be sure that we use those fifty minutes effectively, that I have a plan" (Steven Homer). Similarly, the effort to maximize her classroom time with students has caused Julie Nice to reject some teaching techniques that work well for others: "I'm evaluating whether this is the best use of the class time right now. . . . I do a lot less [of small groups] than I used to. I'm not sure I'm right about that, but it's just . . . my own meager attempt to assess the value-added of how we spend our time. . . . I'm just going to go with the feedback I get from them indirectly and directly and my own sense of is this the best use of their time?"

Motivate and Engage Students

The teachers we studied make engaging and motivating students a core goal for their class preparation. "Surprise. I like surprise. Every now and again.... Sometimes I'll go to class early and put a word behind the screen, and then I'll press the button and lift the screen, and use the word behind the screen as the starting point for the discussion. So surprise, drama, flair, a little performance, without insincerity or inauthenticity.... Leaving them with something tangible, I think that's exciting for students" (Patti Alleva).

Nancy Knauer connects her efforts to make the material relevant to her goal of being student centered. She says, "Assume that you're going to be met with some skepticism by students as to why this is relevant and why they should care and you have to sort of answer those questions." Bridget Crawford strives to influence the overall mood of the class: "Part of the fun and the challenge of being a classroom teacher is to make that a learning and exciting experience.... It's not just a box that can be checked because [the students] do have to learn a lot of it on [their] own."

Meredith Duncan and Julie Nice seek to spark interest by making their courses as current as possible. "If I've read something and it was interesting a few months ago or a year ago, I put it in the file because I like to use current things that they will be able to relate to—movies, books, things like that, and so I can use those as examples" (Meredith Duncan). "At the end of the day I believe if I'm connecting what they're learning to their lives and real time, it's better for them ..." (Julie Nice).

Other teachers find creative ways to make their courses come alive for their students. Nelson Miller, for example, finds newspaper articles addressing topics relating to the particular material he is teaching, gives them to students in advance, and has students present the articles to the class. Playing the role of management, Roberto Corrada structures his Labor Law class so that the students learn how to unionize; the students know that, if they succeed in forming a union, they can negotiate the course structure and grading. Beth Enos and Andy Leipold contact the attorneys who handled the cases they teach. In class, they share the attorneys' original insights about the clients, the judges, or case strategies and theories. Two of Leipold's students spoke of this practice in glowing terms: "He'll call and say what was this client like? How did you meet him? What was he like in person? Just a really interesting backstory.... It's such an interesting idea, and I don't know any other law professor that does it." "He did that, it seemed like, for every case, and so one time he wrapped up and, like, we were waiting for the—you know—him to tell us about the lawyer he called. And so finally someone said, 'Professor Leipold, did you talk to the lawyer on this case?' He [said], 'I tried, but I couldn't get a hold of him.' We were . . . so let down."

Teachers also engage students by attending to them on an individual level. "Prof. Gerken also manages to keep track of who says what in every class and distributes 'air time' accordingly" (student of Heather Gerken). "I sit with my list of students and I contemplate who do I need to hear from, who hasn't been present enough in terms of verbal contribution to class?" (Paula Franzese). "I think about the students who don't—haven't—participated that much, you know. Can I bring them in more?" (Roberto Corrada). In Cary Bricker's regular meetings with her coteacher, she says, "We'll talk sometimes about individual students who are having problems, and ways to deal with that, so that goes into the prep as well."

Organization

For many of the teachers we studied, preparing an organized class is a critical goal. Heather Gerken says, "I spend a great deal of time on my classroom notes so the discussion is organized and coherent." "I want to be organized. Disorganized teaching . . . gets in the way of learning" (Don Hornstein). "I try to use frameworks for everything. I'm going to give them the beginning of the course, the GPS, the framework for the whole course. Then I'll have frameworks for each system. . . . I use Starbucks as an example . . . Here are the coffee drinks. . . . Here's the food. You know exactly what you're getting, whether you're in Spokane or Greensborough" (Steve Friedland). Hiroshi Motomura also carefully plans his teaching in a way that makes the organization transparent: "I actually have a folder called 'Today,' and then I put whatever map I want on the manager map. I also start the class with just the daily agenda on a word document, because I used to write that on the board, and now it's just clearer to put it this way."

Reflect on Teaching

The teachers we studied reflect about their teaching before and after class. Bridget Crawford's preparation efforts start with an evaluation of how things went the last time she taught the topic: "I mostly think about what didn't work the last time, so I've reviewed my notes and tried to come up with new ideas." Beth Enos also includes reflection on her teaching as part of her class preparation process, engaging in reflection both after each class session and as she prepares: "I also take notes from year to year. So I go over my notes from the year before about what worked and what didn't work." Similarly, one of the reasons Andy Taslitz redoes his notes every time he teaches is that "it forces me to rethink what worked, what didn't work; what can I experiment with?"

After each class session, Taslitz tries to evaluate his efforts: "If there's not a class immediately after my class, I just ask a few students to stay . . . and I ask them, what'd you learn? . . . Are you confused about anything? . . . From that feedback I may go back to my office and do a different exercise or plan to address the class differently the next day."

Meredith Duncan also reviews each class session right after it ends so she can identify ways to enhance the next class: "Somebody gave me really good advice when I first started teaching: that there's nothing that you can say today that you can't fix tomorrow. And so I think about what I need to fix." Bridget Crawford also evaluates what may have gone "too well." Because students had been confused about a topic one semester, Crawford prepared a detailed handout she gave students the next semester: "There wasn't a single question. . . . To me that tells me that I presented it too clearly and didn't show them the murkiness of this particular tax rule . . . I zoomed out all the messiness, and so then I know I need to change it."

Paula Franzese explains her efforts to reflect on her teaching:

I think, as well, I know that I spend time after each class for an hour or so, thinking about what just happened. Did I meet my intentions for that class? I have a set of intentions before going in, a set of principles that I would like to establish, and also a set of lawyering skills I'm hoping to encourage, and I think about what went right, what didn't; who made a really good connection that I want to build upon for the next class; where was there a lingering concern where I did not adequately address? . . . I think, also, about how my students interact with each other, during role-playing or small-group simulations and then—it's the sweetest thing—I've noticed my students' capacity for kindness towards each other. . . . I take lots and lots of notes. I have a binder, and it contains all of my supplementary materials, but it will also contain my own personal journal of sorts. It contains my notes on points that I need to get back to; it will contain the names of certain students who raised questions that I think are particularly resonant so that those students will forever be associated with that particular point."

Conclusion

Patti Alleva's preparation process illustrates many of the mental and physical steps the teachers we studied take when preparing for class. She asks herself a series of questions:

- [Are] there any questions or issues from the last class that need to be clarified?
- What learning do I hope to facilitate today?
- What are the concepts I hope I could encourage learning about, what processes, what skills, what subjects?
- What order should I present the materials to ensure deeper understanding?
- How should I transition?
- What are the trouble spots?
- What are the subject areas that the students are going to stumble over in my estimation?
- What areas will students resist?

- If I was a student in the class, what three things have I just taken out of the class?
- Are there new things I should be doing, that I haven't done before, that will be better to improve the learning?
- Where are we in the course?
- How's the overall learning going?
- Have any students been missing class with any regularity?"

In addition, because she begins classes "with a summary of where we've left off . . . regaining, remembering where I was so I can now incorporate it as I think through the whole" is also part of Alleva's preparation process. She then focuses on "doing supplemental research and reading obviously new cases, looking at other case books, looking at treatises to supplement my casebook."

Once she has a plan for a class session, she rehearses it: "I lay out on my desk, my book, my notes, my overheads, my handouts, literally, so that I can walk through the class from start to finish. I know at which point I'm going to go to which overhead. . . . It doesn't always come out that way, but at least I have a plan going in."

7

How Do the Best Law Teachers Engage Students in and out of the Classroom?

Four Core Behaviors

The classes of the twenty-six teachers we studied sometimes seem almost magical, suggesting that good teaching is more art than science. Overall, these teachers share four core behaviors in the classroom. They (1) consciously structure their class sessions to achieve their learning goals, (2) show they care about students, (3) make classes relevant, and (4) are extremely effective with their chosen teaching methods. In addition, they extend their teaching outside the classroom, effectively handle teaching challenges, and begin and end classes and courses well.

Emphasize Goals

Most of the teachers we studied provide their students with explicit learning goals at the beginning of every class. For example, Nancy Levit writes her goals in the center of the whiteboard before class starts, and, while she writes and erases many things over the course of a class session, the goals remain front and center. Nelson Miller's goals are on one of the first PowerPoint slides he shows; he also reviews the goals verbally, explicitly addressing strategies for learning his course material, talking to students about their approaches to learning the subject, mnemonics, and, more generally, about the students taking control over their own learning process.

Emphasizing goals causes these teachers to make student learning the central, defining activity in their classrooms. For them, teaching is not about what they teach; it is about what their students learn. "You're not teaching if they're not learning" (Julie Nice). Hiroshi Motomura expresses the importance of student learning in an instructive way that is typical of the teachers we studied: "Teachers should not let their experience and expertise blind them to the fact that they are there for the students. What matters is what the students are learning, not how impressively the teacher is performing. In the best classes, the teacher may seem to be doing very little that is noteworthy, but the students are."

Students appreciate that their teachers focus on explicit goals:

- "You feel like he not only commands the attention in the room but that at the end of the day you will hit upon the point that he wants you to hit upon" (student of Andy Leipold).
- "There's no way you're going to remember every single detail [about evidence] for the bar, let alone at real life. But you will now

know what's important, and you'll remember how to figure it out, and you'll know also I should look at these advisory committee notes because they probably do have some bearing" (student of Andy Taslitz).

- "Class is not about 'professor show time'" (student of Ruthann Robson).
- "He prioritizes the learning experience over the material being taught.... [He goes] out of his way to make sure that people are learning. The point [is] to teach the students, and to check with them, and to ask questions, and to be available, to be fully willing to go all the way back to the beginning of the conversation" (student of Hiroshi Motomura).
- "She not only conveys the information, but engages the class to the point that we internalize the information.... She incorporates our ideas and most importantly our doubts into the discussions, when she could have ... just stated the rule" (student of Susan Kuo).

Focus on Student Learning

The emphasis on making sure their students learn specific goals causes these teachers to check regularly for understanding and improvise new ways of explaining concepts if their initial efforts do not succeed. "I'm a big believer in repeating. Either repeating what a student has just said ... or repeating what I've just said.... I'm also a big believer in slowing it down, if I need to.... I'll say, 'Did everyone get that?' If not, I'm going to try it one more time. I'll try to say it again and say it again" (Patti Alleva). "He asked, 'Are you all getting this?' or something like that, and he just saw all our faces ... he was, like, 'All right, let me explain it a different way,' and he actually took the time to go back and try to re-explain the concept just to make sure that we were all getting it, even though nobody said specifically, 'I don't get this'" (student of Don Hornstein). "He has a way of checking in with the class that I really appreciate. . . . When he explains something in class, he will literally pause . . . and be, like, 'Does that make sense?' And then he'll pause for like a minute, and then he'll, like, look at everyone in the room. And you know what? [After] that pause . . . there are a lot of questions" (student of Hiroshi Motomura).

Organized and Structured

Outstanding teachers have a clear structure for their classes. "I put the material in multiple contexts. I give a roadmap for each class, and an overview of the next few classes. This helps students to follow the discussion and anticipate the relevance of what comes next" (Steven Homer). Paula Lustbader begins class sessions with a roadmap of the topics for the class on the board. Nelson Miller's class sessions are carefully structured; he appears to have thought through the questions of sequence, priorities, the match between teaching methods and his goals, what he and his students will each be talking about in class, and the use of visuals. As he moves through the classroom, even his position in a wide variety of spots in the classroom appears to be the product of conscious choice. Patti Alleva believes in providing both large-scale and small-scale structure: "I am a big believer in context. . . . I begin most courses . . . by going over the syllabus, creating the framework in which we are about to group proceed. [I provide] minioutlines as we go, taking minichunks of the larger piece when we hit the chunks."

Julie Nice provides what she calls "coding. Which is basically kind of like what a social scientist would do if they had a body of research material and they're looking for patterns. . . . I'm trying to show students how to find patterns of argumentation. So we take a case and code it for types of argumentation. So, right now, for example, it's such a hot topic with all the Prop 8 stuff, we did same-sex marriage. And we coded what are the possible arguments that could be made for defending a ban on same sex marriage or opposing it—and where do we see those arguments in the various cases that we're reading?" Similarly, in her classes, Heather Gerken identifies important terms, regularly summarizes, cues students on where they are and where they are going, and relates the class discussion to scholarly arguments and law practice. Likewise, in her classes, Ruthann Robson provides clear signaling, such as indicating when she is shifting the discussion to different topics and connecting the conversation to previous material.

Students repeatedly commend the outstanding quality of the structure provided by their teachers. They appreciate how having a structure helps them learn:

- "[His] teaching style conveys the information in a way that you can organize and use" (student of Philip Prygoski).
- "I feel like a skill that you develop in law school is being able to not only have the ability to use details and really dense material but also to see the big picture at the same time. . . . I don't think I've ever really had a an experience in any other . . . classroom where I've been so transparently involved in the process of utilizing the details and also seeing the big picture at the same time" (student of Hiroshi Motomura).

- "She is able to break really complex concepts, especially with Con Law, down so they make sense, and her organization of the class and the topics is just phenomenal. She creates the road map on the board" (student of Julie Nice).
- "He always told us which step we were in and mapped out where we would go next" (student of Rory Bahadur).
- "Her lectures are always clearly organized, which aids in the understanding of the material. In particular, her PowerPoints and blackboard outlines show the direction of the class and the interrelationship of concepts" (student of Susan Kuo).
- "[She] gives points she wants you to take away from each class. She provides a clear map—theories, concepts, cases—and she does a great job introducing things, then coming back and wrapping it up" (student of Bridget Crawford).

In many of the classes we observed, teachers provide structure by reviewing key points from prior class sessions at the beginning of class and/or reviewing the key points at the end of class. "At the very beginning of class her recaps would gradually get you into that class and it would remind you how the things interclick. . . . You would build what you're learning today onto what you learned in the last class. And because of that, your notes would be clear and concise because they would really flow" (student of Nancy Knauer). "One thing that really helped me was at the beginning of each class he would spend the first ten minutes reviewing the main points we had done the previous class" (student of Roberto Corrada). "I think one of the best things Professor Friedland does is at the beginning of every class he always talks about where we've gone. So we review; we talk about what we've done, where we're going, and the day's materials as well" (student of Steve Friedland).

Students note that the structure teachers provide in class helps them make connections and see a course's framework. One of Roberto Corrada's students analogized learning in law school to putting together a puzzle, explaining that "a lot of teachers give you all the pieces but never show you the full picture.... He goes over it almost every day in class. This is the picture. Then he shows you little pieces of the picture, but he always relates it back to how the whole picture comes together and how all the little pieces work together" Meredith Duncan's students similarly appreciate her willingness to help them see the connections among the concepts they are learning, "One thing that I really like is a lot of times you kind of get so into the case that you lose the big picture idea, and she makes sure that you always know where exactly this fits into the big picture. So, like right now, we've been doing conflicts of interest. She always makes sure that you know these are the rules for concurrent conflicts, and these are the rules for successive conflicts."

Flexible

Although these highly effective teachers are structured and organized, devoting many hours to their class preparation, they are also extraordinarily flexible while they are teaching. They have no qualms about going off script to ensure that their students learn. Paula Lustbader points out how flexibility supports her philosophy that teaching is collaborative: "What they're giving me in class then helps me decide where I'm going to go in the next five minutes.... It's that give and take ... 'Tell me where you guys are. Tell me what you understand about this. Tell me what you don't understand.'" Similarly, Julie Nice notes:

If I am teaching a really good class, I am with the students in the moment, and it's not total improvisation, but I try to get as close to jazz as I can in there. . . . It's one of my rules of teaching: work with whatever they give you. . . . I'm not saying they're in charge because I very much feel that we're the conductors while we're up there . . . [The highest] compliment I think I've ever received on a student evaluation is a student who said most days in this course felt like a trading floor of ideas. And to me, that's what I'm trying to achieve. And if I'm truly committed to that, there has to be room for this organic collective process to really emerge. It is not always successful, but I believe that my least successful trading floor of ideas, or jazz classes, are still better than my early teaching: fully canned, prepared set of notes where I'm so focused on what I want to impart to them that they're not as actively participating in the learning process.

Students deeply appreciate their teachers' flexibility:

- "She's just 100 percent there. She's not like 'What was that? What was my plan? . . . She's completely in control of it, but she will go somewhere else . . . and still seamlessly bring it back" (student of Ingrid Hillinger).
- "She knew exactly what information and lessons she wanted to impart in every class, but she was not rigid in her teaching. She would constantly adjust to the class as it went, whether it was to pursue a new idea a student had raised, to try another approach when the class was having trouble understanding a concept, or to make sure that all the students were participating" (student of Heather Gerken).
- "His lesson plan's very fluid. He's not, sort of, like, stuck in the 'We're going to cover this, this and this.' He's sort of following the

class and so, because his lesson plan is fluid, I think that it helps the students, sort of, like, learn and adjust better" (student of Andy Taslitz).

- "[She] takes risks . . . able to improvise . . . just flows" (student of Ruthann Robson).

Demanding

As noted in Chapter 5, the focus on student learning doesn't mean that the teachers we studied make things easy for students in class. Bridget Crawford keeps expectations high by bringing the discussion back to the texts, asking students to talk about "theory, theory, theory." She never lets the students wander off topic long or far; her unspoken message is "interesting conversation, but we need to return to the topic." When Crawford's students are working in groups, Crawford circulates—listens, looks at those in the group, and says things such as, "Push that!" "Let's sharpen that." Heather Gerken explicitly tells her students she is pushing them as she does so: "Now I am going to push back on both of you" and she asks them to articulate the arguments if a particular issue were litigated. While she acknowledges that "this is hard," she also encourages students by saying, "If you crack this nut, you should get tenure somewhere." She regularly follows up with students: "Good. That was the functional argument. Now give me textual argument." While she is polite and affirming, she doesn't hesitate to challenge her students, often saying, "Just to disagree with a little thing . . ."

Class participation is a must in these teachers' classes, and the students are happy to live up to the high expectations: "When you go to Hornstein's class, you know that he's going to engage the class in general, and you know that he's going to ask questions and demand, like, a certain level of participation. . . . And so you go there with the need to be able to answer him" (student of Don Hornstein). Andy Leipold's students are also eager to prepare for his class, a view we heard expressed by the students of most of the teachers we studied. "I think as a whole, students prepared for that class more than any other class I had because out of respect you wanted to show the same enthusiasm back to him when you were answering" (student of Andy Leipold).

Like all of us, sometimes these excellent teachers make mistakes. For example, Larry Krieger explains his greatest challenge as a teacher:

> My bad days and mistakes in teaching usually amount to the same . . . problems. . . . [Sometimes], I talk too much. This happens because students ask good questions and they are interested in the answers (and I often have what I think is a good answer). The problem is, it becomes very clear to me (and this is not rare) that other students really are not interested in the answer, and would rather get on with the business at hand, as they see it. I usually find the question and answer germane to the topic at hand, but I am trying to learn that that is not good enough. Coverage is potentially infinite, whereas class time is not, and answers to questions usually involve expanding coverage at the expense of class time for activities, which result in much more actual learning. I often tell students to see me after or e-mail me the question, but I don't do that enough and, as a result, I end up with a lot of faces drifting off and checking out. I don't know how many more years it will take me to get this lesson, I really don't.

Show Caring

Our study reveals that, while technique influences student learning, law teachers' attitudes and relational behaviors are even more critical to the learning process, as Chapter 4 details. Every day in class, the teachers we studied connect with their students on a personal level and show their passion for teaching and student learning. These teachers show their caring and passion in a wide variety of ways, such as listening carefully, visibly delighting in students' insights and questions, teaching with energy and enthusiasm, being encouraging and empathetic, and being flexible. Patti Alleva articulates her overarching goal during class sessions in a way that typifies the people we studied: she strives to create "positive learning environments" and explains that she accomplishes her goal, in part, by "putting myself on the line, making myself vulnerable." One of Hiroshi Motomura students expressed how much he valued Motomura's willingness to do the same: "It was also really important for me that he shared a personal impetus for studying his substantive area . . . [by] showing us a picture of his family and [because] many of his students come from immigrant families."

Classroom Encouragement

All the teachers we studied strive to encourage their students in class. "Getting [a] good answer from . . . and praising them . . . this is extremely important to me" (Philip Prygoski). Similarly, Steven Homer notes that "whenever they participate, I always try to have them end on the right answer if they can." Nancy Levit notes the positive effect on students when she attributes good points to particular students: "It gives them the comfort, the security, the safety of the environment. . . . They feel more free to take risks. . . . Attributing ideas to the person who mentioned the ideas in the first place, that's particularly helpful because that makes them feel engaged. And if someone else is getting credit with idea ownership, they want idea ownership too, and so you get more players."

In the classroom, teachers encourage students in a variety of ways. Heather Gerken talks to students like colleagues, saying things such as, "When you are clerking for Justice Stevens . . ." She also names what they say and calls them theories, as for example, "Mr. Trevnick's theory," and she writes those "theories" on the board. Paula Franzese delivers extensive praise throughout the class: "Yes," "Good," "Well said," "Excellent," "Brilliant," and "Very, very good!" Andy Taslitz thanks students for their contributions. Beth Enos uses phrases such as "such good thinking," "love that," "good work today," "good point," and "good question!" Andy Leipold responds to a student insight by saying, "That's a nice point. I hadn't thought of that."

A key aspect of these teachers' empathy is how they respond to incorrect student comments in class. One of Julie Nice's students explains that "she'll work with you and not make you feel like you gave a poor response for a question, but she really helps you work for it and find the answer with her." Similarly, one of Don Hornstein's students notes, "If there's something that we don't understand or something that we do need to say, then he'll be open to it, even in class. If we say something that is completely and totally wrong, which happens from time to time, he doesn't make you feel like you're stupid for opening your mouth." One of Susan Kuo's students reports that "Professor Kuo is always willing to slow down and cover difficult issues. She never makes students feel like a liability." Similarly, one of Andy Leipold's students says, "He'd roll up his sleeves and he'd be like 'Ms. Nelson, why don't you help me with this one.' . . . You wouldn't really be terrified because for the rest of whatever, twenty, twenty-five minutes, he would work through it with you, and there's really no wrong answer with him, even if there is. . . . He works with you the whole class period so you don't feel on the spot or that you got it wrong. It's just you and him working through it."

Listen Carefully

These teachers model careful listening in the way they position themselves in the classroom." You have a question and you raise your hand. . . . He'll usually step behind and, like, come over to where you are and, like, look at you directly and be, like, 'Yeah, so what's your question?' . . . He's actually interested in what you have to say. . . . He does it all around the circle, all around the class" (student of Andy Taslitz). Bridget Crawford's classroom movement is quite similar; when she listens, Crawford leans in and nods her head. She appears to really enjoy the students, the subject, and their contributions. She tells students to honor their reactions and emotions, and she picks up on students' reactions and asks them about those reactions, saying things such as "Kate, would you say something?" and "Can you give a concrete example?" Similarly, when his students ask questions or respond to his or their classmates' questions, Andy Leipold's body language and facial expressions are focused, laser-like, on the student so that the student feels as if he or she and Leipold are the only two people in the room. Other teachers we studied listen attentively by turning toward and sustaining eye contact when their students speak.

Teachers also show they are listening carefully by summarizing and repeating what students say. "When it's his turn to jump in and to have his say, he's very good at saying, you know, and 'Kari had a good point ten minutes ago when she said this, and I like what Sean had to say, because here's what that brings in. And then, Mike, you responded—,' or 'Zack, you brought in—.' So he'll have his say, but he'll give a lot of credit to students. . . . A lot of professors won't do that, and then you get a sense of, well, they're not listening" (student of Roberto Corrada).

Excited by Student Insights and Questions

The teachers we studied show their delight in student success. In the classroom this appears to create a triumphant cycle: the students make great points, the professor gets excited, the students offer even better insights, and so forth. For example, Nelson Miller responds to the students' presentations in class with enthusiastic compliments, for example: "Very good, Sheena." He encourages students, saying things such as "Answer please," "Sorry to interrupt," and "Shane has all the answers today." Susan Kuo is similarly encouraging and affirming in the class, saying things such as "Wow, really interesting question!" "Great!" "Super duper!" As one of Hiroshi Motomura's students recognizes, this process is also a matter of professorial mindset: "His philosophy is that anything that's really important in class should first come out of a student's mouth. That's what he told us pretty recently. . . . Sometimes I just want him to say . . . 'No, that's not right.' But he never says, 'No, that's not right.' He's really good at finding, like, the one kernel of truth in a totally wrong statement."

Students relish and remember this positive feedback. For example, Heather Gerken's students reported that Gerken says things such as "That's a great idea," "That needs to be said—you should write that paper and I'll write it with you," "That's a home run!" when they ask a good question in class. These students note that Gerken's encouragement in class is powerful. She inspires them, gives them confidence, and makes them feel valued. Nancy Levit's students similarly appreciate her excitement about their insights: "I can tell that when somebody raises their hand and makes a comment that she really appreciates that you prepared for class and that you're making comments and you're engaging in the conversation . . . She [says] 'Oh, that's a good comment,' or something, or she'll send you an e-mail after class and say, 'I appreciated your comments,' or something like that." Another Levit student said, "I know I'm not afraid to ask a question in her class for fear of looking stupid."

To the students, it is striking that their teachers recognize student insights even when an idea conflicts with the professors' ideas. "If you have just a legally sound argument that is . . . completely opposite of whatever he was thinking . . . he'll still accept it. He won't, like, just bash you or anything like that. He'll actually appreciate you thinking through this and actually coming to this conclusion" (student of Andy Taslitz). "He will really take something you offer in class and really expound on it and continue to go on. I think he's really great at doing that and keeping me very involved and engaged" (student of Steve Friedland).

One of Paula Lustbader's students summarizes the value of these teachers' visible appreciation of student insights. "It's not a competition. She's happy. She's happy to see you learn. When you're learning, she's happy. When you're getting something, she's happy. I don't think anything makes her happier than to see the light bulb go off. I really mean that. If other professors that I'm thinking of saw a light bulb go off, they might not show it; there might not be the praise; there may not be the recognition, or the acknowledgement."

Energetic and Enthusiastic

In the classroom, the teachers we studied also show enthusiasm for the subjects they teach and for the entire teaching and learning process. Paula Franzese infuses her class with high energy, enthusiasm, fun, and passion. She conducts a fast-paced class covering a wide range of topics with a very high rate of student-teacher back and forth. Similarly, Rory Bahadur moves throughout the classroom, modulates his voice to show enthusiasm and passion, imitates movie characters with reckless abandon, and generally exudes tirelessness. Nancy Knauer frequently expresses enthusiasm for her subject: "So exciting today," and "Isn't that great?"

Students experience their teachers' classrooms as positive, exciting places, see their teachers as energetic and enthusiastic, and believe their professors' enthusiasm helps them learn:

- "She's superphysical, like she uses the entire front of the room to explain what she is saying. So she is making a distinction between two cases or two things; one of those distinctions will live on the left side of room and the other distinction will live on the other right side of the room. As she is tying them together, she will literally be running back and forth and pushing the hair out of her eyes. . . . When I would be studying for her final, I'm remembering her physicalizations of the issues of these cases like the left side and the right side of the room" (student of Julie Nice).

- "I didn't really want to take tax, but it was one of the things I knew I should take. And her enthusiasm about it, like blind enthusiasm, . . . made you get into it" (student of Nancy Knauer).

- "I think it's the passion that comes through. He'll say something, and then he'll just become so emotional about it, and he'll kind of look at all of us and go, 'Well, doesn't this just incense you? This should incense you.' That passion just makes . . . you want to care about as well" (student of Don Hornstein).
- "His passion, definitely in his passion for the law, his passion for fairness, his passion for equality, it's imputed in everything he says and everything he teaches us. . . . His eyes just light up in class whenever he's talking about these things that really move him. . . . You can just see that he feels it all" (student of Andy Taslitz).
- "She brings a contagious enthusiasm to the classroom" (student of Susan Kuo).

Humor and Fun

We observed many classrooms filled with laughter and fun. Students of about half of the teachers we studied confirmed our observations. As one of Patti Alleva's students explained, "I don't know if she had a bad day in the three years I was here. I certainly never saw one. She made it fun with everything she taught; she made it fun, and she made me want to learn, and she made me retain everything she told me because it was a damn good time." Roberto Corrada's comfort with humor in his classroom has another positive effect for one of Corrada's students: "[A] smart example of the amount of respect that he shows for a class is that . . . he encouraged people to use a little bit of humor in class. . . . I mean we're there to learn, yeah, sure, but I just think he created an environment where people weren't scared to crack a joke every now and then, and the class would have a good laugh, and then we'd kind of get on with it." One of Paula Franzese's students reports that "students enjoy the process" of being in Franzese's classes, and asserts that "it's hard not to learn the material when it is so fun to learn."

Significant and Relevant

A defining characteristic of the teachers we studied is their effort to make their classes significant and relevant to their students, as Paula Lustbader explains: "Students learn what they're motivated to learn. . . . And they're learning because they care deeply about something. . . . Something brought them to law school. . . . How they learn is really connected to why they're learning, because otherwise they won't stay for another half an hour to try and figure that out, because it's too abstract; it's not connected to why I came to law school."

Students argue that this emphasis on helping students connect to the material makes the learning, even in case-focused courses, "fundamentally different" (student of Julie Nice):

> She . . . rarely talks about one case alone. She is talking about one case and its relation to one case that came twenty or thirty years before it and its relation to a case that might come after it, or the case that's pending . . . or a smattering of cases about this issue. . . . And then on the board she is triangulating, trying to constantly place a case in the contexts, in a historical context, in a . . . context, and then in a personal context, where she's constantly saying, "How would you feel if . . . ?" and you're talking about *Plessy,* and talking about *Brown.* And relationships with her own students, triangulating with this is where I come from. I'm from the Midwest; this is where my people are from. Where are

your people from and how are you relating to these cases? This is how the justices are relating to the cases, and why is that? The amount of cases she'll talk about at once and keeping everybody on the same page is amazing.

—STUDENT OF JULIE NICE

Another of Nice's students asserts that "she has that ability to take whatever it is that we are supposed to be learning, that law, that basic law, and make it relatable to us, and we can involve our experience."

Cary Bricker makes it clear that the process of making the course relevant is just as significant in her experiential learning courses as it is in doctrinal courses: "First of all, the person who's doing the learning has to have some belief in the outcome of the learning; they have to have investment. . . . For example, I mean the most discrete, the most concrete example, is I do a lot of teaching trial advocacy, where the result is a full-day jury trial for a set of jurors from Sacramento, from the community." Speaking about the students in her Federal Defender Clinic, she adds that students have many "discrete tasks where the outcome is effective representation of indigent clients. So they have to believe in the outcome; they have to believe in the clients; they have to believe in the methods of communication."

Materials

In their classes, the teachers we studied use significant and relevant materials that engage their students. For example, Beth Enos brought the *Harry Potter* contract to her Contract Law class. Her students note, "I'm going to be more interested in the contract if it's about Harry Potter." "She would have us bring in our own contracts, like, for adhesion contracts, we had to bring in one, and I think maybe even the very beginning of the year we just had to bring in any contract just to show that . . . all of our life is basically agreeing to different kinds of contracts, and so she kind of brought it home that way." Similarly, one of Nelson Miller's students comments, "He'd always bring in his newspaper article . . . and it was showing you that what we just learned is really applied outside of the classroom."

Students also appreciate these teachers' use of supplements and casebooks. Students of Meredith Duncan explain the value: "Every single one of her classes that I've had she has also had a [required] supplement. . . . So in Criminal Law we had a casebook that had true, real crimes that had been committed that comported with what we were learning. In PR, same thing. She had a true casebook, and then she would read in my PR class. She would read things that had happened here in Texas, where attorneys were disciplined. So it is a way to take this theoretical framework and apply it. . . . It really did teach me to learn, because, instead of just learning about these theories in a bubble, it allowed me to see how they were applicable to my everyday life as an attorney." "In Criminal Law, our first year, she had a supplemental book that had detailed stories of the defendants in most of the criminal cases. . . . But she's just able to humanize the cases and, I think, make you think outside of the sterile facts that are sometimes listed in the opinions, and I found that to be a much more in-depth way to think about a criminal law issue or a professional responsibility issue."

Andy Taslitz's students believe the casebook he authored played a significant role in their learning: "There were lots and lots of questions, and so through kind of thinking about the questions. . . . You don't realize it, but through kind of reading all these materials, cases and materials, and then all the questions, you're formulating your own framework. . . . To me that was the big picture that really helped me."

Bridget Crawford's students similarly cited Crawford's self-authored supplement as an important factor in helping them relate to and learn the material. One student described the supplement as being "like gold," asserting that the supplement "explained material better than anything . . . better than any other classes I've been in." Another student explained that the supplement included "examples, charts, visuals, cartoons, outlines, check lists and was really clear, helpful, and organized."

Creating and Using Examples

In his "Teaching Philosophy" Statement, Steve Friedland makes it clear that he, like other teachers we studied, seeks to create examples and tell stories that maximize students' ability to see the relevancy of what they are learning.

> I try to use examples and exercises that create relevancy. This is
> especially true in a course such as Property Law, which involves
> subjects such as land possession and ownership with which
> the students might be unfamiliar. Thus, I ask students to find
> easements in the real world, or to look at their own leases—past or
> present—to determine which provisions they would like to change
> after studying landlord-tenant law. . . . Students also remember
> stories better than unadorned information, and I have had
> students use a story to recall the information associated with it.
> In teaching Constitutional Law, I use the fascinating story of
> Gordon Hirabayashi, who was sent to jail as a Japanese-American
> who violated the World War II curfew on the west coast of the

United States. He tells the story of being released and sent to a detainment center a thousand miles away, on his own, without escort, despite the rationale for his detainment being his possible involvement with espionage. It is a poignant part of his story that students remember.

In teaching Professional Responsibility, Meredith Duncan looks to the disciplinary reports for Texas, the state where her law school is located, for examples that help her students see the relevancy of what she is teaching. She starts her class sessions by reading from the list of recent lawyer disciplinary actions so her students know the consequences of the issues they are discussing. Duncan's students get the message; several said they would never want Professor Duncan to read their names to a future class.

Julie Nice also uses examples to help teach professional values. "She encourages her students to wrestle with legal ideas both from the position of a lawyer looking for the legally significant tidbits, but also as human beings struggling with the oft-ignored subtexts of liberty, equality, equity, and justice. This allows for her to teach with passion and to help students make concrete connections between the abstract of the law and its ground-level implications" (student of Julie Nice). Philip Prygoski takes his examples from current events and his sense of issues students might encounter if they were to choose to practice in his field, Constitutional Law. Prygoski explains that he motivates his students by his efforts to "tie the material to real life, to tell the stories, to talk about current events." As one of his students expounds, "The class is always forward thinking . . . based on what you know now of the constitutional law. What's going to happen in the future with gay marriage? What's going to happen in the future with divorce?" Another of

Prygoski's student says, "I mean, when he discussed the constitutional implications, he would relate it to everyday life. I mean, I don't care if it's mud flaps on a truck dealing with interstate commerce, and I remember that, and I thought, well, that's interesting, because you know everybody that's driven knows what a mud flap on a truck looks like. So I mean, just taking common everyday things that we see and observe and that's part of our being, part of our life, something we can relate to, and turning it into, or making it a part of, a constitutional subject matter."

Don Hornstein often draws his examples from local issues: "[A] lot of the cases [Hornstein discusses] are local, relevant examples. Like, a lot of the cases are from western North Carolina or East Tennessee, South Carolina. These are all places that we're familiar with. So that gives us more of a personal interest" (student of Don Hornstein). Andy Taslitz uses media depictions of criminal practice for examples. One of his students explains that Taslitz "made the material accessible. . . . [He] connected to the lives that we had come from. . . . He used a lot of movie references, TV references that—'Okay, yeah, well, I've seen that,' and 'Oh, that's what this was reflecting.'" Similarly, Bridget Crawford's students remember her examples, such as the "tax implications of casino tips, Oprah's cars."

According to Susan Kuo's students, finding contemporary examples of the concepts she is teaching is one of her regular teaching practices: "She normally has a more contemporary example of what we are talking about so it sticks. Being able to relate something to a recent event that you may talk to a friend about later makes application a lot easier and immediate. That way, [it] is not just a concept but also something you can apply in a regular conversation."

Connect to Practice

Making connections between course material and its law practice implications is a defining teaching strategy among the twenty-six teachers we studied. In Larry Krieger's externship prep class, which Krieger created for students who would be working as externs in prosecutor and public defender settings, students learn the nitty-gritty of handling particular types of cases. His students leave the class feeling ready to handle actual cases. "He shows you how to put that in a specific instance where, say, it's a DUI, and he'll go to the statute. He'll pick it out. He'll split it up into the elements, and then he'll go from there. He'll be, like, 'From there you list what you need to prove that first portion of why their normal faculties were impaired and proving why they were behind the wheel.' Then he just goes through that, and then you have these homework assignments, and through that you do your rendition of what you think you're supposed to be doing, and then he goes through them and tells you a more efficient way to do that. It is more efficient, and, in the courtroom, you can't be writing full paragraphs, and he shows you how to do that on a half of a page. That way, when you take that into the courtroom, like, you will actually be prepared and you won't be searching through these two-page documents" (student of Larry Krieger).

Steven Homer and Tina Stark connect their legal writing classes to students' future work. "I justify assignments not only in terms of the course but also by explaining how they prepare students for practice" (Steven Homer). Tina Stark's students say things such as: "Her method of teaching was like being in practice." "We understand why we are on first name basis—Stark is preparing us for practice." "[She] teaches contract drafting in context."

Hiroshi Motomura tries to put his students in contexts "where, in some sense, I can imagine their palms sweating but in a different way from being a law student. The most extreme version of this is when I walk into class and pretend that I'm a client and ask them to interview me based on what they read, which is really hard and very challenging, but it really gives them a stake in this in a different kind of sweaty palms. It's a lawyer sweaty palms, not the law student sweaty palms." While Motomura describes himself as "a very theoretical person," he also reports that he tries "to view it in a way that an attorney would look at it, which is: 'What does this case mean for me and my client?' 'Does it hurt my brief? Do I have to distinguish it?' as opposed to 'What are the facts of this case?'" One of Motomura's students describes another Motomura teaching tactic, in which Motomura says to the class, "Your uncle sends you an e-mail. You, as a law student, are the only legal resource they have in their network. Here is their immigration situation. How are you going to help?" The student admits that "his questions would sometimes be disarming, but they were realistic questions and the challenge forced us to act on our feet and assess just how much we understood."

Julie Nice finds different ways to bring authentic practice experiences to her courses. "She makes everything very practical. Her later classes, her finals, are actually amicus briefs you have to write on the position. . . . During the Prop 8 trial, she cancelled class for the whole week, and our class was to go to the actual trial and to sit in on the trial and watch it, and she said, 'If you can't watch it, there are courtrooms that will show it, so make sure you watch it somehow if you can't make it to the trial.' That really . . . brought [the issues] to life for me" (student of Julie Nice).

An important learning activity in Andy Taslitz's Criminal Procedure class is watching a videotape of police interrogating a suspect, as one of his students describes: "It was, like, four hours long. I mean, I sat there. I just thought, 'Oh, just be a half an hour.' I started at six o'clock and at 10:30 I was still watching this poor guy, you know, 'Can I get some water?' And I wanted to watch it because I knew—I was so excited when we got to talk about it finally.... I looked it up, and I saw what actually happened to that guy later.... It's not just the book anymore. It's real life." Taslitz also involves students in criminal law practice simulations. "Two people were for the prosecution side and two people were for the defense and each side had their own kind of set of facts, and we had to conduct, basically, a plea negotiation, and so, while it was focused on kind of the substance of criminal procedure and the rules, it also kind of gave us a very interesting experience dealing with other parties. And that's, you know, something that we're going to have to do in practice. So it was kind of the best of both worlds, and then we spent [time] in class talking about 'Here are things that went well,' 'Here are things that didn't go well' in our individual sessions, and kind of, from a practice standpoint, how his experiences can help us to maybe handle the situation better or do things differently if we're in that situation in the future" (student of Andy Taslitz).

In Steve Friedland's class, students appreciate that he "bring[s] the courtroom to the classroom ... In Evidence class, you get the opportunity to apply it by being called on to respond to objections and things of that nature. So it's really just very interactive and forces you to think on your feet. He tells us his goal is to make sure that every student is comfortable when they first step in the courtroom" (student of Steve Friedland).

Nancy Levit's "Teaching Philosophy" describes the wide variety of lawyering activities her students attempt in her classroom. "In the first year Torts course, my students do intake interviews to

learn to humanize clients. I may ask students to take minideposi-
tions of expert witnesses, argue motions for summary judgment,
engage in negotiation exercises or settlement discussions, or participate in a mock appellate moot court. This does more than make
classroom conversations sparkle; it introduces students early to
their professional roles. Students need to see law in action, and
they also need to understand how deeply they are affecting human
lives." One student's report of her experience in Levit's classes is
typical: "You get shoved out of the box a lot with the 'Okay, if you're
a plaintiff's attorney, what are you going to tell your client?' Wow!
Nobody really says that in class. Nobody asks me to think like an
actual attorney. I can brief cases all day long. I'm old, and I been
doing this a while, so that's no big deal, but having to think as the
attorney and give a response, what am I going to tell the client?
Wow! I didn't know that."

For Meredith Duncan's Professional Responsibility students,
the lawyering skill focus is statutory construction and application,
and her students discover and appreciate the practical implications of both the professional responsibility doctrine and the skills
they have learned:

> Like she really parses statutes, and if you haven't taken statutory
> interpretation, or you're just not used to reading rules, I think it's
> helpful, because the way she teaches you to read statutes helps you
> in every class whether [the language is] 'they may' or 'they shall' or
> 'they _____'whatever terminology is used. It helps you figure to
> how those questions could be couched on an exam and in real life,
> and there's been at least two people I know that have had PR-related
> issues in the summer after we took the class and were able to
> effectively go to their bosses and say, 'Here's what happened. Here's

what the rule says. Here's what we should do.' And I think . . . regardless of how you do on her exams, the ability to apply those in a real life—to recognize the problem in the first place and then to . . . really go through the process of solving it—speaks more for her teaching"

—STUDENT OF MEREDITH DUNCAN

Ingrid Hillinger's students encounter a critical lawyering activity on the first day of Bankruptcy class:

I remember on the first day of Bankruptcy class she came in and got the class started by telling a story about, you know, you are the attorney and the client comes into your office, and he's got terrible financial problems. And he's telling you about this, but he says that he has one asset that he knows he still has is his insurance policy. And he asks you, 'Well, so if I died, who gets the proceeds of my insurance policy, my family or my creditors?' And she brought it all together for me there. . . . She knew that if she told the person the truth, he'd walk out the door of her office and blow his brains out. But it was the combination of letting you see that. You had to be able to—you could find a way to figure out the neat interesting legal thing about how 541 fit together with 362 and all the rest of that. But at the bottom there were real human beings, who were going to be sitting in your office, and how did that come together? . . . Real people's lives are going to be influenced by what you do, and I don't think she ever let you forget that."

One of Rory Bahadur's students reports that "he would use real-life application with teaching legal concepts. For instance, when we started talking about . . . proximate cause, actual cause, he used a real-life example from a case that he litigated when he was in private practice. He brought in the pleadings, some motions that were filed, and kind of walked through the arguments that were made, and you know, rather than you just talk and read cases, you can actually see how these concepts apply in the real world in a court, and I think, I mean, I still remember that very vividly, and that was one of the things that I thought was very valuable in how he taught."

Excel at Chosen Teaching Techniques

One universal characteristic of the teachers we studied is their skill in using their chosen teaching techniques. They use a wide variety of teaching techniques, including cooperative learning techniques, visuals, role-plays and simulations, real-life experiences, papers, drafting exercises, and storytelling. Almost all of them use active learning methods, and they excel at having their students successfully experience a wide variety of exercises. Their discussions engage the whole class, and their small group exercises create mechanisms for their students to engage the material, provide peer feedback, and teach each other. When they use Socratic questioning, they ask challenging, carefully crafted questions that engage students in thinking on a wide variety of intellectual levels. When they ask their students to write or think, they provide compelling prompts and give their students sufficient time to engage the task. If they lecture, their lectures are clear, thoughtfully planned, and punctuated by examples, stories, or visual aids.

A few examples from our observations of particular class sessions illustrate this point:

Julie Nice: At the beginning of class, Nice delivered handouts to each student, greeting them. She briefly reviewed recent articles in the field and provided an overview of the doctrinal area to create context for the cases the class would be discussing. She then created groups and gave each group a section of an opinion to distill the best arguments. She gave the groups five minutes to complete the task, providing a one-minute warning and asking each group to choose a spokesperson. Each group then articulated and evaluated its assigned argument, while Nice captured key ideas on a whiteboard and asked follow-up questions. Throughout, Nice displayed passion for the subject, and both Nice and the students used humor. Nice gave frequent positive reinforcement for student contributions. Student engagement was high throughout the class session.

Roberto Corrada: He arrived early to class and used the time to write an outline on the board, overviewing where the class would be going that day, and he made efforts to connect with the early-arriving students. Throughout the class session, the students were central. One message he consistently communicated as he taught is that the only difference between him and his students is that he has been studying the material a lot longer. He used a wide variety of teaching techniques, including cooperative learning groups, Socratic-style questioning, guest speakers, and lecture. He knew his students' names and used them regularly. He was comfortable with students disagreeing with him and with silence, waiting patiently for his students to speak and finish their points. He often avoided standing at the exact front of the room. He achieved widespread engagement and comments from most of the students. He explained the rationales for his teaching choices and acknowledged the demands on the students other than the demands of his class.

Hiroshi Motomura: This class took place on the day that the first year students' major writing assignment was due for their legal writing class. Many of the students had been up all night finishing their memos. Motomura called on students by first name, often calling on two students at a time. He asked follow up questions to both students for depth and detail, and he directly answered students' questions. Motomura used several visuals, which were projected on a screen—an outline of the subject matter, the text of a statute, and a mind-map computer program. During class, Motomura and the students used the program to chart an analytical framework. Students were actively engaged throughout.

Cary Bricker: The lecture was team-taught. Twenty-one of the twenty-two students engaged themselves throughout the class session. Both the students and the teachers frequently used humor. The teachers made excellent use of brainstorming throughout the class session, and they captured student ideas on a flip chart. They also drew a simple and effective graphic on a flip chart and then made use of the chart throughout the session. Both teachers made great use of silence, allowing students time to generate responses.

Patti Alleva: Alleva began the class with music, asking her students to "listen, think, feel." Alleva read a short excerpt from the book students read for class. The particular excerpt had powerful, emotional content that grabbed the students' attention. Alleva then facilitated a large group discussion; she asked questions and used silence to give her students time to reflect. Alleva captured nearly all student comments in writing, and both Alleva and the students commented about students' comments, attributing particular insights to particular students, listening to each other, and nodding. Alleva then set up a small group exercise. In particular, Alleva clarified who would be in each group (she used already-established groups), the time allotted (she projected a watch on the screen, counting the time), and the task (she provided the question and directions on a handout). She gave a one-minute warning, and then took reports from the groups, following up with questions and making some comments that applied to all the groups. The entire session was characterized by deep mutual respect and intense engagement.

Philip Prygoski: Prygoski used a modified version of Socratic questioning in which he tried to diffuse rather than produce anxiety in his students by acknowledging the uncertainty and unsettled aspects of the law he was teaching. A critical component of Prygoski's teaching appears to be the many links he makes among the topics the class is working on that day and all the topics the class has discussed before this class session and will discuss afterward. Constitutional law in Prygoski's classroom therefore felt like a story that hangs together. He emphasized doctrinal themes, common constitutional arguments, and the many possibilities for drawing analogies. He called on students frequently, asking them questions and prodding them in an encouraging way to develop arguments that moved beyond mere opinion to viable argument, and his incredibly vast knowledge of the subject meant that the students understood that their contributions had to be grounded in the cases they were studying.

In her "Teaching Philosophy," Julie Nice provides an additional, helpful insight into her teaching. She explains her way of teaching students the skill of synthesizing at higher levels of abstraction in this way:

I use three techniques to help them develop higher analytical skills, which I refer to as coding, mapping, and doing "mash-ups." Coding simply requires identifying the reasons given by parties, legislatures, or courts, then sorting them into types of arguments and tracking the arguments in the designated materials. Mapping applies this same technique more broadly, tracking how the various arguments have fared over place and time. I emphasize the importance of coding and mapping in practice, specifically stressing that developing professional expertise requires identifying and understanding the arguments in play (not merely the primary case holdings), and tracking the development of these argumentative trends in their chosen practice area. Nearly every day I use what I suppose now might be called "mash-ups." This refers to asking them on the spot to compare across doctrines, courses, and, sometimes even disciplines. Rather than resist the randomness of the mash-ups, the students seem to relish discovering that they are able to retrieve and relate information stored in their brains. Such tracking of the law's development, both within a specific doctrine or policy context and across doctrines or contexts, serves the invaluable goal of reinforcing the historical interplay between law and society, politics, and the economy.

The students recognize the excellence of their teachers' classroom efforts:

- "She started many of her classes, you know, trying to elicit responses or guttural feeling responses in Criminal Law or Professional Responsibility: 'Does this feel right to you in your personal experience?' . . . So I think that I find that I internalize things a lot better and remember things better in her classes because I've

actually thought and developed my own opinions about them."
"She allows for students to discuss the topic, but she'll respectfully correct students when they're wrong and also question the
students' opinion regardless of where they fall . . . ideologically. . . .
She finds that perfect mix between talking to the class or questioning" (students of Meredith Duncan).

- "[In her Contract Drafting Seminar we] really dissected
  contracts . . . as to what [they] mean and how to rewrite them and
  [we] had to rewrite them so that they're better. And then each peer
  reviewed them and gave you feedback on what you wrote, and
  I just thought, to me, that was the best way of learning—learning
  how to write and to review and to just think really clearly"
  (student of Beth Enos).

- "Professor Motomura does a great job of starting what sounds just
  like a conversation and then kind of seamlessly, and sometimes
  not even apparently, guiding it to a fruitful discovery. . . . What
  otherwise would be kind of a seemingly choate conversation,
  becomes extremely clear because of his reliance on mind manager
  to really illustrate the connections between everything that's
  happening." "The Socratic that we know from *The Paper Chase* is
  this froth, horrible, emotional, not very educational. . . . but, at the
  heart of it, the conversation is what's important, and what Hiroshi
  really does very well is have it be a very collaborative learning
  experience, having a conversation, inviting feedback, talking
  about building these mind managers. The mind managers aren't
  built when you walk into the classroom. They're not PowerPoint.
  They are kind of a sedimentary history of our conversation in
  class, and he sends them out immediately after class" (students of
  Hiroshi Motomura).

Emphasize and Use Active Learning Methods

Almost all of the teachers in this study regularly ask their students to write, think, speak, reflect, talk to a peer, or work on a task in a small group. In their teaching philosophy statements and interviews, they express considerable consensus that students learn best when they are actively engaged. As Paula Lustbader explains:

> [Students] learn best when they're doing, when they're engaged. . . . Active, engaged learning has always been one of my big things, and that's one of the things I do to help students learn. I build on a lot of active learning, which doesn't mean . . . that I have all these rigid role-play exercises. It could just be: 'Stop! Write something down.' It could be: 'Talk to your neighbor for a minute,' which is why I move them halfway through the class so they have other people to interact with. . . .
>
> I make sure that no more, typically, than five to ten minutes am I talking at them about anything. And no more than maybe fifteen minutes before they're actually having to do something. . . . My primary method is problem oriented . . . so I try to start everything with a hypothetical either that I have generated, or I'll have them generate it. . . . By having them do the hypotheticals, they get that connection ('Why should I care?' and 'It's relevant to my life,' and 'It has meaning.'). And they remember it in a much more profound way.

Andy Taslitz doesn't use the term "active learning" to describe his approach to teaching, but his description of his many teaching techniques focuses on active learning:

I use a lot of problems. . . . If the students don't apply it, how it's going to have any real meaning for them? So I use a lot of problems. I always have a few role-plays and two kinds of role-plays. One could be in class. I give more of them that they have to do out of class. And then they have to produce some written product. And then the class will focus on, you know, so how did the negotiation go? What did you do to prepare for the negotiation? How did the counseling session go? . . . Did you look at the ethical rules? So, you know, we'll spend time talking about that. So I do a fair number of role-plays.

I always have some writing exercises, and it depends on the class, how many I might give or the nature of the writing exercises. So, [in] my first-year class, the writing exercises are mostly very short and they're focused on basic, really basic, skills like fact application, stating a rule, figuring out the policy underlying the rule, interpreting a statute and engaging in acts of statutory interpretation, although I also have them occasionally draft the jury instructions, something like that. With some of my upper-level classes I'm more likely to have them do real lawyer tasks. So I'm teaching free speech this semester. They have to draft a judicial opinion. They have to take a deposition."

In identifying her teaching methods, Paula Franzese talks about teaching through multiple senses:

[I use visuals by] pointing to the materials in the casebooks, highlighting those materials, having the students speak to what moves them from the written materials. . . . Then I go to the auditory reinforcement. I think, to anchor information, it has to be repeated at least three times in three different ways. So I'll go to the more oral component, the auditory, by speaking to the premises, and then I ask the students to commit to that engagement by then restating or reciting the premises. So this is an off-laptop or off-note-taking component of the class.

You saw the role-playing; I simulate responses, and then [they] have to state in their own words what they would say to their clients to try to explain a given document, keeping it as simple as possible. . . . Thereafter, we go to yet another iteration of the same sorts of materials using my supplement, which is my short [outline and] is an opportunity for the students to listen . . . to [what is being said about the material] but also work through it, but to write down to fill in the blanks . . .

That tends to allow the materials to congeal and also gives the students an opportunity for their own purposes to see it put in one framework that represents a visual framework so that they can then make it their own. . . . I do try to humanize in terms of anchoring information. I use a lot of metaphors; I use analogies; I use stories. Sometimes I'll even use songs to try to render the material more accessible.

Roberto Corrada explains his thoughts about the importance of active learning:

Problems are a very effective way of having students try to transfer their knowledge of materials from cases and particular fact patterns to other facts . . . I use . . . what I call ill-structured problems. . . .

If all we're modeling is how we think about things we already know the answer to, we're doing a huge disservice to our students. Because mostly [students] are going to be in situations as lawyers where they don't know the answers. So what we need to model more is how we handle situations where we don't know the answer. How do we model that? What's the first thing we look for? What are the kinds of questions we ask when we don't know what the answer is going to be?

For Corrada's students, active learning classes are whole-class simulations. In his Labor Law simulation, Corrada structures the class so that his students can form a union to negotiate the terms of the class, such as whether the class will include a midterm and whether class participation will count toward students' final course grade. The students must have themselves certified as a union by the National Labor Relations Board, and Corrada has worked out an arrangement for the local office to conduct a union certification vote. To spice things up, Corrada deliberately violates his students' unionizing rights on his course web page so that his students can make a National Labor Relations Board challenge.

Hiroshi Motomura emphasizes his belief that students learn by doing and talking. "I like to think that I don't say anything in class. . . . But I now do a lot more minilecture[s] [for] summary and by way of introduction . . . I'm trying to put students in role[s]. I'm trying to give them lawyering tasks streamlined for the constraints of the sixty-five-minute hour and the forty-minute or even the hundred-minute, forty-person or even hundred-person thing. . . . So putting them in lawyering situations, counseling a client—What would you tell a client to do? How would you write the brief?"

We observed Beth Enos using a wide variety of active learning methods, including think-pair-share, lecture, Socratic-style questioning, small-group projects, having the class complete a chart as a class, and peer grading. Students wrote on the board, created their own exam-like hypotheticals, and gave each other feedback.

Students asked many questions. Nearly all of them, if not all of them, spoke. Enos emphasizes the value of students being actively involved:

> One of the most effective classes I ever taught was one when I had laryngitis and I couldn't talk. And I had to teach two classes that day: my contract drafting class and my first-year Contracts class. And in each class, I wrote out a series of things that I wanted them to do because I just couldn't afford to skip class right then. So I thought, "Well shoot, we don't need to cancel class. We're going to do it." And so I wrote out very clear steps about what I wanted them to do during class. I could whisper but I couldn't talk . . . and they worked in groups throughout the class. And I could go around to the different groups and help because then I could whisper and help individual groups with what they were doing. And I got to the end of class, and I thought that was the best class I ever taught, and I didn't say a word.

The students of these teachers seem to understand what their professors are trying to accomplish, as one of Motomura's students describes: "I would characterize my learning in Hiroshi's classes as the epitome of active learning. I cannot think of one day when class was a lecture for us to passively take notes. Each day would be a mix of exercises: class discussion, brief oral arguments, policy debates, class exercises, building upon our class diagrams on mind manager, or asking questions with guest speakers. The variety of ways in which we engaged the material helped us to gain constant exposure to the same immigration concepts but through multiple lenses. The classes felt much less like a lecture and more like a workshop." Similarly, one of Friedland's students says, "He actually made us, in class, not only learn the material, but every day he would make us stand up and talk to our neighbor and actually do the process of what you would do in court."

Use Silence Well

In their classrooms, the teachers we studied use silence to let students think and reflect. Our classroom observations of Professors Heather Gerken, Ruthann Robson, Roberto Corrada, Patti Alleva, Ingrid Hillinger, and Cary Bricker specifically mention their use of silence or the long wait time between their questions and when they start taking student responses.

Students also notice their teachers' effective use of silence:

- "He's remarkably comfortable with silence, with actually letting that sit, and letting students process, and all that stuff" (student of Hiroshi Motomura).
- "[She] provides some moments in class where she allows the students to have a moment of deeper comprehension, deeper thinking. . . . It just gives the students the time to reflect on what she's been speaking about and understand the specific area where we're looking into a broader sense and how it affects the law" (student of Patti Alleva).
- "Professor Robson steps back and lets everyone discuss." "Few professors teach where they let the ideas flow around the room without intervening—Ruthann Robson does that" (students of Ruthann Robson).

Facilitate Community and Collaboration

The teachers we studied excel at creating a sense of community in which students listen to and respect each other's contributions.

Most create small-group learning activities that students see as critical to their learning. One of Paula Lustbader's students captured the value of creating community:

We did like a lot of group work and from that we were able to create community with the people around us. But I think that really worked towards creating a safe environment. I think what makes law school so intimidating [is] you're in a room of a hundred people that you don't know. If I was in a room with a hundred people that I knew, I probably would have spoken a lot more in law school. But the fact that it was a hundred strangers . . . really made me feel intimidated. Being in a room that I felt comfortable, being in a room where I knew I had at least a common bond with [classmates], besides . . . being accepted to law school, really made the environment much more safe to be in.

But the group work also made it such that we learn collaboratively. We were able to work off the knowledge that other people had. Instead of having [the professors] being the sources of knowledge, we were able to learn from others.

Paula Lustbader's students experience the classroom community as personally transformative, and they develop a sense of community that continues long after their class is over: "To me, as I learn now, it's not just obviously a sense of community, but also her sense that the study of law, and maybe the practice of law, is about collaboration. That's ingrained in me, not just the practice, but really in life." "If it wasn't for Paula, I've always been the person that likes to kind of be by myself and learn and just work by myself, but after the ARC program and after my first year, I now collaborate as much as I can, get other people's opinions, and go forth from that."

All of the teachers we studied foster peer respect:

- "The nature of my learning was what I would call 'joint': an engaged and combined effort between myself, Professor Nice, and the other students in the classes" (student of Julie Nice).
- "He wants you to work together. He calls on multiple people to piece together an answer, and then he has everyone kind of recite back the piece that they each individually know . . . with Professor Friedland you feel like you're kind of working towards a common goal and you can kind of see the process a little bit more" (student of Steve Friedland).
- "I've seen her transform a group of eighty people into a single community of learners that all speak a single language" (student of Patti Alleva).
- "I learned a sense of belonging and treating everyone with respect in the classroom, that eventually each one of the people around you would be a colleague, and to treat them how you would want to be treated, basically. Those you wanted to work with—and then you worked in small groups together, and so you learned to work together in a classroom" (student of Rory Bahadur).

Many of the teachers create community by structuring cooperative learning experiences, such as Roberto Corrada's having students work in a simulated union in his Labor Law course. Corrada also sets up a discussion board on his TWEN course web page and, as one of his students reports, succeeds in getting his students to teach each other using that discussion board: "If we had questions regarding those readings or assignments, he would recommend—rather than e-mail him with the questions . . . he would say, you know, put your questions on there and let other students answer it. . . . It was part of our class participation grade. So, for those of that didn't like to talk in class, it was a really good way to get out there."

Beth Enos is more typical of the teachers in her use of cooperative learning: "We do quite a bit of in class work on problems, often in small groups. I walk around the class and talk with the groups. The problems they work on usually come from me, but I also ask them from time to time to make their own hypotheticals to share with their group. In all my classes, students work frequently with each other. To increase their exposure to other ideas, I have everyone in all of my classes switch seats periodically to sit next to people they haven't worked with before."

Similarly, in his "Teaching Philosophy," Larry Krieger states, "I also employ collaborative/group work as much as I can. I often have students break into pairs or small groups in class to discuss or practice a skill; I provide time to then take questions and comments/ observations based on what they experienced in their interactions. It is humbling, but quite clear to me, that the classes in which students speak the most and I speak the least are the most effective and successful for the overall goals of the class."

Cary Bricker describes her success in getting students to collaboratively reflect on their law practice efforts when the students are working as externs. "A lot of the time we'll do reflection where one of the first things my colleague or I will ask them [is], 'You had a bench trial. What worked? What would you do differently?' So there's that self-reflection discussion, and other people add in, 'Well I had this experience; this worked.' So there's this community learning."

The students greatly value these experiences. One of Rory Bahadur's students wrote in his student evaluation: "Group exercises were engaging, informative and fun." Two of Tina Stark's students were equally laudatory. "Stark," says one of those students, "sees the value of having us interact with each other. She breaks up the cliques . . . I became friends with other people because of the class. . . . I learn more when working with other people. I get different perspectives." "Tina Stark recognizes the important of working together and the need to work together." One of Nelson Miller's students asserts that his experience working in groups in Miller's Torts II class "breaks up the class a little bit, and it makes the class more interesting and the subject matter more interesting when you're working with other people."

While some of these teachers explicitly create cooperative learning exercises, others create a sense of collaboration that operates to foster great whole-class interactions. Many of Heather Gerken's students cite her ability to get students to listen to and respect each other. Gerken "deliberately and intentionally gets students to talk to each other—cultivates that in a room of 120." In Cary Bricker's class, we observed that she had created a classroom culture in which students and the teacher collaborated to provide feedback and make suggestions as each student practiced cross-examination. Similarly, when we visited Ruthann Robson's class, we saw that students regularly interacted with each other, looked at each other, and offered each other suggestions.

High Student Engagement

Regardless of what teaching techniques they used, the teachers in our study all managed to generate very high levels of student engagement, and the students noticed. For example, one of Steve Friedland's students stated, "He kept us involved in the lecture because he would involve students." Steven Homer's students even appreciate Homer's "everyone must participate" policy, as one student explained:

He's, like, "Nope. Everyone is going to talk, and I am flipping through my cards until at least everyone has said yes or no." He was just so fair to everybody in that way. And I think it changes—I keep going back to this, his expectations for the class and for us, but it just felt like the expectation was so clear, again, and everyone knew I'm going to say something, and you knew too that even if you didn't know he was going to help, he was going to support you in some way, like you said, building confidence. He was going to at least try to work you to the right answer. It's not like he's calling on you to make you look stupid or make sure you read. It was more to make sure everyone had practice in speaking. Because he knew—he even said in the beginning, "I know some of you aren't comfortable speaking, so that's something you need to work on."

Our classroom observations consistently noted a high level of student engagement. For example, in Bridget Crawford's two-hour-long evening seminar, students were talking to each other, making contact with their classmates, and referring to each other by name. Being in Tina Stark's class felt like witnessing a very engaged supervising attorney working with eager associates. Steve Friedland asks many—more than a hundred—questions during a class session. Using a combination of calling on students and taking volunteers, Friedland has widespread participation from both women and men and both students of color and white students.

Heather Gerken's students comment upon her ability to engage many people in class as a defining quality of her teaching: "Heather Gerken managed to get greater diversity of students participating than in other classes." "She made sure she knew all of our names from the start, took time to get to know us as class progressed (even if that meant holding more office hours than anyone else at the law school), and wouldn't let anyone get away with not participating in class. Far from creating an intimidating classroom environment, this 100 percent participation policy made the class more vibrant and engaged. Of course, it helped that she would restate even our least perceptive comments so that they sounded sensible, even astute."

Other students make similar comments:

- "She forces you to stay engaged . . . teaches to the whole class" (student of Paula Franzese).
- "You have to be really prepared to make class feel like a conversation, but it does feel like a conversation among all of us and her, and she's just one part of it, which is amazing" (student of Nancy Levit).
- "He had this whole system where you sign in and then you circle yourself if you were willing to be on call that day. And there's a carrot with that . . . you can get your grade bumped up by . . . a plus or minus or whatever at the end if you signed in a number of times. . . . It was nice that he acknowledges that some days people just can't be prepared or this is like a particularly scary topic that you don't feel comfortable with. . . . It made me at least want to be prepared and want to participate on all the days that I could" (student of Hiroshi Motomura).

Most of the teachers use Socratic-style questioning as an important teaching tool to engage their students. Overwhelmingly, the teachers expect all students to speak in class regularly, and, regardless of whether the students have volunteered, call on students:

I call on almost every student almost every day. This pushes the students to prepare for class. I believe students' first professional responsibility is to contribute to making class time as useful as possible. [What] I want them to see is that "contributing" is more than allowing a few students to dominate the conversation with what interests them; "contributing" means working jointly as a community of learning that maximizes what everyone learns. Related to this, I call on students to balance participation. I have the good fortune to teach at one of the most diverse law schools in the country, and by including all the diverse voices in the class, students learn that legal problems can have multiple solutions, and no one subset of students holds a monopoly on useful ideas.

—STEVEN HOMER

Similarly, Ingrid Hillinger asserts, "Calling on students randomly encourages class preparation . . . I want my students to have a sense of accomplishment and personal satisfaction." Paula Lustbader makes the same point: "I call on them randomly, not in a harassing, Socratic thing, but it's waking them up. It's like, 'What did you think? What do you think?' And then they jump in and they get engaged. So I think that's how I help them learn."

The teachers use different ways to engage their students. For example, Patti Alleva reports that she asks students to "'take a minute; write something down". . . . Then, I'll call on rows randomly, and they'll read or discuss what they've written down. I find that to be a way to get everybody involved." One of Meredith Duncan's students talked about her engagement in Duncan's Criminal Law class: "I did more self-reflecting in that class than I have done in almost any other law-school class. . . . She always brought it back to theories of punishment and why we punish and does this make sense and do you agree with this theory or this rationale that leads to this rationale? And getting to think about the law in that way,

I think, made me think about it in a deeper way than just this is what the statute says, these are how the cases interpret it."

Beth Enos uses voting to encourage her students to be more engaged: "I might ask the student a question and then immediately turn to somebody else and say, 'Do you agree with that? What do you think about that?' Or I'll say, 'Does everybody agree? Do we have a dissenting opinion here? Well what do you think about that?' I have them vote a lot in class. 'Who thinks this party should win?' 'Who thinks this party should win?' And I make them—they have to—raise their hands. I'll catch the person who didn't do that, and I do that partly to make them see their different opinions. It's not just a right answer. And I think that's especially important at the beginning of first-year Contracts because they all come in thinking there's a right answer. And it's good for them to see visually. They can look around and say, 'Oh, well, you know, not everybody's in agreement.'"

One of Enos's students articulated the value of this technique. "[My] favorite thing [in Enos's class] is the votes. . . . 'How many of you all think it should have come out for this guy?' 'How many of you all think the other one?' Then, we talk about it some more, and . . . we'd have to do the vote again. And so in every other class where you're doing Facebook or writing e-mail and you know you can totally excuse yourself mentally from the class, you absolutely couldn't do that in her class. And, you know, we weren't even tempted to because you were there, and she wanted to know what you think and, you know, what your vote was. So you had to be active."

Andy Leipold asserts that student engagement is the key marker of effective teaching. "When I teach a class where I do nearly all the talking, or where my questions to the students are weak, easy, or mechanical, it's a bad day at the office."

Welcome Diverse Perspectives

For the teachers we studied, student engagement also means that the students who talk feel comfortable to express a wide variety of views on the subjects the class is discussing. Students appreciate such inclusivity:

- "The class discussions were especially positive in this course. I heard many different perspectives and things I would not otherwise have thought of" (student of Patti Alleva).
- "He is able to draw out people's thoughts—and not just answers— you know, people's thoughts, in a very meaningful way, without putting pressure on them. . . . I love hearing lots of different people with lots of different ideas. . . . I think in that class more than any other, you really get a diversity of ideas from the students" (student of Andy Leipold).
- "There was constant dialogue among students. It was clear Prof. Nice wanted to hear everyone's perspective on the cases we read, and she did not want to merely rehash the facts/case holdings" (student of Julie Nice).
- "[In Contracts class], we had law students with parents that were on welfare versus law students with parents who were multimillionaires. So, you know, you had this very diverse group, and all the sudden there's this defense of unconscionability, and so, the people with the parents of welfare were, like, 'Absolutely, this is a great defense, you know? That is absolutely unconscionable.' And people who grew up in more of a privileged background, like, 'No, that's ridiculous.' Beth really mediated that well. It never got out of hand, but she allowed it to flesh itself out and to really kind of get some really interesting conversations" (student of Beth Enos).

- "He's very open to the different viewpoints. As long as you were prepared and you were trying, he wanted to hear what you had to say" (student of Philip Prygoski).

These teachers make sure that the students with whom they disagree still feel heard. One of Heather Gerken's students reports that in Gerken's Constitutional Law and Law of Democracy courses Gerken "honors the conservatives," despite the fact that she actively worked on Barack Obama's presidential campaign. One of Nancy Levit's students similarly says, "I have a sense of what her ideology is, [but] you would never have known in the class.... [She made] each student feel accepted, feel like it's an open forum to discuss ideas and not have any judgment or any disrespect toward that person's viewpoint—was just really amazing."

Creative

Many of the examples in this and prior chapters illustrate the teachers' creativity. Among other things, they sing songs, recite poetry, take students on field trips, use science fiction simulations, show videos, play games, use props, and do art exercises.

Steve Friedland uses handcuffs, fake weapons, and even a target of a human figure to "help the learning process." Tina Stark uses demonstrations for similar reasons. "I wear my best pearls to class. I take three people—one buyer, one owner, one escrow agent—to all appraise the business deal of selling the pearls. Students are in three groups in class and brainstorm what are the business issues for each—escrow agent, buyer, and owner?" Bridget Crawford uses tennis balls and Barbie dolls in Tax.

Patti Alleva uses a recurring demonstration to illustrate a key point. "I tell the students it's critical to develop as a lawyer, both sides, or ten sides of a problem, to see ten different perspectives, to argue back and forth. So, play tennis. You get the first shot, hit the ball over the conceptual net, then run to the other side, and I will literally run in the classroom to the other side, and hit the conceptual volley back again, and, oh wait, there's another reply, another way to see this, hit it back, run to the other side.... I just run around, and do it. And it's funny, I don't know why, but students focus; students remember the playing-tennis thing."

Bridget Crawford has taken the demonstration idea one step further, writing a "'tongue-in-cheek, one-act play' to teach a particularly difficult case. Students take different parts; one is the narrator, one is the appellate judge . . . [We] have the person speaking in the voice of the plaintiff, like, 'Well I want to argue this'. . . . I ask for hammy volunteers so it's fun."

Paula Franzese gives a "gift of the day": one student each day is selected to be awarded a gift in the following class session. The gifts are cupcakes or some small trinket, and they come wrapped by Franzese. The winner selects the next day's recipient. Nancy Levit also strives to shake things up every once in awhile.

> Over the years, this [goal of shaking things up] has meant:
> playing Constitutional Law Jeopardy to study the holdings of
> various decisions; examining Chinese binding shoes and reading
> two pages of Jung Chang's *Wild Swans: Three Daughters of China*
> regarding the practice of foot-binding to discuss the cultural
> construction of gender; having students role-play and cross-
> examine an expert witness in a medical malpractice case; in
> Criminal Law, viewing a clip from *Defending Our Lives* (the Acad-
> emy Award-winning film for documentary short subjects) to
> explain the phenomenon of battered women who kill their

abusers rather than leave them; asking students to bring in their worst antilawyer joke and using the caricatures to spark a discussion on making clients happy.

Ruthann Robson helps her students understand a wide variety of religious perspectives in her First Amendment class. "We do religion in the last five weeks, so before they start meeting, they get assigned into three categories. One, they have a recognized religion; second is a quasi-want-to-be religion; and third is nonreligious. They have to come up with a role for themselves and post on TWEN, like what religion they are or are not. I assign the categories . . . alphabetically and then everything that they say in class and in their group work . . . has to be from that perspective."

Many of the most creative activities are also practical lawyering exercises. In Beth Enos's contract drafting class, she has each student choose a contract the student wishes to become an expert in and draft a practice guide for that type of contract. At the end of the semester, Enos edits the practice guides and combines them in a bound set of materials she gives to the students as a parting gift. Andy Leipold takes his students on a tour of a jail so they know the stakes of the criminal procedure cases he teaches.

Because these teachers take risks, sometimes things do not go well. One of the teachers, to whom we have not attributed this story upon request, describes a great idea that he unsuccessfully tried multiple times:

> I often learn from my failures, but one time I didn't. I came up with an idea that I still think was my best ever. I tried it four times, reworking each time, and failed miserably (based on analysis of student evals and informal polling of students). I teach

Administrative Law. One day, I thought, "You know, I give students all these rules at the beginning of class: how much the midterm and final count, how much participation counts, and what that looks like, etc." At the same time, I thought, "One of the staples of administrative law is teaching students about agency rules and regulations and procedures related to those." Huh! What if, at the beginning of class, I have the students form a commission, take comments, per the Administrative Procedure Act, and promulgate the rules for the class. Brilliant! The students would have a context and they would have a voice and would really learn APA procedures for rule making. Wrong! I still don't exactly know why, but, despite trying this four different times in four different ways, students never really connected up the two ideas: APA rule making and student rules for the class. Most evals said it was an enormous waste of time! Just give us the class rules and get on with it! This comment was consistent across four classes. And, by the way, there were never any positive comments about it. I finally gave up the ghost. Maybe the students actually learned rule making better, but, despite that, I'm not going to keep doing something students virtually unanimously dislike as being a waste of time.

Another teacher, to whom we also have not attributed this story upon request, reports a very similar experience with an idea he tried, with only good intentions, in his first-year course:

Experiments are essential to becoming a better teacher. But sometimes experiments backfire. Given the flood of criticism about law schools not preparing their students for actual practice, I decided to introduce many skills exercises into my 1L class.

I discovered several things. First, students always compare their treatment by their professors to similar treatment by other professors. They resented what looked like my giving them far more work than other teachers in different sections. That matters less for electives, where students have some choice in whom they select as a teacher. But in required 1L classes, the resentment can be palpable. Second, it overloaded students with information before they were ready to assimilate it. That interfered with learning doctrine rather than aiding it. Third, 1Ls still have trouble accepting that they are learning skills as much as information. They are too tied into their undergraduate experiences. They do not, therefore, fully get the point. Moderating my efforts to, for example, use two role-plays touching on skills but mostly as a way of illustrating and reaffirming doctrine proved much more productive. Baby steps, not big jumps.

Clear Explainers

The teachers' expertise in their fields, combined with their gift for teaching and sensitivity to students, means that these law teachers are skilled at explaining concepts clearly and, in many instances, in multiple ways.

- "[She] uses her intelligence in terms of emotional intelligence to communicative intelligence, to pass it along to you at your lower intellectual [statute] so you can comprehend it. . . . You're talking about a lot of different sort[s] of IQs and EQs working at the same time and she's operating . . . everywhere" (student of Nancy Levit).
- "When she says something in class, she doesn't just say it one way and move on and expect everybody to understand it. She will stop

and literally use the words. . . . And she'll use illustrations. She uses slides and PowerPoints . . . also draw[s] diagrams. . . . I think she's very cognizant that not everybody learns in the exact same way and the same verbiage. The same language may mean nothing to me but may teach somebody else" (student of Meredith Duncan).

- "Some teachers just repeat the same thing at you and if you don't get the concept, you don't get the concept. She'd stop, break it down, and talk about it in a different way. So even if you didn't get what was on the exam in one way she would make sure you got it another way" (student of Nancy Knauer).

- "[He] is one of the best professors I've ever had of breaking down very complex situations into very, very basic building blocks and it's sort of the same elements and he can break them, each—any—problem down into the same elements that are very familiar and recognizable and then to show you how to put it back together to understand the problem" (student of Andy Leipold).

- "Just something very simple that he breaks down and tells you, this is how [performing lawyering skills] is going to work. This is what you want to get out of it. He doesn't hide the ball, just sort of substantively guides you along" (student of Larry Krieger).

- "She is able to peel away at the cases and get through all the different layers that each case is composed of. It's almost like an onion. She is able to peel away one layer, the second layer, and she explains it so clearly that at the end you pretty much know exactly where you started, and you're down at the core, and you know exactly what that case stands for" (student of Julie Nice).

- "I don't consider myself [an] exceptional law student but I feel like I leave every class able to explain that to someone else" (student of Don Hornstein).

Use Visuals and Technology Well

Many of these teachers consciously integrate visuals and technology into their teaching. "Visual supplements, whether it is the board, . . . I like filling in the blanks, that's something I do. Diagrams, key words, colors. . . . overheads, myself, using my body, my face, motions, to help people learn. . . . And I physically project the casebook pages; they see my markings, and I want them to see my markings. I want them to know I respect the text, that respecting the text and reading the words is incredibly important" (Patti Alleva). Similarly, Nelson Miller uses videos, graphics and even body movement to add to students' visual experience in his classes. Susan Kuo uses technology to enhance class discussions, employing clickers, PowerPoint slides, and Blackboard and TWEN to get everyone involved. Paula Lustbader uses art projects, charts, and the whiteboard to add visual components to her teaching.

Both Andy Taslitz and Ruthann Robson regularly use video. "He shows different clips from different movies that are very popular, that a lot of us can relate to and have seen. . . . It's something that you can see and feel so it's not just theoretical" (student of Andy Taslitz). "Prof Robson brings in videos into criminal procedure topics to illustrate points and cases, and then Robson brings it back to the topic being studied" (student of Ruthann Robson).

Andy Leipold uses videos and websites, sometimes even to create new problems for the class to discuss. "He's good about bringing in other mediums too, for his class. . . . He'll show . . . a video with this . . . new technology that Canadian police are using and [will ask], 'Well how does this relate to search and seizure [law in the United States]?'" (student of Andy Leipold).

Some of the teachers we studied use PowerPoint; others find it unhelpful. "I'm using PowerPoint now because I think they react better to that, but I now also think I've learned not to put my slides as the lecture. It's really just the guidelines. It's the structure to help structure for them where we're going, what we're supposed to get out of class, and it also reminds me of where I should be going" (Steve Friedland). One of Meredith Duncan's students explains that using PowerPoint is a part of what makes her effective: "She is visual in her presentation, both with her PowerPoints and you see her in class. She'll put one box here, and then she'll walk across the room and put another box to kind of give you—if you're a visual learner—kind of give you a way to have a different perspective on what she's trying to present. I think it's really helpful in some of her flow charts on the PowerPoints—are also very good, and later on, when you're studying for finals, to be able to look at it and kind of remember some of the things and some of the pictures she was trying to paint in her lecture." Bridget Crawford's students appreciate her use of PowerPoint slides too. A highlight for one student is that she "incorporates slides about who has evaded tax—celebrity status—juicy examples help engage us."

Other teachers choose to write on the board to give the class a visual sense of challenging concepts. "I try to not do very much in the abstract, just verbally. I will go to the board and even if it's messy, even if it's element ABC connect, connect, I always try to give a visual cue to underscore the point we're trying to make or the thing we're trying to show" (Paula Lustbader). Paula Franzese insists that PowerPoint "is too passive." She argues that writing on the whiteboard "is dynamic because three things are happening: 1) the student is listening; 2) the student is jotting down; 3) the student is also participating visually so that what they are jotting down replicates what I have been writing down. It's a simultaneous expenditure of energy, and, ultimately, I think it requires a little more active listening on the students' part and also a little more active teaching on my part."

Storytelling

A number of the teachers use storytelling as a teaching tool. One of Don Hornstein's students characterized him as "just a wonderful storyteller," adding that Hornstein "really brings the cases to life, and he seems to know some background detail about just about every case, and that kind of adds life to what is kind of just regular case opinion." Meredith Duncan explained her approach to storytelling: "I'm self-deprecating, and I share stories about my family and funny things, and I try to tell memorable stories. I do it at least once or twice a week I think, tell a story of something that happened as an illustration, and I have students who come back and say, 'I still remember the guy who knocked down the guy's door and 9-1-1 said you can't shoot them through the door.'" According to one of Andy Taslitz's students, "The thing that I remember the most is he'll tell a story, an anecdote from either his own life or somebody else he knows, to help you remember the concept we're discussing. You know, there are several stories that I remember from Criminal Law where we're discussing a particular crime, and he'll explain a situation where he knew somebody. . . . They're very funny stories that stay with you definitely during the exam and then beyond."

Repetition

Several of the teachers also use repetition as a teaching technique. Both Steve Friedland and Patti Alleva, for example, list repetition among their teaching techniques. Students appreciate the repetition:

- "He would tell us everything three times. He would tell us where we're going to go, he would tell us what we need to go, and then he would tell us what he just told us. So every day we would hear it again. We would constantly review" (student of Steve Friedland).
- "Very fast pace in class . . . but all the repetitions help. . . . No one complains because Franzese provides structure, scaffolding" (student of Paula Franzese).
- "I think he really repeats key points several times throughout, you know, not just the class but throughout the week or, you know, for exam purposes. You really know what's going to be tested. You really know what the important points are" (student of Don Hornstein).

Use Variety

Nearly all the teachers in our study consciously use a wide variety of teaching techniques. Rory Bahadur explains his approach: "Each of my classroom presentations is designed to cater simultaneously to three different learning styles, experiential, collaborative and visual. . . . As a result, I develop exercises for group work in class which teach and reinforce the substantive areas we are covering while catering to three different, broad, learning styles. Even if the existence of learning styles is currently controversial, utilizing a pedagogy that presupposes their existence creates an effective, multimodal teaching environment." Heather Gerken has a similar approach: "I vary the structure of the class. I often have competitions in class—best team gets a pass for the next day. I write on the board—this gives students time to think. I ask them to turn to neighbor and discuss a question, and I ask them to write two sentences with an intelligent response (I will mock them if they are longer). I'll ask them, 'What's the one question no one is asking that your neighbor likely has?'"

Paula Lustbader describes the variety of techniques she uses to foster her students' learning:

> I have seven groups, so seven times we're going to get a bite at this apple to be sure that we're all on board. And like today . . . I gave them all the same thing to do because it's complicated interpreting the model penal code, interpreting *mens rea* stuff. And so the groups would come up and present something, and then we would debrief it and get that cleared up. And then they would sit down and then the next group would come up, and they came at it a different way and reinforced and debriefed and came back down. So seven times, they got it. They should get it. . . . I use art for those purposes. . . . I have them do free writes. I have them stop and think for a minute. I have them summarize something. I do have them [answer] When was I the most engaged in class? When wasn't I? What was I doing to encourage that? . . . I have them do a lot of fill-in-the-blank things so there's also worksheets that they have to fill out.

Andy Leipold similarly notes, "Begin with a short summary of what you covered yesterday and where you are going today. Structure the class so that sometimes there is lecture, sometimes there is discussion, sometimes there is a video clip, and that not too much time passes before you switch among them. Every audience likes to relax the brain for a few minutes, so tell an interesting story. Summarize a bit at the end."

Students appreciate that their teachers use a variety of teaching techniques:

- "I also like the different mediums he uses. He uses PowerPoints, he uses our textbook, he uses videos, slides. We write practice questions so we're more prepared for exams. He'll split the class in half and one will take one side, the other take[s] the opposite side, and then we can argue against each other. It just keeps you interested" (student of Steve Friedland).
- "In the first week of Immigration Law, he asked all of his students to respond to a short questionnaire about our learning styles, our expectations for the class, and our personal interest in the subject matter.... This simple questionnaire ... made us, as students, much more aware of our learning styles.... He would create diagrams and charts for the visual learners. He had us split into teams and make arguments on the spot if it helped other classmates to learn by listening or to think out loud, and he gave us some sample discussion questions to prepare the night before class if some of us were not as quick on our feet. It was amazing to me that Hiroshi took the time to thoroughly present the material in such a customized, varied way" (student of Hiroshi Motomura).
- "[She] uses a variety of styles and approaches for different students. Students are not able to slip through the cracks" (student of Tina Stark).
- "One of my favorite parts about watching her teach: she will say something in four different ways all in the span of, like, a minute and a half. So if you didn't catch it the first way, you might catch it

the second way, and if you didn't catch it the second way, you might catch it the third way" (student of Julie Nice).

Extending Learning beyond the Classroom

The teachers in this study frequently extend their teaching and learning efforts beyond the classroom. For example, as noted earlier, Roberto Corrada convinces his students to ask and answer questions on his course web page. Andy Taslitz uses elaborate course web pages: his web materials include dozens of examples, numerous legal documents, problems, and other learning materials.

Several teachers use office hours to make deeper connections with their students and to help students who are struggling. As Steven Homer says, "The third place [where learning happens in his courses] is here in this office. I try to do everything I can to encourage them to come." Our observations of his office hours showed that students were present for the entire ninety minutes of office hours. Homer helped students work through questions they had about their writing, organization, and analysis. He answered questions directly when appropriate. Other times, Homer asked a series of follow-up questions that led to students developing thoughtful responses to their own questions and productive paths forward.

Patti Alleva uses "café hours" to extend her students' learning. "I do these voluntary open office hours. . . . The students know . . . I'm going to be sitting up in the lounge . . . for an hour, having a coffee with myself, but anyone and everyone is welcome to come and talk about anything in the course that's bothering them or that they're excited about."

The teachers' office hours are very productive in large part because they make themselves so accessible, as noted in Chapters 3 and 4. One of Meredith Duncan's students describes this phenomenon in a way that is typical: "After class, like, it's hard to actually get to her because there are so many people. . . . Because she is approachable you'll get ten people down there asking questions."

Steve Friedland pulls students aside or uses e-mail to try to reach the students who are struggling in his class. "He'll pull people aside before and after class. For people who show up late, he'll shoot them an e-mail, 'Is something wrong? If not, we need you to be here on time'" (student of Steve Friedland). Friedland's out-of-class assignments also include a lot more than readings: "I think a lot of the learning occurs outside the course, so I'm going to try to give them things that are not just reading assignments but also different kinds of assignments, like we're going to go to the jail in Criminal Law. In Evidence, they have to watch a case, and they have to watch lawyers in action."

Hiroshi Motomura also has his students visit the courthouse. "He had students visit the immigration court and listen to asylum merits hearings. He arranged for the class to tour the immigration detention facility in Aurora. This was all worked into the regular classes and casebook study that one expects to see in law school" (student of Hiroshi Motomura).

One of Andy Liepold's students recalled the experience of touring a jail as part of Leipold's Criminal Procedure class and was struck by Leipold's behavior during the tour." One of the things that stuck in my mind more than anything else about that tour was when we toured a cell that was occupied, and at the end he [Leipold] asked the guard to be sure and tell the inmate who lived in that cell thank you. And the guard looked at him like he was crazy. You know? They're like 'What are you talking about?' He's, like, 'Well, that's his space. . . . And we're all just going through and gawking at it, and we would like him to know that we appreciated it.' And it was just, you know, that understanding the implications of what we do—if you're a prosecutor or if you're a defense attorney where that actually puts that person."

One of Nelson Miller's students was similarly struck by being able to witness Miller in a lawyering context. "I participated with him on a . . . nonprofit incorporation project where I learned practical legal skills of how do you form a nonprofit by working on it with him, so he supervised my learning and modeled what that looks like. What do you do when you're talking to a client? Well, I sat in a room with him while he talked to clients, and I watched him and learned from him."

Paula Lustbader argues that learning outside the classroom is most likely if the professor gives her students specific exercises to complete. "I actually think more learning goes on outside of class if you give them directed exercises, if you give them focus questions so they know how to prepare for class. . . . We've been doing chats on our TWEN site so they can talk to each other about it, giving them a hypo and then posting a grading rubric so they can evaluate, but of course I've spent time talking to them about how to use the grading rubric."

Addressing Challenging Issues

One of the opportunities created by the chance to study twenty-six great teachers was to find out how they handle many of the issues of concern to law teachers. Those issues include a wide variety of problematic student behavior, such as students who appear to have come to class unprepared, say incorrect things in class, inappropriately use laptops in the classroom, have become excessively cynical, try to dominate the class discussion, or become stressed in class. Other issues that came up during our study process included how these teachers approach questions for which they do not know the answer; what they do to minimize cheating; how they respond when a class session does not go well; how they balance the recurring issue of coverage versus depth; and how they facilitate respectful and open discussions of sensitive issues.

Addressing Problematic Student Behavior

In some respects, the teachers address all forms of problematic student behavior in the same way—calmly, respectfully, and authentically. They do not yell at, or humiliate, students who engage in undesirable behavior. By and large, they operate under the assumption that students act in good faith and want to do right and do well. If the teachers do encounter a behavior they do not appreciate, they are likely to say so, often in a one-on-one conversation with the offending student. At the same time, the teachers are conscious that their public reaction to such behavior will have effects on the rest of the students in the class, and they are unwilling to do anything that interferes with the learning process of the other students.

Unprepared Students

Andy Taslitz treats unpreparedness as a signal that the student is struggling in some way and therefore offers help. "[When students are unprepared] I try to be encouraging, offer extra help." Heather Gerken and Roberto Corrada have adopted similar approaches. They calmly communicate that being unprepared is not acceptable and promise to call on the student again in the next class session:

- "I was called on and was not prepared . . . Gerken said, 'I'll come back to you,' and then e-mailed me after class." "If she asked you a question and you didn't answer, she would ask easier questions . . . she would stay on you. . . . [You] have to be prepared" (students of Heather Gerken).
- "He didn't berate you if you did not answer his questions . . . But he also would point out, like, if you weren't prepared, he was, like, 'I'm coming back to you next class'" (student of Roberto Corrada).
- "She made it clear on the first day that if you were not prepared, you could come and tell her and you could avoid getting called on that one day. You didn't know if you were going to get called on, so you were running a risk if you were not prepared that day, and you could skate if you didn't get called on. . . . We had one student in one class who was not prepared and got called on and got busted, and Nancy just had a moment of quiet and kind of raised her eyebrows a little bit . . . and said . . . 'Come see me after class,' and that was all there was. Nothing more needed to be said" (student of Nancy Levit).

Ruthann Robson describes a similar but more elaborate approach and uses progressive consequences: "Here's my rule. . . . I call on people, and if I call on you and you're not prepared or absent, then you know you're going to get called on in the next class. If you're not prepared for that, you get called on in the next class. If you get called on a third time, three strikes and your name goes to the academic dean and the dean of students for counseling. . . . In the first years that [approach] would cause a lot of anxiety about preparation, so [I explained] . . . what preparation means . . . Preparation doesn't mean you have to be able to answer every question."

Student Laptop Use

Meredith Duncan and Heather Gerken ban laptops in their classrooms; none of the students complain. Other teachers who discuss laptops do not ban laptops but are quite direct about their dislike of inappropriate laptop use during class, as Ruthann Robson explains: "I have to say, 'If you want to do that in class, you're paying to be here—go for it.' On the other hand, I will walk around; I will call someone on it . . . One thing that happened in Criminal Pro: I went around and someone had their e-mail open. [I said,] 'If that's what you're thinking relates to this class and the exercise we're trying to do, why don't you read this out?' I think you can stop that kind of thing by being humorous."

When the musician Michael Jackson died, Paula Lustbader used the event to communicate her belief that Internet use during class interferes with the learning process.

I very sneakily, the next day, went into class and said, "God, Michael Jackson passed away yesterday. I mean I've been crying all night. I've been watching all the old things. I pulled out my *Thriller* album, you know, and it's so sad. It was just so sad."

And I said, "How many of you learned about that during class? Raise those hands proudly." And 85 percent of them raised their hands, and I'm, like, they walked right into it didn't they? And I said, "And how many of you could concentrate on what else happened in class that day after you heard that news?" You can't be on the Internet. I am so ADD that I have to turn the e-mail thing off if I'm working because any time there's the beep, I'm on it. . . .

I gave them this long rap and I said that it's disrespectful to me; it's disrespectful to your colleagues; it's really doing you a disservice . . . And so then, what was interesting is then we did an art thing. . . . One of them came up with a hypothetical statute that said, "Anyone who's on the Internet during class is disrespecting the teacher."

Paula Franzese's approach to the laptop issue is more holistic; she strives to build in breather moments so that she can retain her students' focus. "I call on lots and lots of people during the course of a class because I can tell, a laptop can be a great asset but can also be a great distraction. . . . I will sometimes build digressions into class simply to allow for us to collectively take a breather rather than lose students individually."

Dominating Student

One of Roberto Corrada students reported on an incident involving a student who "liked to monopolize time with questions that could have been asked outside in office hours, where it seemed like almost every time she spoke the entire class would sigh because it was, like, oh . . . 'Why is she saying this?'" The student vividly recalled how Corrada had handled the issue, saying, "But I respected the way that he dealt with that because he was never rude to her or he never shushed her or skirted her questions. . . . And even if that's not happening to you, if you see that happen to someone else, it changes your perception of the class and the teacher's perception to questions. He was always very respectful of her and would say . . . 'Well, this is the general answer, but you know, if you have any more questions, you can stay after class and I'll speak to you about it.'"

One of Bridget Crawford's students reported that, in the first three weeks of class, some of the male students challenged her repeatedly. Crawford, according to the student, "managed them well, did not engage." Instead, Crawford "would say, 'This is beyond the scope of this class.'" The student reported that after a few such episodes no one challenged her. The student concluded that Crawford "gives the impression she can be mean but doesn't want to."

Excessively Cynical Student

One of Julie Nice's greatest concerns is students who have become excessively cynical. She has developed specific techniques for addressing these students.

> As much as a problem for a teacher that doesn't care, it's a problem for a student who's really gone all the way to cynicism. It's very difficult. I unfortunately think that's fairly endemic in legal education, in part because we do it to students. I think [legal education] is very coercive and toxic in the classroom.
>
> I'm very overt with them about that. I say, "Oh, that sounded so cynical. Please say something more so I don't have to think what you just said means you've gone all the way to the dark side, because if you've gone to the dark side I don't think you can learn, and I don't think you care, and I don't think you can contribute." . . . Those are very tricky moments because I'm saying something very negative about what a student just said, but I'm giving the student a chance to say more.
>
> I rarely believe that students want to be cynical; they hate that feeling of hopeless[ness], so I'm trying to throw them a little lifeline to say something more. . . . Every now and then I'll have a student who will cross their arms and shut down. When that happens, I follow up with that student. I'll shoot them an e-mail and say, "Please, I want to talk more about this. I want to understand

more. Maybe I misunderstood you, or maybe you're saying what I think you're saying, and I want to see where it comes from, and what that means for you, and how you'll try to fulfill a path in law if you've already sort of defaulted, given up." . . . Mostly, I think they take the lifeline. They don't want to be cynical. They're feeling defeated; they're feeling demoralized.

How They Handle Questions They Cannot Immediately Answer

Many of the teachers we studied respond to questions they cannot answer immediately in the same way. "She's not afraid to say, 'You know, that's a really interesting question. I don't know, but let me look into that, and I'll get back with you on that next class.' . . . She did that a handful of times in both classes, and I found that refreshing as opposed to some professors who felt put on the spot, the deer in the headlights, and then they'd spew for five minutes and be completely wrong" (student of Meredith Duncan). "If you ask a question that he doesn't know the answer to . . . he'll go as far as he knows and then says, 'You know, I'll look into it,' and then, the next day, the first thing that he does the beginning of class is says, 'Now this is the answer to. . . .'" (student of Andy Leipold).

Class Sessions That Go Poorly

When a class session goes poorly, the teachers are equally candid and model the type of reflective, self-directed thinking they hope their students develop. "I try to share my concern that I think something's not clicking, or I don't feel like I'm expressing myself, or 'Guys, what's going on? . . . Let's think about what just happened; share with me.' [I] use the beginning of next class to make corrections" (Patti Alleva).

Susan Kuo tells the story of a particular class session that did not go well:

One time, to my great mortification, . . . I had to go back in and apologize to the class for mishandling a situation. It happened in South Carolina just the day before an instance on the news. There was a police officer/cruiser . . . chasing an African American suspect . . . and you could hear them talking and they used the N word several times. . . .

I warned the students (the students were the ones who sent me the video). We were having a discussion about race and racial profiling and any kind of racialized views of the defendant would that come into play when determining reasonable suspicion or probable cause . . . This had been on the news the night before so I played back part of it, and students were, "Oh, heck, we've seen this all before." But then another student started giving hypotheticals based on this, and he kept using the N word. . . . This was at the end of class, and the students were getting very, very agitated.

I did not handle that as well. I kept trying to bring him back. "N word aside, let's talk about what happened here; analyze this." What was interesting was it was that speaker who came to me after class. I was in my office sulking because I had handled it poorly and [was] thinking about what I would do the next day to fix it. He said, "Professor Kuo, I feel like you need to protect me because I said some things in class that students are angry at me for, and they are telling me they are angry for, and I don't know what to do." I said, "I will protect you but also the class."

I went in the next day with a "I'm very sorry, I did not handle this well, and I could have handled it better. We need some ground rules about how we are going to function in this class, you know, lay some ground rules on how we are going to work out conflict." I felt better after class because several of the students who had been upset with me said they appreciated my coming back in and discussing it. . . . You can't stop [students] from saying things like that, but you can act upon it in a more productive way that makes people feel validated—not only the speaker but also the listeners.

Balance Coverage versus Depth

While some of the teachers we studied did not weigh in on the coverage question at all, those who did overwhelmingly reported that they choose to emphasize depth over breadth of coverage. One of Roberto Corrada's students explains Corrada's approach to designing his syllabus in a way that reflects this orientation to the question of coverage: "[In] first-year Contracts class, . . . he picked a manageable amount of substantive material and emphasized that over and over again, kind of realizing, probably, from a lot of the studies that he does on pedagogy, that even the best students won't retain a lot of substantive information six months out, and so trying to learn all of contract law is not as beneficial as teaching the core principles and trying to teach them well, and teaching you the skill set of thinking like a lawyer, as opposed to massive amounts of substantive law that you will certainly forget and almost certainly be changed by the time you graduate."

Sensitive or Controversial Topics

The common thread in the comments below is that the teachers we studied do not eschew controversy; instead, they find ways to encourage dissident voices, calm discussion, and foster respect among their students.

Heather Gerken, for example, strives, in her Constitutional Law class, to "build trust through the structure." She explains that "by the time we get to controversial topics, there is trust, which is important, especially for conservative students." She strives to "give them space to discuss." She focuses on arguments and reminds students about important cases, when necessary to focus the discussion, asking questions such as, "What did we learn from ____ case?" She also describes another strategy for helping students voice unpopular views. "I have students take on roles of Supreme Court justices . . . [I] ask students to give the best argument according to the justice's views. . . . [It's] easier for students to speak in another's voice. I also tell students, 'Defend your justice.'"

Ruthann Robson creates what she calls a "safe zone." In her seminar on Sexuality and the Law, she and her students agree upon a cue for the safe zone that allows students to take a time out if they become uncomfortable about a topic. Her students appreciate that she creates an atmosphere in which students are comfortable expressing nonconformist views "[She] pushes it further than most normally take [the discussion]." "Robson finds the energy of the class, and gives students permission to 'go and come back if you need to.'"

Susan Kuo describes how she approaches controversial topics in her classroom:

> I think I get away with a lot and, for better or worse, I've learned to use my size, my gender, my race, all of these things, and my age or my appearance of age to my advantage. . . .
>
> I am able to go through the race issues and, for me, I think, being Asian, I feel that some of the students feel that I can speak with some kind of authority about race issues but without

putting them in that black/white confrontation, not neutral but in a safe place for them. Also, I think, [because of my] size and gender, they feel less threatened by me. It's one of those times when I feel like I get the benefit of the doubt on some of these issues that, for example, a white male would not, especially a large, white male. . . .

Mostly when I'm teaching a rather uncomfortable subject—I not only do that in Crim Law but also Crim Pro—I see these issues come up in courts and certainly with the seminars that I teach that are on race, law, and social justice seminar, I spend a lot of time preparing those ahead of time. . . . I spend a lot of time thinking about it and, typically, I would use myself as an example of one [of] the hypothetical[s] they were are working off. . . .

We had a few tense moments this year about the *Getz* case in particular. . . . I had a student from New York who was basically saying, "Well, you guys don't understand what it's like to be on the subway with those kinds of people and how they are scary." The reaction of the other students—"those other kind of people"— now what does that mean? It was a very racialized statement she was making. I don't leave those statements to flop like a fish. I say, "Exactly what does that mean?" . . . One way that I've addressed it in the past and continue to do, especially in Crim Pro, is that I have a good faith clause at the beginning of class with students.

Kuo also acknowledges that she has not always handled controversial issues so well:

Some topics are hard to teach because they elicit strong emotions. Perhaps the classic example is rape doctrine, a staple of the first-year Criminal Law course, although some professors choose not to include it. . . . I had a bad teaching day when I allowed the students' obvious discomfort with the subject matter and unwillingness to engage in discussion to dictate coverage. Rather than exploring the cases and accompanying materials in greater depth, which would have meant addressing the tension in the room, I vaulted directly into our theft readings, propelled in part by my own relief at the change of topic. My haste, however, was a mistake. The students seemed disinterested in learning about theft, and, as it turns out, at least some, if not many, were still ruminating over rape. In the last seconds of class, one of these students raised her hand and asked, tongue-in-cheek, "If someone rapes a prostitute, is that theft?" This quip not only earned uproarious laughter from the bulk of the class as they began traipsing out, but also prompted another student to shout angrily across the room, "You guys are so stupid!"

Caught by surprise, I was unsure of how to address the situation. I returned to my office and fretted about my inability to cultivate an environment sensitive to the statistical likelihood that the class included rape victims, perpetrators, and alleged perpetrators. I also thought about what I wanted the students to glean from our coverage of rape. I did not want the takeaway to be that rape was a subject of levity. I wanted, among other things, for them to consider how social norms have shaped the enforcement of rape law (and vice-versa). Ultimately, I decided to include a question on the final exam seeking student perspectives on rape-law reform and the element of nonconsent. At the start of the next class session, I spoke briefly about the importance as well as the challenges of teaching rape law. I notified them of my plan to test them on an aspect of our study of rape law and, to ensure adequate time for reflection, supplied them with the actual question.

The net result of my attempt to address my earlier teaching mishap was a stack of well-considered responses to my question. Some students criticized rape law reform; others offered suggestions for improving our laws. All conveyed an understanding of the policy concerns surrounding the controversial and divisive topic of rape. By using the final exam to prompt more thoughtful engagement, I was able to make rape doctrine an important aspect of the students' study of criminal law. A more general takeaway from the experience, in addition to its sharp reminder to remain vigilant for signs of disquiet in the classroom, is that teaching blunders should be addressed head on and that mistakes should be put to rights.

Beginning and Ending Class Sessions

The teachers start and end class sessions in a variety of ways. As noted earlier in this chapter, many of the teachers we studied begin individual class sessions by reviewing the key concepts for the previous class session, articulating the goals for the current session, and describing what the class will be doing during the current session. Don Hornstein, for example, says, "I orient the day with what we have been doing. . . . I do some review, even if it's, like, two or three minutes, four minutes, just reminding them what we did. But I definitely find that necessary. I just don't assume that, given all their other classes and everything else . . . they remember yesterday's class as well as I do. So I get them back into the vocabulary and back into the intellectual train of thought."

Other teachers start with a current newspaper story, as does Tina Stark: "Students need to look at business . . . the *Wall Street Journal* is required. We start the class with five to ten minutes discussing current issues in business." Paula Franzese starts by expressing her enthusiasm for the course and her expectation that her students feel the same way; we saw her starting her class, saying, "Property connoisseurs!" and she does the same thing after the break. Heather Gerken does "a 'speed round' at the beginning of class where we walk through the class from the previous day, doctrine and theory . . . [and discuss] what pushes the doctrine."

The teachers almost never conclude class by simply noting that the class time is over. Many foreshadow what the class will be learning in the next class session. For example, Rory Bahadur chooses to use the last five minutes of the class to consolidate the students' learning. He often asks his students to write down what they have learned in class that day and says, "I leave five minutes at the end of my class usually for a recap of the class, for example, anyway. [In] a recent class, . . . I didn't have time for a recap, so at the beginning of the other class, I gave like a mock quiz on what we did in the last class." Bridget Crawford uses endings to review the key points of the class session: "I try [to wrap things up], and, if I run out of time, I tell them I will start the next class with a quick overview of the four things we just covered."

Beginning and Ending Courses

The teachers are particularly thoughtful about how they start and end their courses. Each identifies a very specific set of goals and designs activities to take advantage of those magic moments when they have, arguably, the greatest degree of student attention.

Course Beginnings

For some, the first day of class is a moment to create community. For Cary Bricker, creating connections among her students is a way to help students feel comfortable being vulnerable during the course, and a lesson about good lawyering:

> We have them stand up in groups of eight and tell a story of their own lives to us with a lot of eye contact. So much of what I think makes an effective communicator in a trial context is taking the jury and putting them where they need to be. So they're watching the car accident or they're watching the mugging if the prosecutor or whatever, and it's the emotional connection that I was talking about before where if the lawyer believes in the case then the jury's going to believe in the case.
>
> Well these are personal stories that . . . these students . . . really believe in. So, the idea isn't to have them come in and give confessions, even though we have many, many who cry when they present. . . . But that's how we start that class. Now that's very purposeful. It's both to break the ice so that they're all going to trust each other more, because once you've sort of talked about something somewhat personal, in that . . . and we say "what happens in Vegas stays in Vegas" and we mean it. But it also teaches them and everybody sees [and thinks] "Oh wow! I felt that, you know. I really felt that emotional connection with that story and with that person." And then I do say . . . "Those are your openings. Those are your closings. That same commitment and emotion. Don't lose that."

Paula Franzese connects with her students by making it a point to share her perspective on teachers. "The very first class, I make that promise to them, and I tell them that teaching is a sacred trust, and I tell them that for better or worse we never forget our teachers. I tell them about my infatuation with my first-grade teacher."

Bridget Crawford's approach is to make a connection using humor and fun in her big classes. "I usually give them a song on the first day and a song on the last day. . . . I, they, write a new one each semester. It depends. Or, it's a poem; one time it was a parody of *Hamlet* 'To Tax, or not to Tax, that is the question.' "

Others teachers welcome their students, provide an overview of the course, and plan a defining learning activity or interaction that sets the stage for the rest of the course, as Steve Friedland explains:

I try to start each course with a problem. I want to draw them in. I want them to see what's going to happen here. This is what we were talking about: boring material versus exciting.

Evidence—I'm not going to start with the statute. I'm going to start with objection, response, ruling. And in Criminal Law I'm going to start with 'Okay, here's an issue; here's what happens out there. How should society deal with it?' Then I surely put up what I think is what I call a course framework. It's at least one way for understanding a lot of it. Crim Law has certain elements over and over again. . . . So I try to orient them to GPS, this is that big global picture, and I give them an idea where we're going in each course.

I try to look at it as a travel log. 'Here are the thirteen countries we're going through. It may feel like three days, but look we're going to have some fun doing all this stuff.' So I try to make it like that to create a preview. We're going on a cruise, and I'm telling them about the malaria and all the other things out there and the Legionnaire's Disease, and the bad food, and we're going to get bad weather. . . . I try to show them that there's going to be some good stuff.

As noted earlier, Hiroshi Motomura often starts his courses by asking his students how they prefer to learn. "I ask them two questions. . . . One of the things I ask them in that context—and I give them an example of what I mean—Are you a visual learner? Do you like to see the big picture, or are you a detailed person? Do you read? What do you do when you are in class? And I get different sorts of answers. . . . I want to get specific answers as to certain people. . . . In a class of forty, I might get five to ten responses that are extremely specific that I need to make note of. But, for the other people, it's a question of sensitizing them to the fact that there are other people in the class that learn very differently."

Philip Prygoski provides a careful overview on the first day of class. "I start my courses by giving them an overview of where we're going. I mean, I told them last week, and I told them again today, I said, 'Look, we're doing really only three things in here: judicial review, separation of powers, and federalism.' And [in] Con Law I, I went through. I said, 'Read Articles one, two, and three carefully. We're going to go over the three articles pertaining to the three branches.'"

Course Endings

As explained in detail in Chapter 8, several of the teachers do some sort of review to end their classes or otherwise acknowledge, in a serious and respectful way, that their students have questions about their final exams. Rory Bahadur's ending for his Torts class has become a revered institution at his law school. On a Saturday shortly before his final, Bahadur has his students write an answer to an exam-like hypothetical and, then, using a rubric he has created, provide peer feedback. The day ends with a massive feast; Bahadur has spent the previous day preparing a barbecue pork dinner for the entire class (for those who do not eat pork, he provides chicken or a vegetarian dish).

Others prefer to end the class with a ceremony or, like Bahadur, a party.

Paula Lustbader ends with a game that is also a review and then, after the exam, hosts a barbecue at her home. "We play charades to review the whole course substantively.... The students have different crimes that they have to create a whole scenario, and we split them up into about eight groups. And they'll come in and do theirs and the rest of the class has to do the analysis. They have to issue spot and do analysis.... And then ... I talk to them about they may have thought they were on the short bus, but they are on the express bus. And they're going to do great things, and we always pray they will find their right work.... And then right after their exam—their exam ends at 12:30 in the afternoon—and they come to my house for a barbecue as closure."

Heather Gerken ends her seminar classes with a meal in her home and her larger classes with fun—a poetry slam. She says, "With seminars, I invite the class to my home for wine and cheese. With Con Law, [we] have a review the day before the exam. In Con Law and Civ Pro ... [we] have a poetry slam where students write one bad poem about the topic."

Hiroshi Motomura ends his Immigration Law course with the Woody Guthrie song based on a true story about deportees from the 1940s. He also likes to remind students how much they have learned and to reinforce the idea that each student can and should individually make sense of the course. "I'm often convincing them of both how much content and knowledge they've mastered, how many skills they have mastered, but also how manageable it is that they can actually see this forest.... I tell them.... 'At the end of the day I want you to keep outlining your outline until it keeps getting briefer and briefer and you bring it down. Here's [a] one page overview of what we've done, but you can organize it in lots of different ways.'"

Steven Homer also ends his class encouraging his students. "I try to give them a little pep talk.... I share with them how special it is for me to watch them grow as lawyers and what that experience is like for me.... I [also] have some practical advice, 'I always take a pen with me' and that kind of stuff. I always tell them 'Never tell yourself you're stupid because you are new at something. Never tell yourself that you're stupid because you're nervous about something.' These are radically different things."

Nelson Miller and Patti Alleva end their courses on more thematic or big picture points. Nelson Miller tells his students, "some of the friends in my practice whom I met as opposing counsel ... have become friends. [It's] as if to say to them, 'You too will join a community of professionals.' And you will have this meaning of the subject itself, and you'll have it within the community of people of whom you respect and value even as they do you." Patti Alleva tries to leave her students with a new way of looking at the course, with what she calls "a slight shift of perspective." For example, in Civil Procedure, "we talk about justice ... and I do a quick run through of all the subjects and rules we covered in brief.... I try to show them how all of them relate to fairness. So that in the end it's fairness that matter[s] most in some ways, whether you're trying to apply, interpret, and live these rules."

Conclusion

At the end of their courses, the teachers we studied have spent themselves in the effort to teach, to connect, to make a difference in the lives of their students. For some, all that is left for them on the last day is tears. "[On the last day], I always cry. I tell them it was a joy to teach them. I ask them to stay in touch" (Tina Stark). "In the end I can't say anything. I get too teary" (Ingrid Hillinger).

8

How Do the Best Law Teachers
Provide Feedback and Assess Students?

Assessment

The exceptional teachers we studied integrate feedback and assessment to help students learn complex course material. As Julie Nice states, "I don't know how to do assessment other than as another learning opportunity." Paula Lustbader echoes this point: "They learn by doing. They learn by practicing again. They learn by getting a lot of feedback and tweaking and coming back. . . . They learn different ways. Not just that different students learn different ways, each student learns from different stimulus."

Many of the teaching behaviors, expectations, and personal qualities depicted earlier in this book also describe how these excellent teachers assess students and give them feedback. They are committed to helping their students succeed, as Nancy Knauer shows: "Ultimately, how well our students perform is a reflection on us." The teachers we studied want students to learn important knowledge, skills, and values, grow into their professional roles, and develop confidence. Ingrid Hillinger illustrates her approach and commitment to student learning in her "Teaching Philosophy":

> In addition to demanding class assignments, students have to complete three drafting exercises of ascending complexity and difficulty. They have to do them in teams. The drafting exercises are designed to develop certain skills, (e.g., statutory analysis, code methodology, drafting, and risk identification), and to reinforce certain concepts, rules, and techniques. These drafting exercises permit students to apply what they have learned to a new fact pattern. They reinforce information by testing it. They also give students the opportunity to apply what they have learned—both information and skills. I make individual comments on each drafting exercise. I also hand out a detailed general comment sheet. . . . These exercises are especially helpful and important to students who do not test well. Those students learn they too can be good lawyers.

Commitment to Student Learning

The teachers we studied vary considerably in the kinds of assessments they offer and the feedback they give, but they are deeply thoughtful about integrating assessment as part of learning. In talking about giving students practice and feedback, Nelson Miller observes, "we all know the value of that . . . frequent assessment is critical to development."

Ruthann Robson explains how she approaches assessment and feedback: "Testing is an important part of teaching—the ultimate feedback for a teacher, as well as the feedback/grade the professor gives the student." She also talks about how she guides students after giving them a long fact pattern. "Figure out the structure of it [so] that you're not driven by the narrative; you're driven by the structure. Organize. This is the structure, this is how to organize it. Some organization has a logic to it, some does not. You could do this first or do that first, it doesn't really matter." For first year students, she also connects what she does in her doctrinal class with students' skills-based courses. "'You are doing this . . . like you are doing in your memo.' I think for a portion of students, that's really terrific. They make that connection."

Steven Homer articulates how he seeks to help students learn by setting challenging but attainable goals. "You can't just be: 'I am never going to be satisfied. I'm tough and demanding and you'll never please me. But go on, keep trying.' It has to be justified. So I write a lot of comments on their stuff to really give them a feel for what my interaction with it was. How I felt about it, what I saw, what I saw them doing, the diagnosis of that. I frame a lot of the comments in terms of 'I can see you're trying to do x and it's successful to this extent; now to take it to the next level. . . . I can envision for you a better paper, a more successful paper.'"

Cary Bricker shows how she provides multiple forms of feedback and helps students develop self-assessment skills as part of their learning. "If we're doing role-plays, for example . . . client interviews and client counseling . . . [the students] do the interview and then first reflection ('What worked?' 'What didn't?' 'Did you connect?'), a series of questions. So the students have to give feedback on their own performance, and then we will give some constructive ways of really creating that relationship with the client."

Nelson Miller's students take periodic, multiple-choice quizzes. On a weekly basis he tracks students' individual scores and "collective responses on single items so that I know when . . . too many students are missing the same item." He tries to figure out "what have I done, then, in instruction or failing to instruct, or what are they're doing, perhaps, in misunderstanding the concept or its application that we can correct together?"

One of Andy Leipold's students commented on his commitment to learning. "His goal is to have everyone do well [on assessments]. . . . He wants everyone to walk away from the class knowing more and having learned things from him."

Opportunities to Practice and Get Feedback

Many of the teachers provide students with multiple and varied opportunities to practice and get feedback during the course, even when they teach large classes. Enabling students to practice their learning in and outside of class, they offer practice exams, midterm exams, writing assignments, hypothetical problems, small group projects, and role-plays. "I give oral hypotheticals. I give them written hypotheticals. I make and provide them with multiple-choice exercises" (Meredith Duncan).

Patti Alleva uses small group exercises, role-plays, reflection moments, short writing assignments, and "'checkpoint exercises' . . . realistic questions or hypotheticals that implicate all three learning domains: doctrine, skill, and values." Susan Kuo talks about her course-long approach: "To more accurately gauge student understanding, I use in-class exercises that call for students to apply

WHAT THE BEST LAW TEACHERS DO

what they have learned and to practice making legal arguments. . . .
When possible, I try to correct misunderstandings about the material as we go, rather than waiting until the end of the course."

The teachers also communicate their feedback in different ways.
They deliver verbal feedback during class, write comments on students' work, hold individual and small group conferences, disseminate sample answers, distribute scoring sheets, facilitate peer reviews, and engage students in self-assessment. Many teachers give multiple kinds of feedback. Noting that "feedback is critical to student learning," Andy Taslitz writes about how he offers practice and feedback in three different courses:

> Feedback can be hard in large classes. Nevertheless, I take several
> different approaches. In my first-year Criminal Law class, I give
> two short essay examinations, followed by written individual
> comments, student meetings, a sample answer, and an optional
> group review session on each exam. In Evidence, I periodically
> assign multiple-choice questions, then spend much of a class
> period reviewing them, not only to identify the "right" answer but
> also to discuss the approach to taking multiple-choice questions.
> In Criminal Procedure, I use an at-home role-play negotiation,
> with students submitting their agreements and a brief analysis of
> the legal issues and negotiating process, then spend a class period
> just discussing that exercise. But the exercise is designed to review
> all the major course issues covered up to that point.

Students appreciate having the opportunities to practice and
learn from their experiences.

- "I liked that Professor Corrada tested us throughout the course. It
  helped me feel like I was really learning the material as I went and

I was more prepared for my final exam" (student of Roberto Corrada).

- "[She] puts you in the position of lawyer—you are ready to take her exam even midway through the course" (student of Paula Franzese).

- "Every single week there was some sort of drafting exercise, which was phenomenal. . . . You'd get . . . copious feedback on what you did, which of course makes you that much better because you have another one coming up" (student of Beth Enos).

- "In Immigration class we had problems assigned to us and people were on call . . . and then, afterwards, he'd e-mail out the answer to the class, going through the whole problem. . . . I don't know how else you'd learn it other than to do these kind of small check-in and feedback type of assignments along the way" (student of Hiroshi Motomura).

- "Excellent use of technology and questions to make the class interesting and constantly provide feedback" (student of Susan Kuo).

Practice Exams

Many of the teachers we studied give practice or midsemester exams. Rory Bahadur surprises his students by giving them a fake exam on the first day of class. "And then I tell them 'In ten classes, you will be able to answer this exam.' Ten classes later, when we're done with the intentional torts, I give them that exam again under exam conditions. And it surprises them how much they've learned in the ten days."

Others teachers use practice exams in the classroom or make them available to students in other ways. Bridget Crawford says that she provides practice exams so students can "self-assess their substantive learning." She administers "a practice midterm that has no impact on grades. I want students to know early in the semester if they need to 'step up' their classroom preparation or studying." Heather Gerken makes a similar point. "I give practice exams. I make all available and give them one, with sample answers with annotations. The best students take the practice exams and come to talk about them. I am happy to review practice exams and tell students the ten things they got wrong."

Students in Paula Lustbader's course take increasingly complex, cumulative practice exams every week. "[The students] start off with just a very simple problem, and it's a very simple IRAC structure. . . . The doctrine gets a little more challenging; there's more grey facts, and they're having to really start to develop. . . . At the beginning there's more explicit sample answers, and then, as we go, there's less" (Paula Lustbader).

On her course website, Susan Kuo puts up sample exams: "[The students] can actually think of it as a sample of what to expect, and then I give them sample answers." Roberto Corrada expands on giving sample answers: "I go back and I take a sample A answer, B answer, and C answer to the four final exam problems, and I put them online for the students to see, and I don't tell them why one got an A, one got a B and one got a C, but . . . there's something to learn in comparing them and trying to figure that out. . . . I think students can learn a lot from models and so I try to create models for them. When I put those things up, the most hits I get on anything are those, so I know students are looking at those things and trying to figure out what makes this good and what makes this not so good."

Nancy Knauer takes the opposite approach to giving sample answers to practice exams. "I will not give them a sample answer because they're not going to try. They're going to look at it and say, 'Yeah, that's what I was going to say.' So I really want them to try to write it out, and then I will edit that for them."

Students learn from taking and evaluating their classmates' practice exams, as Rory Bahadur explains: "At the end of each topic . . . I give them a mock exam . . . [and] have them grade each other's. . . . When I have students write the exam under exam conditions, and then I have them switch with other people, and everybody has a rubric . . . students suddenly understand. We then come up with a list: 'The top ten things I could do to fail Bahadur's essay exam is . . .' and they generate that list and I never have to tell them what I was thinking because they realize it for themselves."

Students in Nancy Levit's class receive four kinds of feedback on midsemester and practice exams. "[I give a] midterm in every class with intense comments written on them. A model answer or answer key for me, but also students' best papers because the answer key, as I explain to them, has to be the universe of all possible right things they could say and nobody's going to get all of them. So seeing what a peer good answer would be is an important form of feedback, as is coming in to talk. You do one thing and you get four forms of feedback. . . . I offer to do one more midterm for each of them and offer to evaluate a written practice final for each of them" (Nancy Levit).

Students value having opportunities to learn from taking practice exams and seeing sample answers. Students praise Heather Gerken and compare her favorably with their usual experiences. "She reads your [practice] exams and gives feedback—some professors don't even read—she would read and provide typed comments to everyone." One of his students talked about the value of the model answers Andy Taslitz gave out: "He'll take it under time conditions and give you his sample.... It's always magnificent."

Other students similarly observe how much they learn from having practice exams:

- "He was open to me to go and print out an essay question, write it out, and I would go to his office.... He and I would sit down, and he would go through my answer, and then he would pick apart my answer. And then we would discuss it, and he would tell me, 'Well, here you made the wrong argument' or 'Here you didn't make the right argument,' and that helped me, and I did that throughout the semester" (student of Philip Prygoski).

- "When it got closer to final time, [he] posted online different examples of what was an A paper, a B paper and a C paper in his class, and I mean, like, let's be honest, grades matter in law school, they matter to everybody. And the thing about first-year law school, what you're trying to figure out, is how to change your writing style to meet each professor's specific needs.... You could read those sample exams and see what he wanted from you.... It was fair, you know?" (student of Roberto Corrada).

- "He gave us a practice writing exam for Criminal Procedure. I think he did it for Evidence as well, where he'll give you a question, you'll respond to it, and he'll go through it thoroughly and read it for you, which is helpful if you haven't had him as a professor before, and most professors don't take the time out to do that. You see their thought process and their grading process during the exam, but he takes the time to give us practice so we can reach that level of high expectation that he sets. He can give that feedback to us so we can better improve ourselves" (student of Andy Taslitz).

Writing Assignments

Many of the teachers in our study provide students with extensive practice and feedback on writing assignments. Tina Stark comments on her multifaceted method of teaching students contract drafting: "I have extended office hours. [On a draft] I come up with a list of standard comments—very detailed. [I] cut and paste them in with individual comments.... For [scheduled] conferences, students get detailed comments ahead of time. I also offer shorter, fifteen-minute conferences before major assignments are due. Students do a draft, come to a miniconference, and we go over portions."

Larry Krieger provides prompt feedback on his writing assignments. "I have students turn in a copy of their preparation in the first class each week, and return it to them with detailed feedback from me by the end of the week while the material is still fresh. I try to get the assignments back within three days every week, and the first half of the course I'm successful." He alters this approach later in the semester: "They don't need the feedback as quickly. They know they don't need the reassurance." Similar to other teachers, he recognizes the challenges of providing effective, detailed feedback:

I am finding I have probably worked too hard to give students individualized, written feedback on a regular basis. That is ... close to an ideal thing to do, but it is a huge time demand of course and so not many of us do it. For some learning, it is critical (feedback on written work product, especially involving professional writing or other skills), but it can be overdone if, as in my case, it keeps me from expanding the seats in my classes or programs. It seems that students learn as much as they want to learn, and for many, the written feedback is more than they want on a regular basis. I have been asking for feedback and input on this from alumni of my courses, and the mix thus far has been consistently about 25 percent saying they value the feedback every week (my preferred frequency), and about 75 percent saying they could do without such regular written, personal feedback. They tell me that when I go over the assignment in detail, orally for the entire class, they get all or most of the same input (which saves me a lot of time), and that even if not doing that, other critique, comments, and responses to student questions in class gives them most of what they needed. I do not take this to mean I should not do any individual written feedback; some of the work clearly needs personal input. But I do think, with more consideration, I will be able to decrease the frequency by perhaps 70 percent, thinking case-by-case how to assure the needed learning happens in other concrete, participatory ways in class.

Beth Enos requires her students to prepare each other for transactional practice in her Contract Drafting course: "In addition to weekly drafting assignments, [students] complete a project that is 50 percent of their grade. Each student chooses a particular type of contract to become an "expert" on. The student puts together a packet of drafting information on that type of contract. The packet includes an original article, a helping document of some sort (glossary, checklist, flowchart, or something like that), an annotated sample contract, and an annotated bibliography. The sixteen projects are then copied and compiled into a reference manual for each student. I hear from students and graduates every year that the reference manual is a much-used and treasured resource in their practice."

In his "Teaching Philosophy," Steven Homer also considers how the feedback he gives students will help them later as practicing attorneys. "I pay very close attention to my students' written work, by commenting extensively. Here as well, I worry that it is too much—I know they can absorb only so much. I don't expect them to take it all in at a single sitting. Rather, my hope is that they'll use the comments as a reference, since the comments represent individualized teaching tailored to each student's strengths and weaknesses. I err on the side of extensive feedback because the reality of practice may well be that they receive no feedback at all. I want them to have a detailed measure of their progress, and to appreciate critique not as a fault-finding endeavor, but as an opportunity to examine their strengths and weaknesses."

Students express their gratitude for the written feedback they receive:

- "If you have any opportunity to have her working with you on your writing, whether it's on law review or research and writing project or even a law-school exam . . . she will sit down with you and walk through every line of your law-school exam and explain exactly . . . why this or that needed to be improved. And I don't think you can have an interaction with her on your writing and not come out writing better" (student of Nancy Levit).
- "[Having to write journals] was really annoying at the time . . . but . . . he actually wrote little responses to them, and it was very individual and very personalized. . . . You know he paid attention and cared about everything we did" (student of Larry Krieger).
- "[She] gave really detailed feedback, like, fix this—everything from substance to errors in punctuation" (student of Ruthann Robson).

- "[After writing up a role-play outcome], he'll write comments on it so even if you don't go and see him after class, you know . . . what did you miss and what could you have done better" (student of Andy Taslitz).

Students also appreciate when their teacher empowers them to do better, not just adopt the teacher's approach or style. "She has the capacity—the gift of articulating what you are saying in three sentences. 'Here's what I think you're saying, and here's what I think you mean to say' and then helps you get there in your voice" (student of Heather Gerken). "I felt that she really worked to understand what you were trying to say. She wouldn't just leave it at not understanding something and telling you that" (student of Ruthann Robson).

In addition to providing helpful comments, some teachers also engage students in conveying feedback to their classmates. Cary Bricker notes, "I find their comments are at least as good as mine when we are in our seminar. They make some very insightful observations." Hiroshi Motomura illustrates the approach to peer feedback he uses in his seminars: "Everyone writes a one-page comment on everyone else's draft. . . . I model that after song-writing workshops that I've been in. . . . [I am] sensitive to the fact that students are not used to sharing with other students. But . . . the thing they find the most helpful and rewarding was getting feedback from other students and learning to give feedback to other students." One of Hiroshi Motomura's students waxed enthusiastic about the peer feedback experience: "Perhaps the best part of the class was the exchange of drafts between the students for critique and commentary."

Meetings with Students

Many of these teachers use meetings as another way to give students practice and feedback. Some require individual conferences with students. Others offer students the opportunity to meet face-to-face to discuss the students' development, provide feedback, and assess how well students are learning. Paula Lustbader discusses how she conducts meetings after students take one of the midsemester exams in her course. "I meet with them for about twenty minutes, but before they meet with me they have to go through the grading rubric and a sample answer of the first issue so they can see what they were supposed to be doing and then come in and tell me where they think they're having challenges. But I also ask them to tell me what they're doing right. Can they see it? Can they point to it?"

Talking about her Professional Visions course, Patti Alleva articulates how she engages with students during their required individual conference. Before she meets with individual students, she provides them a list of questions, including "'How can we make the course better?' 'Are you getting things?' . . . We literally discuss their learning, and I can provide feedback during this midsemester status conference." Philip Prygoski invites students to meet with him individually or in groups. "I set appointments whenever they want them. . . . I also tell the class, even the big ones, that I will look at and fake-grade any old exams they want to write up. So if they want to write them up and bring them in, we'll talk about them, and I always tell them, 'Look, we'll deal with substance as well as writing on this' and we spend a lot of time doing that."

Students value meeting with teachers to talk about their performance and feedback:

- "I struggled on multiple-choice questions. . . . And he really sat down with me and really helped me think through solving multiple-choice questions. Something that I think is going to help me in other subjects tremendously" (student of Andy Taslitz).
- "She goes through all the comments . . . [and] makes sure you know/understand the material" (student of Tina Stark).
- "I really enjoyed working with her after every exam. I didn't enjoy taking the exam, but actually afterwards, discussing what I wrote with her and going through the different things that were salient to me at the time that I realized weren't really accurate legal analysis. She would step through that with me, and I would explain what I was thinking, and she would explain how I should have thought about it. I really appreciated that she really took the time to understand my learning style and work with me individually on that" (student of Paula Lustbader).

Positive Feedback and Constructive Criticism

The teachers we studied tackle balancing positive and constructive feedback in different ways. Some only convey positive feedback; others are sparing with praise; and some intentionally balance affirmative and constructive feedback. "When I give a feedback letter . . . I will write it, and then I will write the first paragraph about what the strengths are because we really do focus on the negative" (Ruthann Robson).

Cary Bricker elaborates on how she structures critiques: "It's a four-step process. . . . The main thing is a headline where you're telling the student what it is that you're going to be critiquing about. . . . Tell them verbatim what they did. It doesn't help to generally say, 'You know you used leading questions, a lot of leading questions, and that really wasn't persuasive, okay?' ... [Instead, you say] 'You asked the following six questions' and you give it back to them verbatim. Then you come up with a fix, a prescription. 'This is a different way of phrasing the questions so that they are open, and the focus is on the witness, where it's supposed to be on direct, and not on the lawyer, where it's supposed to be on cross.' And then, if you have time and it assists the entire class, then you can give a rationale."

Students are motivated by the feedback, even though some teachers focus almost exclusively on what they are doing well, and others balance positive and constructive feedback.

- "He's very giving with praise as well. If you wrote something correctly, he will tell you, you know, 'This is written really well'" (student of Andy Taslitz).
- "I've never heard her say anything negative to any students that would discourage them even if I myself might have had some [negative] thoughts. . . . She is just so positive and I think that was very helpful. . . . You are going to come back feeling capable" (student of Cary Bricker).
- "When I got a paper back, it was so detailed in comments. . . . There wasn't just negative comments; there were positive comments, and what you could do better. It was just filled with comments and what you could do better, and not just a grade on the top" (student of Steven Homer).
- "Every day you stand up and say something—he gives you positive— and a little bit of encouragement to try to improve in different areas, and so you're able to develop. . . . You can see [your] growth. . . . [You] realize, 'Okay, I can handle this. I can be criticized and not feel like the world is going to fall apart'" (student of Larry Krieger).

Challenge

A number of the teachers we studied mention how challenging their assessments are. Steven Homer explains his thoughts: "I have the reputation of being the hard grader. And especially early in the first semester I am a little stingy with the high grades.... because I want them to see...that the law will demand from them more than they are used to giving." Heather Gerken speaks about challenging her students: "I take pride in writing very hard exams. I find that all students get the basic material, and [I] want them to really push themselves. Exams will have 300 points—the top students will get a 156."

Bridget Crawford expands on the theme of being demanding in her "Teaching Philosophy." "The greatest compliment I can receive as a teacher is that I am, and my examinations are, tough but fair.... In asking students to apply doctrine or policy to new scenarios, I want students to reach beyond the familiar. I want them to walk out of an examination thinking, 'That was really hard. But I handled it in a way that I would not have been able to before.'"

When we spoke to these highly effective teachers' students, we did not ask about the difficulty of their teachers' exams and graded assessments. Nevertheless, over and over, students volunteer these comments, speaking with awe about how much they need to exert themselves to do well in these teachers' courses. In speaking about what made Ingrid Hillinger an exceptional teacher, several students first commented on the rigorousness of her exams, and then four students volunteered that they received their worst law-school grades from her. Nevertheless, they found her to be extraordinary. Other students were similarly impressed by the rigor of their teachers' assessments:

- "You have to be very thorough. I mean it's not, like, oh, you'll get As. You have to work really hard. You . . . have to really put everything into your exam and your papers" (student of Don Hornstein).
- "Everybody also knows that they're the hardest exams in this school" (student of Andy Taslitz).
- "Generally people think that when you take some of these smaller seminar classes . . . it's an easy A . . . and it was anything but that. I mean I think overall the class probably did well, but we really had to work hard for it" (student of Roberto Corrada).
- "He's student-centered without being easy. So many of the student-centered professors . . . tell you the answers and they give you a multiple-choice test. His tests scare the bejesus out of me. . . . It was really hard. There was a lot of stuff, but you know he taught it to us all. We knew it all. We were prepared for it, but it was still—you had to work for it" (student of Andy Leipold).
- "She has tough questions on her final exam, and she admits that from the beginning, that she's going to ask you very smallest details that she's made sure to discuss in class. And she will teach you to the very last page of the book too. So she presents a lot of information. She presents it very well, but you'll know everything about the subject when you finish. And then she expects you to know it on the final exam. . . . There's no shortcut" (student of Meredith Duncan).

Fairness and Transparency

The teachers in our study emphasize fairness and transparency when speaking and writing about assessment. They intentionally connect what they taught with what they assessed. As Philip Prygoski stresses, "You got to test what you teach. . . . Try to make the exam match the course as much as possible." Don Hornstein makes similar points: "I try to be really transparent. . . . I work on that because I think it's a really important part of teaching. . . . I tell them what type of exam it is. I tell them how I construct the exams."

Students compliment their professors for being fair and transparent about their assessments. As a student of Roberto Corrada stated, "The teachers that I take the most away from are those that are fairly transparent in the reasons why they are teaching us certain concepts." Similarly, after talking about how challenging Ruthann Robson's exams were, one of her students observed, "I always felt that her exams were fair. . . . She read a portion of them three times to check for consistency." Other students echo these points:

- "Her final was very difficult, but it was also very fair. . . . [A] huge part of me taking her class again was the fact that her first final I took with her was fair and I mean it's a difficult final" (student of Meredith Duncan).
- "He's not trying to trick us. I mean it's so straightforward. The material on the exam, the material on the papers is exactly what he teaches" (student of Don Hornstein).
- "Exams were open code. Very fair. [They] were based on everything we'd gone over. Not easy teacher but fair" (student of Bridget Crawford).

One of the ways in which teachers show their commitment to being fair and transparent is their method of evaluating students. Several teachers use rubrics, or explicit grading criteria. Some apply these while grading and also share them with students in advance. Meredith Duncan discusses how she provides feedback to first-year students after they complete a midterm: "I have a rubric that I provide to them, a reading rubric, and I fill it out after I've graded the exam and give it back to them." Cary Bricker portrays how she gives students evaluative criteria in her Federal Defender course: "In my syllabus we lay out the grading criteria.... These are the [seven] principal criteria that we rely on. That's their main guideline and then some other things as well. So I guess this is a rubric to some extent.... So if they come to me later and say, 'Why did I get a B?' and I will say 'Well, because of four through seven.' We also sit down with them periodically, once a year, and say, 'These are areas where you are showing strengths and these are areas where you could put some more work into it.'"

Paula Lustbader wants her students to use the multiple forms of feedback and detailed performance criteria she provides to develop the ability to self-assess. "For each exam, I hand out after they've written it and turn it in on the TWEN site. Then it gets posted, a critique sheet ... a grading rubric, and sample answer, and a list of things they need to do with their exam in looking at that.... But my goal is for them to be able to do some self-assessment."

Steven Homer links evaluating students' work with the demands of their future clients. "I am really, really picky about late papers. I am super hard on that. And I tell them, 'It's not to torture you. It's because I take it really seriously. Clients take it really seriously. And so now is the time to develop the time-management skills to get stuff in on time.'"

Students appreciate understanding how they earn their grades:

- "Two of us went to question a grade. We didn't think that she calculated correctly. Tina checked it out and explained, corrected.

She wants us to question her, to understand the material and her grading" (student of Tina Stark).

- "She used really detailed grading sheets . . . Had very useful grading matrix" (student of Ruthann Robson).
- "She really, really is focused on making sure that her students are going to learn and get the most out of the exam process, and I think that's an amazing trait just because of the work involved" (student of Nancy Levit).

Multiple and Creative Approaches

Many of the teachers use several graded events to determine students' final grades. They intentionally design their assessments to be congruent with course learning goals. Larry Krieger explains his approach in his "Teaching Philosophy": "The test counts 40 percent of the overall grade (which I consider sufficient to encourage a serious review), the weekly assignments 60 percent." Tina Stark articulates her rationale for assessing student participation: "Twenty percent [of grading] is on homework and class participation. Participation is essential because students need to speak the language in front of others . . . to express transactional concepts in words. It's important for them to explain the concept to the client or talk about as part of negotiation. I want them to show me their thought process, not whether they got it right."

Bridget Crawford relates how she used clickers (electronic response devices) in calculating students' final grade. "They only count negatively. 'If you don't click at least 5 percent of the time when I ask a question, then you will get points taken off your final.' . . . Psychologically, it sits better with them with they are losing points as opposed to gaining points."

The teachers are also thoughtful about how they motivate their students, given their law schools' mandatory grading curves. Julie Nice describes the challenge and her efforts to help her students focus on learning: "I do my very best to try to get them to forget about the relative comparison of their performances and stay focused on their own development. But as you know, that's a very difficult challenge. I think for every student, at the end of the day, a lot of their stress and anxiety is about how they're going to do relative to other people. It's how we grade them; it's a curve. What I try to convince them of is that they will feel a lot more confident and it will help their performance if they focus on their own learning and how are they improving and how are they progressing. I go back to the old adage; it's the only thing they actually can control."

Several teachers have adopted creative approaches in terms of what counts toward students' grades. Steve Friedland offers students a chance to gain bonus points. "The extra credit is up to five points. You can write a poem; you can make a video; sing a song, anything about Crim Law. And I get some amazingly creative stuff." One of Roberto Corrada's students was grateful for having the opportunity to write a grade appeal. "He gives you a midterm with your grade, and he gives you a week to go back and write . . . a petition for review if you felt that he had gotten something wrong. And typically I don't do that because most of the time I just trust law professors when it comes to things like that. . . . I actually looked at it and there were things that I thought that he was wrong, that I thought he either misunderstood what I was trying to say, or that he hadn't given points where his outline suggested that he should have, and so I wrote a one-page . . . petition to him, and he ended up changing my grade."

Final Exams

The teachers in our study design final exams in a variety of ways. Some teachers require students to memorize material. Others offer take-home exams. Some use a combination of essays and multiple-choice questions. All were thoughtful about their choices. "To me the exam is itself a capstone learning experience . . . a vehicle for them to really to demonstrate their knowledge and skills but also that they will learn what they know and how well they're able to use what they know in this particular vehicle" (Julie Nice).

Expressing appreciation for Philip Prygoski's exam, one student said, "Something that's so great about his final exam too [is] that he has an opinion question, and so you're not only just forced to learn a bunch of cases but think about what you think about it and talk about it and present an argument . . . I don't think I've ever had any other class where I had to actually formulate an opinion about a topic and then write about it in an exam."

From the content of fact scenarios, description of tasks to be completed, and information they give to students, these teachers have thoughtful, learning-focused reasons for each of their choices. Ruthann Robson elaborates on how she designs her exams. "I have different levels of difficulty in the answers. Always have a mix of questions. Some multiple-choice questions—to help them get inside the doctrine. Closed-book unless in seminar class because they need to be able to do that on the bar exam." Steve Friedland describes his final exam: "In-class multiple-choice, objective, final exam. Five days or four days before, take home with short answers and a long answer. Limited amount of space they can answer, like three or four pages. . . . I want to, one, challenge them, but I also want to serve other purposes. I want them to learn from the exam. So I'm trying to have them review the course, learn. And then I'll have some tougher questions, but it's not having a whole exam where they feel like they can't write. I want them all to feel like they put down what they learned."

Emphasizing that it was "not fair to require them to memorize the Model Penal Code," Susan Kuo revealed her "cheat-sheet" method. "I let them bring in one piece of paper, regular size, and they can write whatever they want in it. . . . It gives them a security blanket. And I always remind them, though, if you do this right, if you study correctly, you won't have to refer to your security blanket, except in utter panic mode. . . . So many of them say, 'I didn't look at my cheat-sheet once.' . . . I'm, like, 'That's the way I want it to be.'"

A student of Andy Taslitz comments on having access to materials during the exam: "Our exams were open note . . . which you would think would make the tests easier but it doesn't. And you'd go in there with these huge binders and it's tabbed, it's highlighted, it's color-coded, it's focused. . . . I have indexes and [a] table of contents. . . . I really felt like on his tests especially that it wasn't about getting the right answer, you know? It was truly about the analysis. It was about, you know, 'How did you look at this question?' 'How did you break it apart?' 'How did you kind of apply the logic that we learned in class to answer the question?' It wasn't: 'What's your answer?'"

Some teachers intentionally connect final exam questions to practicing law. "Part of the call of my questions will always be how would you counsel X in view of not only the doctrine, not only the policy, but also in the best interests of the client?" (Paula Franzeze). "I have a traditional exam. . . . I think of how they use this material in practice and then I walk backwards into what the exam would look like" (Hiroshi Motomura). Other teachers deliberately focus on current issues. Julie Nice notes that she uses "real congressional reports, real cases, real everything. . . . Ninety-five percent of it is true, real-life data that I'm using [for] the exam."

Students are grateful to have relevant issues on their exams. As one of Ruthann Robson's students stated, "Her exams were really interesting, fun, use contemporary issues, unique, thoughtful." One of Nancy Levit's students echoed the point: "Even in first-year torts classes, I remember that she would come up with exam questions that were sort of relevant to things that were going on in the world."

At the end of the course, some teachers deliberately devote time to preparing students for their final exams. They hold review sessions, offer extensive office hours, and respond to students' web-based, phone, and e-mail questions. "I give a review during class, an optional Q&A the day before the exam, and have extended office hours near the end of the semester. I believe law professors should be actively engaged in preparing students to take our exams. In this, and throughout the semester, I work closely with academic support professors" (Ruthann Robson).

Students praise teachers for the way they prepare them for their final exams. "We're kind of making an outline together in class. That's basically what this mind map is. And so he's always, like, 'Use the map!' Like on a practice exam on pleading, 'Pull out your pleading map and walk through the map.' And then you know, if you used it correctly, then you'll come up with an A answer. So we have the outline; we made it together in class. And then, also, he's, like, giving us practice questions all the time, and then we go over them as a class" (student of Hiroshi Motomura).

One of Andy Taslitz's students voiced his appreciation for having guidance in how to use time on the exam. "Some questions were worth more. And so he told us in advance. He's like, 'You should allot this amount of time for planning. You should allot this amount of time for writing the answer to this question.' He's like, 'Once you hit that time, you need to move on because you have to finish the exam.' And so for students, maybe, who hadn't had kind of a lesson in how to finish an exam, it was very, very helpful."

A student commented that answering Roberto Corrada's hypothetical practice problems facilitated learning skills transferable to other courses. "He had a word limit, line limits. . . . I could have gone on for pages. But I learned how to concisely say what I needed to say and all the relevant parts in a short amount of time and that's been helpful . . . in other classes because I hear a lot of teachers say, 'Don't go everywhere. Just tell me what I need to know and get it done with,' and a lot of students aren't able to do that. But because he was so willing to take the time throughout the semester and read hypo after hypo after hypo, I feel that I'm much better at that and have taken that into my other classes as well."

Conclusion

Two final comments illustrate the value of these teachers' assessment and feedback. A student's comment shows how feedback can be powerfully motivating: "After the first assignment, knowing he is going to be reading it that carefully made me put much more time on the next assignments. He was taking it really seriously; I am going to take this really seriously" (student of Steven Homer).

Bridget Crawford is eloquent about fairness and transparency: "What does fairness mean? Well, there is the obvious: there is fairness in grading . . . Fairness, I think means, being clear about what you except people to learn, give them a clear opportunity to demonstrate what they have learned, how they've learned it, [and] why it's important. [It's] sort of giving them an opportunity after they've done the demonstration, to review their work. So I think it's very important to be transparent in grading. 'Here's what I asked you. Here's what you said. Here's what the answer should be. Here's why.'"

9

What Lasting Lessons Do Students Take Away?

Chapter 2 offers a definition of exceptional learning in legal education. Our definition synthesizes the views of the law deans, teachers, and students who nominated outstanding teachers for our study (see Chapter 2, Box 2).

Exceptional learning includes both intellectual and personal development. Exceptional intellectual development includes deep understanding of legal doctrine, policy, and theory. Intellectual development also encompasses of a wide range of skills, such as legal analysis, critical thinking, professional judgment, writing, counseling, and advocacy. Exceptional personal development includes self-understanding, confidence, intrinsic motivation, and the commitment to lifelong learning. Professional identity, professionalism, responsibility, and the thirst for justice are part of personal development for future lawyers as well.

By any definition, the twenty-six law teachers we studied succeeded in producing exceptional learning in their students. We have organized the lasting lessons students learned from their law teachers according to the two broad categories in the exceptional learning definition: (1) intellectual and (2) personal development. We offer first the teachers' perspective and then the students'.

Exceptional Intellectual Development

Teachers' Perspectives—Mastery and Development of Legal Doctrine

The teachers we studied teach doctrine. They want their students to learn, however, not only the doctrine itself, the structure of the doctrinal field, and the policy concepts embedded in the doctrine, but also the students' role critiquing, developing, and improving it.

Julie Nice describes her goals for her Constitutional Law students in terms of mastery. She views deep understanding of an area of the law as lasting and transferable as well as a powerful motivator for students:

> I want [students] to have a good overview of Constitutional Law then some really good deep knowledge of how to zoom in and really master one of the doctrines in Constitutional Law and that's a transferable skill. . . . I say to them, "You all know how much depth went into the commerce clause and equal protection, and so you learn two of the templates for structure and individual rights. And now those are the templates you'll use if you need to practice something we did not spend much time on. . . ."

What I'm trying to get them to see is if they were the master of a subject matter that they practice in they would want to have that kind of command. I'm following my subject area. . . . I know where it's been; I know what's happened to it along the way; I could have some guesses about where it's going; I know what I would argue for a client one way or the other. That's the kind of mastery. They feel elated when they feel like they get to that point of mastery.

The feedback they give me later . . . about what they really hold onto are those times where we go into depth and really master something. I think that's what really sticks with them and I think it's because it's more exciting when they are doing it. They feel they are doing something at a higher level.

Roberto Corrada aims to convince students that to be effective lawyers, they need to be more than consumers of legal knowledge; they must discover and develop knowledge as well:

Two pedagogical goals help me to achieve this overall goal of transitioning learning from the law school to law practice. The first goal is to make students take responsibility for their own learning, which is accomplished by enlisting them as "cognitive apprentices" in the law school classroom. The second goal, flowing from and related to the first, is to lead students to the ultimate insight that they are not only discoverers of knowledge but have the capacity themselves to produce knowledge. The lecture format is antithetical to both these goals; it makes students passive learners (insidiously suggesting that knowledge is gathered and collected by someone else, not them, and they are simply there to receive it from the gatherer) and it leads students to believe that knowledge is produced elsewhere. What happens when a law student becomes an attorney with little ability to gather knowledge (and indeed, a strong preference for knowledge gathered by others—in a nutshell or hornbook) and no idea that he or she might be able to change and affect law (as producers of knowledge themselves) for the betterment of their immediate client and society itself?

Meredith Duncan shares Professor Corrada's goal for students to assume responsibility for the ongoing development of the law: "I want them to appreciate that they really may be able to have an impact on developing different areas of law."

Teachers' Perspectives—Analytical Skills,
Communication, Learning to Learn

Meredith Duncan articulates skills that many teachers want their students to acquire. "I want them to also learn that they should be careful in reading, work hard, pay attention to detail, look up words they don't know. . . . I want them to learn how to be able to read a statute and be able to identify the important terms. . . . I want them to learn how to be critical thinkers and critical readers when they're reading things. I want them to be able to figure out what's important and what's not important. . . . I want them to learn how to be efficient writers." Rory Bahadur adds, "I want my students to learn first and foremost that lawyers don't ever have answers. They have arguments."

Cary Bricker wants her Trial Advocacy and clinical students to retain oral and written communication and advocacy skills that will help them in a variety of professional settings. "I want them to come away with a sense of . . . knowing they can communicate in any form. We teach it in particularly a litigation setting, but I want a student to graduate and go to a school board and be the person who stands up and makes a coherent, persuasive presentation. I want them to be an associate in a law firm who's going to ... take this big collection of facts, and isolate legal issues, and come up with legal memoranda that really work, that are persuasive."

Ingrid Hillinger focuses on statutory analysis and transactional skills in her Uniform Commercial Code Article 9 course: "What I tell them on the first day in Article 9 for example, is by the end of this course, whether you've seen a provision or not, you're going to know how to deal with statutory language. You're going to know where to go in the code and what to do there. . . . You're going to have a system and a sense of other laws that sort of impact the system, and you're going to have a sense of what a transactional attorney does, which is risk identification and how you minimize or try to circumvent risk."

A goal for many law teachers is to help their students develop lifelong learning skills. "I want students to learn how they learn, to develop that metacognitive stance. That's just really critical for me. They must go on learning when they leave me" (Nelson Miller). "I want them to think about how they learn. I want them to learn how to learn. I want them to learn how to learn the material on their own" (Nancy Levit).

Students' Perspectives—Doctrine, Principles, Frameworks, and Careers

The students' lasting learning of legal doctrine centers on frameworks and principles, not on detailed principles of the law. For example, one of Don Hornstein's Administrative Law students reports that he was unlikely to retain "the specific details but I'll remember the structure and the overall framework for answering

Administrative Law questions.... I'm sure I'll have to refer to something, but that feeling that you have some facility of material, you know where to start, you have an idea of what direction you're supposed to be going, I think that will definitely stick with me."

Other students learned the principles and policies that are the foundations of particular legal doctrines. "She is careful to remind us that we are learning principles, that every jurisdiction will differ, but that the principles are generally applicable" (student of Susan Kuo). "I still remember most of the things I learned in his classes because he always took care to emphasize the relationships between different concepts and point out the policy-based reasoning behind the courts' holdings. By learning the underlying policy, I was often able appreciate the tensions in the courts' holdings, which, in turn, allowed me to craft better arguments" (student of Hiroshi Motomura).

A student of Meredith Duncan internalized the idea that the application of legal rules can be indeterminate: "She does a pretty good job of emphasizing that ... in some situations, there are no right answers. And so that in the future when you do discuss and you're arguing things, whether it's with an adversary or ... a partner, you know that there are multiple viewpoints that are valid. So I think that's something that will follow me."

Perhaps the most dramatic lasting doctrinal learning for students was the effect studying doctrine with these teachers had on the students' career choices. Many students noted that their outstanding teacher played significant roles in the direction of students' professional lives:

- "Learning from her and working with her had, and continues to have, a profound impact on my life. Substantively, I learned the entire field of election law from Heather—a field in which I now practice, thanks in large part to Heather. She introduced me to an area of the law that I found absolutely fascinating. . . . Beyond the substance and doctrine of the class, however, what has stuck with me was Heather's love of the field of election law. She was genuinely excited to discuss the cases and issues and made it all seem like so much fun" (student of Heather Gerken).

- "Her enthusiasm is contagious. . . . I could see myself as a prosecutor or a defense attorney. I was lucky to have Professor Kuo as my criminal-law professor. It might have just changed the course of my career" (student of Susan Kuo).

- "Based primarily on Professor Nice's teaching, I took it upon myself to write a law review article on a specific constitutional issue. I also was inspired to take on a pro bono case that involves constitutional law. In sum, thanks to her teaching, I have realized that I want to dedicate my life to helping others by working to vindicate their constitutional rights—through defending civil rights, prisoners' rights, the rights of the accused, or others" (student of Julie Nice).

- "The tour of the detention facility literally changed my life. I had not come to law school with any area of practice in mind. . . . When I returned to Boulder after the tour, I had the rest of my working life's path set out in front of me" (student of Hiroshi Motomura).

Students' Perspectives—Skills

Much of the lasting learning for students concerned skills. Students learned to read carefully, pay attention to detail, analyze cases and statutes, and solve problems. Students also developed lawyering skills—writing, drafting, and oral advocacy.

Many students reported that the teachers improved their skill in attending to details and closely reading cases and statutes, as two of Rory Bahadur's students noted: "Well, I think he makes you pay attention to the detail, which I don't think necessarily, in your first year, happens in all of your classes." "I mean, I thought I was a good reader when I came to law school, but I feel like I became an exponentially better reader taking his classes just because every word counts for him."

A student of Roberto Corrada transferred the close reading skills the student learned from Corrada to other courses. "I learned [that] he put a lot of emphasis on paying attention to detail. I remember my briefs expanded over the semester from . . . four bullet points to, like, fifteen. . . . I started seeing things in cases that I potentially would have just glossed over, and I've kind of carried that into other classes. . . . When I read cases, I think I read for a bit more details than I would had I not taken Professor Corrada's class."

One of Stephen Homer's students learned the link between careful reading and persuasive writing. "The most important skill I learned in that class was how to read thoroughly and how to read slowly and how to read carefully. I don't think I realized how much of being able to write something persuasive depends on understanding the source materials that go into it. His ability to really make you focus on sentences as you structure them made my reading ability much, much better."

Students of Philip Prygoski and Julie Nice emphasize that they became better at finding subtle nuances in court opinions. "Before I took his class, I was never as critical and as nuanced in my approach to cases and in doing any school work. It's helped me in other classes as well taking his class originally, but you know, you find yourself able to—and he pushes this—to read between the lines and to go above and beyond the text: why would the court reason this? You're not going to find it in a book. You can flip back and forth all day.... If you spend enough time with him, it starts to click, and you start finding yourself saying, 'Wait a second; what's really going on here?'" (student of Philip Prygoski). "I think she really hones in on the fact of the methods of analyzing cases and arguing cases, and you really learn the different ways to argue a case and to read cases and say, 'Oh, they're using history; oh, they're using precedence; oh, they're using the legislative history,' and I think that is really good and helpful when you practice law because you are going to have to use those tools" (student of Julie Nice).

Other students noted the value of learning strong statutory analysis skills: "Much of what I learned from the Immigration Law class had to do with learning how to analyze and apply what it is, an extremely complex body of statutory law.... I really had not picked up the analytical skills in my first year (were they there to be picked up?), so Hiroshi's careful insistence on unpacking the statutory and regulatory language was extremely important" (student of Hiroshi Motomura). "Paula did an exercise on statute analysis. We went through some sample statutes, and she had some little hypothetical stories that accompanied those statutes, and we just went through in great detail and found what the elements of each statute was and then compared the facts of the hypotheticals and went to see where it broke down or where it didn't quite fit into one of those elements. Doing that exercise has been enormously helpful. I find myself doing it all the time. I've done it hundreds of times since then and that was just the foundation for understanding how to do statutory analysis" (student of Paula Lustbader).

Problem-solving skills were part of lasting learning as well. "He's given me a good framework to work through problems in the future: criminal law, legal, and nonlegal problems. He's taught us different methods. He constantly says experts use checklists, so if you want to be an expert, use your checklist, write everything out, check it off as you go along, and make sure that you're hitting every point that you want to hit. I feel that the things that he's taught us about how to approach questions, about how to approach problems, how to think, is going to stay with me more so than even the actual content of the class" (student of Steve Friedland). "I'm in a clinic, and I had some research questions that I need to figure out and answer. I used a mind manager to map out different bodies of law and different steps of questions to figure out. . . . That's something that I'm probably going to do as a practitioner for years down the line when there's some abstract body of law that I don't know about. By breaking it down into trees, it's easier to understand" (student of Hiroshi Motomura).

Some students learned to deal with legal indeterminacy and to thrive in the gray areas of the law. "He forces you to operate in the gray area and understand that you might have these preconceptions when you walk in. . . . But by the end . . . you open your eyes and you say, 'There are arguments on both side of this'" (student of Philip Prygoski). "I have an engineering background and have a tendency to see things in black and white. The way my mind is structured is I take information and sort it and categorize it and put it in boxes in my brain and regroup it however I need it. She was able to teach me that things are not black and white. Really, the law lives in the grey area. She gave us a general overview on how to approach law school and without that I don't know that I would have succeeded in law school" (student of Paula Lustbader).

Students also expressed appreciation for the role their teachers had in developing their skills in particular forms of problem solving: writing and drafting legal documents.

Stephen Homer's students became thoughtful writers. "He makes me think about what's the purpose of everything I do. What am I trying to achieve with this topic sentence? What am I trying to achieve with this statement of fact?" And editing habits they learned in Homer's class became part of their practice after graduation. "In my office . . . we pass motions around before we file them, and I know that people say, 'Do the Homer thing,' where you take the motion and every word you can get rid of you get a thousand dollars in your head. . . . People are trying to chop out extraneous verbiage before we file things. People actually say, 'Do the Homer thing.'"

Several of Hiroshi Motomura's students learned writing skills that they carried into their immigration practice. "I also took a seminar in immigration issues from Hiroshi, and there I found a teacher who really helped my writing skills. I had thought I was pretty good at writing, being an English major and a librarian, and maybe too old to learn, but Hiroshi took such care with the writing process that I became much better. It stood me in very good stead when I was writing briefs for the immigration court and for circuit-court appeals. I learned more about legal writing from Hiroshi than I did from the official legal writing course." "Learning to write collaboratively turned out to be immensely helpful in my career as an appellate attorney." "I learned how to use scholarship to the advantage of my clients, how to introduce the ideas into writing on behalf of clients, how to analyze the law with a fresh approach and to put it into a context that helped the immigration judges make the decision that helped my clients. I think I was able to do quite a bit of good work, especially for asylum seekers, who almost literally faced the death penalty if they lost their immigration cases. I don't think there is any way I could have done this without what I learned from Hiroshi Motomura. His work has saved lives."

In Tina Stark's Contract Drafting course, students learned skills that helped them get jobs and succeed in practice. Students report that they put "took Contract Drafting with Tina Stark" on their resumes because employers know that students learn important skills in the course. Her students feel that they were prepared to "hit the ground running" in practice because of the transactional drafting skills they learned from Professor Stark. They feel confident they can draft contracts that help clients achieve their goals.

Similarly, students in Beth Enos's Contract Drafting course report that they came away with valuable skills and resources for practice. "Everyone had to select a different area of law. So, for instance, I wrote about construction . . . and someone else wrote about, maybe, commercial residential contracts, and someone else about franchising. So at the end, you'd have sixteen different . . . base contracts [you] could go to and look to and have sort of annotated resources to say, 'Okay, what are the keys?' . . . It's actually on my shelf right behind my desk in my office." "I did an international contract, and I was so glad I'd done that because I've already had to use it a few times. . . . Someone did [an] entertainment contract, thankfully, because I needed that as well."

Students also feel grateful to the teachers for the oral communication and advocacy skills they learned. For example, many of Cary Bricker's students believe that they got their first jobs after law school because they had taken her Trial Advocacy courses. These students feel that they are succeeding in practice because of the skills they learned from Professor Bricker and the confidence they developed during her courses. "I've taken from her . . . a set of practical skills that I can carry into any area of the law that I choose to go into. Not only if I'm standing in front of a jury full of people, but it's also just my interpersonal skills, and being able to communicate with clients, and . . . things that I never thought I was capable of I've taken away from her classroom."

Don Hornstein's students also learned oral communication skills applicable to many practice settings. "I'll forever remember just the way he commanded a room and his public speaking ability, just the way he interacts with people. . . . I think that's something that you can carry with you to any profession you choose to engage in. There's just something about being a compelling figure and engaging people."

Students relate that their best law teachers also taught them advocacy skills that they employ in practice. "I learned to identify my objective and build a foundation for my advocacy using a variety of tools, including connecting the details of my clients' story with the intent of specific statutory or administrative requirements, and how to use that combination in a persuasive manner for the benefit of my client. I also learned there are many ways to address issues and am now able to advocate for my clients through a combination of legislative activity, community engagement, as well as transactional and litigation activities" (student of Julie Nice). "I find that I am more willing than many of my peers to explore and develop untested arguments on behalf of clients, rather than simply resign myself to defeat after a quick review of existing case law or agency memoranda. Thanks to Hiroshi, I think I was the rare student who departed law school a less cynical person than when he entered" (student of Hiroshi Motomura).

Extraordinary Personal Development

Teachers' Perspectives

Many of the outstanding teachers we studied strive to prepare students for practice, not only by teaching legal doctrine and skills, but also by teaching professionalism and values. "I want my students to be competent lawyers, but beyond that, and perhaps even more importantly, I want them to be lawyers (and people) with integrity and compassion. I want them to understand that the parties in cases are real people, and that the choices that the lawyers and judges make have real consequences. I want them to be humbled and sobered by the responsibility they have not only to their clients but to the profession and to the wider community" (Beth Enos).

Paula Lustbader describes her responsibilities in preparing her students to succeed in law school, and to engage in practice in pursuit of justice:

I am deeply committed to promoting a healthy, cooperative, and humane learning environment, both within my own classes and the institution in general. My philosophy is also strongly influenced by my belief that how we teach law students will impact how these students will practice law.... I am ever conscious of my role as modeling professionalism, integrity, inclusiveness, spirituality, and balance, all in the service of justice.

We're preparing them not just to do well in our course, but to do well in law school and in the profession. It's a very diverse classroom and ethnic diversity is rich, gender diversity, and also rich in experience. And part of our goal in this program is to empower these students to keep their voice and to make the difference they need to make in the profession and to serve the clients who are waiting to be served by them.... My job isn't just to make sure they know how to do IRAC. My job is to empower them to make the difference they came here to make.

I want them to question the status quo. I think most of my students come in doing that, and I want to keep them doing that. And to question what's right and what's just. And who's not being heard, who's being silenced.... I want them to find their right work and have fulfilling, satisfying lives.... I want them to believe in their passions. I want them to believe in each other.... I want them to believe that they can be the change agents and transformative.

Patti Alleva also aims to transform students into outstanding people in their professional and personal lives: "In that sacred space in and around the law school classroom, I am privileged to participate in what I hope is the transformative process of helping students to reach new understandings of subject, self, and society that, in turn, will fuel their distinctive contributions to the world at large. Learning as a prelude to doing—and doing with greater depth as a result of learning—is an obvious, but profound, connection that gives our sometimes lonely labors broader significance and practical consequence of the highest order as we help our students to self-actualize in the law and to become the best professionals and people they can be—for their clients, for their community, and for themselves."

Nancy Knauer and Cary Bricker want to empower students in different ways. "Well, what I like best about law school is that there is a degree of empowerment that should happen here and I want my students to read the newspaper differently and to listen to the news differently and to understand their place in the world differently" (Nancy Knauer). "[I] want them to come away with a sense of real self-value and self-worth in a lawyering context, in a lawyering-skills context. . . . But I have a student who comes to me who is utterly terrified of the matter, who thinks they don't matter probably both psychologically and also in the law-school setting. And then they just, through sheer force of will, keep trying and keep trying and keep trying, and by the end of the class, come out with an incredible—it's almost a glow—and . . . they will be really good lawyers because they've shown themselves—the hell with me—they've shown themselves they can do it" (Cary Bricker).

Students' Perspectives

The biggest categories of lasting lessons for students concerned personal and professional development. Some students emphasized personal characteristics such as passion, humility, excellence, and confidence. Other students honed interpersonal values including humanity and respect. Many students learned lessons about professionalism, justice, professional identity, and ethics.

PASSION, EXCELLENCE, HUMILITY, AND CONFIDENCE

Many students were inspired by their teachers' extraordinary passion. One of Andy Taslitz's students expresses a view common among the students. "Whatever it is you want to do, whether it's be a teacher, be a DA, be a prosecutor, be a defense attorney, be a bankruptcy attorney . . . do something that you love because when you do something you love you're always going to be better at it, you know. And he loves this, all of it: the teaching, the writing, the personal interactions with students." Another student explains how Hiroshi Motomura's advice convinced him that law students and lawyers need to develop both skill and passion. "Hiroshi was giving an informal talk to prospective and current law students, and someone asked what advice he could give to succeed in law school. His answer to that question has still stayed with me. Hiroshi said something along the lines of, 'You have to have find the right balance between being a technical expert with the law, and doing what is in your heart. If you focus too much on the technical expertise, you can forget that the law in application actually affects people.'"

A lasting lesson for many students is a commitment to excellence and hard work:

- "He is sending me out with the sense you want to get it exactly right every time. Nine times out of ten no one else will notice, and you'll just have to take satisfaction out of that. But, if you're not doing it right that tenth time out of ten, it's going to make a difference, and it's going to hurt your client, it's going to hurt your cause, it's going to hurt your ability to do your work, and you want to get it right every time. It's really inspiring to see somebody embody that and pass it along." "He was the kind of person that would inspire you to do your best work. . . . I found it very attractive when he would do his finest work. I find this virtuous in someone else that I want to be that type of person" (students of Stephen Homer).
- "She really taught me something that I will take with me for a really long time is try to be master in everything that you do. Try to be good in everything, not just be good but be great in everything that you do. She brings all of her to all of her classes. I take that and I want to bring all of me into everything that I do in life because that's what she does" (student of Julie Nice).

- "I worked really, really hard, just, like, really hard, and you know, you get rewarded for that work. And I think that for me anyway, that's the type of things that stick with me.... [A] good lesson in life, you know?" (student of Roberto Corrada).
- "As long as you're doing your best, and zealously advocating for your client, and you're doing everything you possibly can to put your best foot forward and give them a fighting chance. That's what it all comes down to. You're not always going to be, you know, victorious, but you're going to give it your best. And that's what she's taught me from the word go. I think that makes everybody who has interaction with Professor Alleva, not only a better law student or better future lawyer, but a better person in general, 'cause it affects your everyday life" (student of Patti Alleva).

Students also feel they learned that good lawyers temper excellence with humility. "I feel like he's teaching excellence and humility at the same time. Excellence and humility, excellence and humility, you know what I mean? Like, the more you know and the better you get, the more humble and down to earth and giving and generous you have to be. I mean that's the way he lives his life, you know? And that's what I feel like he's imparting" (student of Andy Taslitz). "She gave me a sense of humility. She instilled me a sense of humility, to always remember that the lawyer is the servant of a greater cause, whether it's the client's cause, whether it's a public cause, whether it's a private cause, that there's something that we are laboring to achieve that's for the greater good" (student of Patti Alleva).

Students feel strongly that they increased their self-confidence through their interactions with these outstanding teachers. For example, "[He] instilled a lot of confidence in me because I think law school by its nature sort of makes you think that you can't" (student of Larry Krieger). "I think he had a knack for building confidence, not just on the individual level but on the group level" (student of Stephen Homer). "I really feel like [she] gave me a running start, and it really gave me confidence.... That little bit of confidence went a really long way in terms of making me feel like I have something to offer and that I had a place within the classroom" (student of Paula Lustbader). "By the time you get done exploring a problem with him, he leaves you with the sense that you knew the answer all along, and you have the confidence to actually implement the solution" (student of Nelson Miller). "She was really able to tell that I didn't have enough confidence in myself and in my capabilities.... She just let me know that "you are talented and you can do this." ... I was ten times more effective than I was the day before because I just needed her to tell me that I could do it" (student of Cary Bricker). "She imparts a sense of confidence in approaching the law, [that] you can sort of reason through it yourself and understand it" (student of Nancy Knauer). "She sees yourself as already being there and she tells you that you are that person already and that is so healthy and so helpful and so motivating because you can see the path that you're walking to be that person but she already sees you as that person" (student of Nancy Levit). "One thing that I think will stick with me for life is that the confidence she gave me" (student of Julie Nice).

HUMANITY AND RESPECT

Several students of Patti Alleva came away with deep lessons about the humanity of the legal profession: "She's the reminder for me of the humanity in the profession, which I think is very easy to lose sight of throughout law school.... That's what I'll take from her." "The bottom line of Professional Visions in the sense that it's not just about laws and rules and applying the facts. . . . We can't forget the humanity of it and that's what it is and if you're not helping do that, then you're not, really not, helping." "We read *To Kill a Mockingbird* and we talked about walking around in other people's shoes. . . . I have represented some murderers, and they have done some bad things, but yet they're still people, and when you actually get down there and look at the person, it's really different, and you just want to do the best job you can for them, even though they did these terrible acts, and you are able to look past that. If I wouldn't have had that class, I wouldn't have looked at it the same way. You know law school is about A and B, not about Alan and Betty."

One of Ingrid Hillinger's students found humanity in bankruptcy law. "At the bottom there were real human beings who were going to be sitting in your office and how did that come together, and of course it's true, whether it's a consumer debt or business debt. . . . Real people's lives are going to be influenced by what you do, and I don't think she ever let you forget that."

Nelson Miller's students relate how they learned about the importance of human relationships in law and life. "I think that sets the stage for training you as a future attorney and how to be a good listener and how to have a personal relationship with your clients. Too often I think we tend to want to be disconnected. This is just a business transaction. This is just a real property sale. . . . Being able to build that relationship . . . lends itself to . . . development as a human being and as a really good attorney." "We don't come to law school to learn the law. We come to law school to be inspired to be better people and to be great lawyers and Dean Miller did that."

Respect and compassion are recurring themes in students' reports of what they learned from the law teachers we studied:

- "I think the big thing I will carry from Dean Miller is to have compassion for my clients and to remember that they are people and to remember the situation that they're in and to treat people with respect and dignity" (student of Nelson Miller).

- "I think, looking ten years from now, and if I was looking back on the lessons I learned from Professor Alleva, they would be revolving around basic decency towards other people, kindness, ability, respect . . . treating people the way you wished to be treated. It's an underlying theme throughout her teaching methods and throughout the way she conducts herself with students and with fellow professors" (student of Patti Alleva).

- "I think I'm going to take away the whole respect of professionalism aspect. I've been in classes where I've not felt respected at all. . . . I think you can accomplish so much more when everyone respects each other. . . . That's one of the things I'll take away from her class" (student of Beth Enos).

- "I think he was . . . a very nice, compassionate, respectful attorney." "I think the thing that I take from him is the care that he gives to us as students and, from what he's told us in the past, to his clients when he was practicing law. I mean if you can carry that attitude towards the people that you work with, you're going to be a success and he just exudes that." "And then I think from a personal standpoint just how to be a humble human being and to not demand respect, being a humble human being that really truly gives respect to people, you can expect that the respect will return." "I think he's just absolutely one of the nicest people I've ever met. . . . I think I'm a better person because I've been around Professor Leipold" (students of Andy Leipold).

PROFESSIONALISM, SERVICE, AND ETHICS

One of Paula Lustbader's students, several years after graduation, recalled what she learned about professionalism on the first day of class:

> One of the things that really sticks with me—one of that messages that she said the first day of law school—is that your reputation starts today, at least in this profession. It didn't hit me as hard then as it does now and how true that really is. . . . So just in terms in how you conduct yourself on a daily level, you do those things that make you happy and enjoy yourself. But at the same time realize you chose a career where integrity counts. And that starts on day one of law school. She told us to look to your left, look to your right and those are the people who are going to potentially refer you your clients in the future.

Students of Patti Alleva say they learned lasting lessons about professional identity: "Before this course I just thought I would graduate law school and be an attorney. I had never even thought about my professional identity." "The thing that really stuck with me is 'internal compass.' . . . Without that class, I don't think I would have connected it to practice as well as I do. I try to . . . on a daily basis to just think of where you are at, and who you are and making those choices of who you want to be and relying on that. . . . She called it our internal compass, and it's what I'll always think of it as." "I learned to really think about who I will be as a lawyer and the decisions I will face, instead of solely learning the law. This course was invaluable."

Stephen Homer's students responded to his modeling of professionalism: "I think he set an expectation of professionalism and he modeled it all day every day. And so for me it demonstrated how to interact with colleagues, how to prepare to come to any job. . . . If I could work as hard as that and be as prepared and organized as that I would be doing really, really well."

Students of Ruthann Robson note that she taught them about how to honor themselves as lawyers: "She helped students integrate parts of their lives, like how to integrate gender identity with the rest of their lives." "She posts creative writing pieces and encourages students to [do the same]."

Larry Krieger's students learned precious lessons about self-evaluation and development from him. "He always said . . . 'You always evaluate your performance before the jury comes back with their verdict.' A guilty or not guilty verdict is not what should send you into a good mood or bad mood. . . . Professor Krieger says never use 'win' or 'lose,' but do evaluate. Did I prepare properly? Did I do everything that I was planning on doing, that I thought I should do? And if you did, then you need to feel good about yourself regardless of what the verdict is and that's something that I always keep in mind when I'm trying cases." "[I learned to try] to constantly improve yourself . . . just to improve yourself, not for anybody else."

The students in our study say they adopted values of service and justice from their law teachers. "I would be hard-pressed to find someone who believes in the legal profession as something as noble as she does. And more importantly the way that she has inspired me to see it that way." "She really emphasized it in Civ. Pro.: the justice system is really about justice and the right outcome. That's one thing I won't ever forget (students of Patti Alleva). "He's really focused on service. I've appreciated that because he's made that feel like that is something you can really do and that's accessible. Because I think I was really frustrated at the beginning of law school with how motivated a lot of people seem to be in going in the direction of only a big firm track" (student of Steve Friedland).

Students of Beth Enos state they learned about integrity and ethics. "She always wants you to become the attorney with the most integrity and really fosters that as well as what you should aspire to be. . . . Contracts is important, but the most important thing is that she teaches you to become a lawyer that has ethical values." "I don't think I could do anything unethical without thinking of Enos. I think that would stop me pretty quickly." "You got the feeling that you would shame her if you ever did something like that."

One student attributes her career satisfaction as a moral lawyer to Hiroshi Motomura's guidance. "I clerked at a litigation firm my first summer, and at a tort firm my second. Both experiences left me deeply upset about what lawyering had to offer. Fifteen years after graduation, I now get to pay my mortgage by doing something morally rewarding every single day. I can honestly say I've never had to do anything as a lawyer that ever left me morally conflicted. This would not have been possible without Hiroshi's guidance."

Many students model themselves, professionally and personally, on their outstanding law teachers. Students of Bridget Crawford, Paula Franzese, Steve Friedland, Andy Leipold, Nancy Levit, Nelson Miller, Heather Gerken, Ruthann Robson, and Andy Taslitz all consider them to be role models.

Other students hear the voices of their teachers repeating critical lessons long after graduation:

- "I hear her voice all the time, when I do trial work and when I do appellate work and that's because of what she taught me. And I'm not kidding when I actually can hear her voice telling me those important things" (student of Patti Alleva).

- "When I read the newspaper, I hear her voice in my head sometimes. I think it's because her classes are so relevant in the world we live in, and so I feel like that's what I am going to take away. This stuff that happens has a huge legal component that I didn't think about before I got into her classes, that is now there and present all the time" (student of Julie Nice).

- "I sort of have this thing in the back of my mind if I am working on an important brief or a memo: What would Homer think? Does this live up to Homer's standards? Because if it doesn't, then I have to do it again" (student of Steven Homer).

Conclusion

Probably the best measure of teaching excellence is by examining the lasting lessons students learn from their teachers—the intellectual and personal development that stays with students during law school and into practice. We end this chapter with a student's and teacher's perspective on the same experience that led to deep learning and continues to have profound effects not only on the student but also on the people the student has encountered since graduating from law school.

"Before I came here, all I wanted to be was a prosecutor. I wanted to put criminals behind bars. Period. And she kind of had me read some books, and taught me and really crafted me in her hands. We've heard a lot that she's very much a believer. But she also believes in the criminal-justice system in that there needs to be ethical prosecution. So she had an opportunity now to affect a young prosecutor and those who work with me at this table know that I try to take a different approach to how I look at cases and defendants and individualize cases. Guess where that skill set came from? Guess who influenced me like that?" (student of Cary Bricker).

"He came to this class and he picks *Surviving Justice*. And the book is a series of stories about Innocence Project clients who were factually innocent, not guilty. So he saw ways that different prosecutors . . . screwed up. . . . And I cannot tell you what a good prosecutor he is. It almost makes me want to cry. He looks to the person and not just to the crime, you know, so they're three-dimensional people. And I just am so proud of him. And it doesn't mean that he won't be incredibly zealous, and he won't get convictions with a lot of time on cases where it's appropriate. But you know he's the kind of prosecutor that you want to be out in the community" (Cary Bricker).

10

Suggestions for Using this Book

Working on this project has been an awe-inspiring experience. Talking to the selected teachers, reading their materials, reviewing their student evaluations, hearing from their current and former students, and observing these teachers in the classroom have deeply moved and inspired us.

All readers can learn from the words and actions of the teachers in this book. Whether you have been teaching for years, aspire to teach, work with teachers, teach a course on legal education, or are just interested in teaching, we invite you to reflect upon and develop your approach to teaching and learning by reading about these teachers.

Of course, one way to use this book is to read it straight through from start to finish. Another approach would be to look at the Table of Contents and then chose to focus on one chapter at a time, based on your interests and questions about teaching. Alternatively, you could dive in at random, opening the book and starting in the middle. You also might want to skim through the book initially to get a sense of the whole, and then return to read individual chapters more closely. You may find it useful to reread portions after some time. We believe there is value in these and any other approaches. We have used these approaches ourselves in learning from other books on teaching.

Regardless of how you read this book, please keep several things in mind:

- Many excellent teachers are not included in this book.
- This book reflects only a small portion of what excellent US law teachers do. We have many hundreds of pages of material from which we drew examples; we could not include many things that even the teachers we studied do, much less report everything all the other excellent teachers out there may do.
- Excellent teachers have a variety of approaches to designing their courses, teaching class sessions, building lasting, meaningful relationships with their students, and providing practice and feedback.
- Excellent teachers are authentic, human, and imperfect; they have good days and bad days in the classroom.
- This is not a how-to book; see the website of the Institute for Law Teaching and Learning (www.lawteaching.org) for access to numerous specific teaching ideas in *The law Teacher,* law journal articles, books, bibliographies, videos, and other resources.

We offer a few concrete suggestions about ways you could use this book individually or in a group. We also suggest ways that the book might be helpful to aspiring law teachers and law schools.

Individual Teaching Development Practice

Use Excellent Teachers for Inspiration

Whether you read through the book starting at the beginning, or study certain chapters individually, use excellent teachers as models. You might pick one or two specific points in the book, such as a teacher's approach to meeting with students or starting each class session, and have that inspire you for a semester. You may also have your own examples of excellent teachers and use them for inspiration.

Consider placing a reminder of your source of inspiration, such as a quote, phrase, or image, in a place where you will see it often. If you have times when you become discouraged about teaching, re-read sections of the book that you found particularly inspiring or recall your own experiences with excellent teachers.

Seek additional inspiration. Find out who students and colleagues think are the best teachers at your school. See if you can talk to those teachers and observe their classes. If there are other law schools nearby, seek out excellent teachers at those law schools and visit them. Invite excellent teachers to observe your classes and give you ideas.

Use the Book to Set Goals

As you read and think about the teaching ideas in this book, identify one to three concrete aspects of your own teaching that you would like to improve during the semester or year. For example, you may decide to learn all your students' names early in the course, as most of the teachers in our study do. If learning names is very difficult for you, you might seek to learn all names, or at least a significant portion of them, by the end of the semester. In future semesters, you might want to learn students' names by midsemester and then within the first few weeks.

In working to achieve your goals, you may find it helpful to consult additional teaching resources, including your colleagues and the literature on teaching and learning. During the semester, periodically review your goals and assess your progress. Modify your goals as necessary, consider new ones if you have accomplished your original ones, and celebrate your accomplishments. Consider noting your goals and accomplishments in your annual faculty-self-evaluation report.

If you use this book to identify teaching goals, remind yourself that most of the teachers in this book have been developing their approaches over many years. You may want to adopt numerous practices of excellent teachers, but, to be fair to yourself, recognize the other personal and professional demands on your time, and make changes in your teaching incrementally over time. Recognize that none of the twenty-six law teachers we studied incorporate all of the qualities and practices set out in this book. In general, setting one to three manageable teaching goals is more effective than trying to make many changes. If you are not sure how to select among many goals, you may find it helpful to talk to students, colleagues, and administrators about their teaching priorities, review student evaluations, and read more of the literature on effective teaching and learning.

Use This Book for Self-Education

Focusing on Chapters 3 through 9, you could study a chapter a week or every two weeks. After each chapter, you might find it helpful to record your thoughts about the material. You could also use the chapters as guides for developing your thoughts about your teaching. For example, you might want to

- develop or revise a statement about your teaching philosophy
- describe a metaphor for your teaching
- draft your views on office hours and share them in your syllabi
- identify things you do to show students you care
- record the variety of teaching techniques you use in class
- design ways to include practice-based material in your course
- find new ways to incorporate diverse perspectives in class and support the students who take such risks
- plan assessment and feedback opportunities
- work out ways to continue developing your teaching
- start a weekly reflective teaching journal (see below)

Use This Book for Guided Self-Reflection

As illustrated in Chapter 3, "What Personal Qualities Do the Best Law Teachers Possess?", all outstanding law teachers are highly reflective. Experts in other fields have also observed the power of reflection in developing expertise. One of the ways to develop a reflective practice is to keep a teaching journal. Use your teaching journal to regularly capture your thoughts about your students and courses. Use practices of excellent law teachers as reflection prompts. You could proceed through the book linearly, taking the time to reflect and note your thoughts periodically, or you could dip into the book at any point for ideas to consider. If you are working on a particular aspect of teaching, you may want to focus your journal on it and any related ideas from the law teachers in this book.

Use This Book for Further Study

Many of the teachers we studied have also written about teaching and learning. They have presented at conferences and conducted workshops. They have written blogs, books, articles, and essays. We learned from and were inspired by many of these outstanding teachers before they were included in this study. We encourage you to seek out and read their works to continue to learn from them. See Appendix D for a list of their writings about teaching and learning.

You may also want to study the complexities of law teaching and learning in much greater depth. The examples from the teachers in this study suggest many areas of inquiry for quantitative and qualitative research. We encourage you to add your insights to the field.

Teaching Development Group Suggestions

Hold a Book Group Discussion

Colleagues interested in teaching could read and discuss the book or selected chapters. Questions for a book group could include:

- Which characteristics of excellent teachers do you find most compelling?
- What did you find inspirational about the teachers in this book?
- What is exceptional learning in the law-school context?

- How do your teaching philosophies differ?
- What surprised you in reading about these excellent law teachers?
- What concerned you in reading about these teachers?
- What examples of highly effective teaching stood out for you?
- What are the challenges to becoming an outstanding law teacher?
- How would you like to be remembered by your students?
- What can your law school do to create a culture of excellent teaching?
- What do you make of the differences among the teachers in this book? What principles are universal?

Conduct Faculty Workshops and Colloquia

Law teachers discussed in this book could be invited to speak at your law school, sharing their perspectives on teaching, and possibly demonstrating their teaching methods. In addition to talking to faculty about teaching, guests could be invited to observe classes or spend time meeting with faculty individually or in small groups.

A group of teachers could offer to organize one or more workshops on practices or attributes of outstanding law teachers, such as relating to students, setting expectations, preparing for class, conducting classes, or assessing and giving feedback. Examples of what extraordinary law teachers do could prompt teachers to collaborate in designing practices effective for their students and appropriate for their institutional cultures.

Teachers could also hold periodic discussions on excellent teaching practices. Different faculty could volunteer to research and inform colleagues about inexpensive, effective resources to help faculty develop as teachers.

Faculty can also seek to include more discussions about teaching in their institutions' professional development programs. As part of regularly scheduled scholarly discussions, internal or outside speakers could be invited to share their works-in-progress on law teaching and learning.

Facilitate Peer Classroom Observations

Reciprocal, nonevaluative, peer classroom observations and discussions could be inspired by examples from behaviors of the law teachers discussed in this book. A teacher might focus on a particular approach to engaging students during class; that teacher could invite a colleague to observe the class, record student engagement, and discuss the class afterward. Teachers could exchange goals for improving their teaching and then work together to help each other achieve them.

Ideas for New and Aspiring Law Teachers

For years students have been learning valuable and significant lasting lessons from the teachers discussed in this book. We encourage new and aspiring law teachers to similarly learn about and be inspired by these teachers. Many of us have become interested in teaching law because of one teacher's influence. Often it is that one teacher's image that we keep in mind as we pursue a teaching position.

We invite new teachers to consider several such examples of highly effective teachers. We believe all teachers benefit from having multiple models. Teaching is complex; no one approach works for everyone. We can learn from and build upon a number of different examples to more effectively reach our students.

At a practical level, reading about excellent law teachers helps in many areas. In applying for teaching positions, knowing more about what such law teachers do can help candidates develop their own teaching philosophies and draft application materials. Having a variety of examples of highly effective law teachers assists candidates in asking and answering questions during job interviews. Such examples provide ideas about how to structure courses, trouble-shoot problems, and work with students.

Suggestions for Law Schools

We encourage law-school administrators to use this book to help build a culture of teaching, much as they already support a culture of scholarship. Simple and relatively inexpensive approaches can encourage and promote faculty interest in excellent teaching. Leaders within law schools can help keep the concept of outstanding teaching at the forefront in administrators', students', and teachers' minds by visibly recognizing and celebrating excellent teachers at the school, providing refreshments for teaching discussions and workshops, and circulating teaching ideas and information about teaching resources.

In addition to supporting and facilitating the above suggestions for individual and group uses of this book, law schools could consider the following practices to try to create a culture of teaching excellence:

Create a teaching-effectiveness committee or task force. We recommend inviting faculty and students to participate in this committee or task force. As with any committee, the group could have an official charge, such as promoting continuing excellence in teaching and learning.

Review existing promotion and retention standards. Are these standards consistent with best teaching practices? Is excellent teaching an important component for faculty advancement? If so, how is it measured? Are teachers given time and resources to develop as teachers as well as scholars?

Review existing student evaluation instruments. Are these instruments consistent with best teaching practices? Are students asked to evaluate teachers based on their experience with those teachers, such as whether students feel they are treated with respect and engaged during class? Are students challenged to work hard to succeed in the course?

Develop a visiting-teaching-excellence program. Among other things, this program could include inviting a professor known for excellent teaching—such as one of the teachers in this book—to spend a few days, week, semester, or year at the school. This visiting teacher could be asked to facilitate discussions and conduct workshops on teaching and learning. The visitor could observe classes and provide feedback to teachers. Other faculty could be invited to observe and learn from the visitor's teaching.

Include specifics about excellent teaching practices in faculty annual reports and reviews. How do faculty engage with students outside class? What are professors' teaching-development agendas for the next year or two? What kinds of assessments and feedback methods do faculty use? What steps do faculty take to continue to develop as teachers?

Pay attention to teaching. Do students know that teaching matters to leaders of the law school? Do the dean and associate deans periodically sit in on classes of full- and part-time professors? Are students asked about teaching? Are faculty asked about how the school can support excellent teaching practices?

Support scholarship on teaching and learning. Many law teachers are interested in learning more and writing about teaching and learning. These teachers may be discouraged from writing about pedagogy, however, if the school does not value such scholarship. Law schools should support rigorous scholarship on legal education. Research in the area of teaching and learning continues to expand, incorporating findings from many fields, including cognitive psychology and neuroscience. Teachers in many fields are developing approaches to help students learn complex material in efficient and effective ways. They are also designing methods to assess whether changes in teaching lead to tangible learning gains. Supporting law professors' research and writing about teaching and learning helps them individually develop as teachers and may lead to improved student-learning outcomes.

Conclusion

Doing this research and writing this book has inspired and changed us as teachers. We are grateful for the opportunity to have seen these teachers in action and hope that these words capture, as much as possible, what makes them so effective. We hope your experience in reading this book proves to be at least half as helpful to you.

Dear_____:

I am in search of the best law teachers in this country, and I could use your help. I have the extraordinary opportunity to conduct a law professor-focused, follow-up study to Ken Bain's wonderful *What the Best College Teachers Do* (Harvard University Press, 2004). So far, I have received close to 80 nominations from a wide variety of law schools including: Arizona, Capital University, Columbia, Denver, Emory, Harvard, Houston, New York, Seton Hall, Southern Illinois University, UCLA, and Yale.

Thus, I am writing to solicit your nominations. In particular, I am looking for teachers who consistently produce extraordinary learning, who change their students' lives and whose instruction stays with students long after they graduate from law school. I am hoping that, if you nominate someone, it will be because you genuinely believe that professor produces such extraordinary learning.

I hope what I produce inspires you as much as Professor Bain's work has inspired me. Over the next three years, I will be:

- soliciting nominations;
- gathering evidence of nominees' excellence;
- paring the list of nominees to the most extraordinary law teachers;
- visiting law schools around the country, sitting in on classes, interviewing the nominees, and talking to focus groups of students and alumni; and then
- publishing what I have found in a book: *What the Best Law Teachers Do* (Harvard University Press, forthcoming 2011).

I have set up a web nomination process (although I will also accept nominations by phone, by e-mail, by regular mail, or in person). To nominate a candidate or learn more about this project, please go to http://washburnlaw.edu/bestlawteachers. Click on the link on the right side of the page to get to the nomination form.

To honor those who have been nominated, I have set up a website on which I will report the name of each nominee, the nominee's institutional affiliation, and a few comments from the nominator. Here's a link to that website: http://washburnlaw.edu/bestlawteachers /nominees/.

Feel free to e-mail me at michael.schwartz@washburn.edu if you have any questions. The names of nominators and nominees will be withheld upon request.

Sincerely,

APPENDIX B
Subject Questions

LEARNING

1. What is your understanding of how humans learn?
2. What do you want your students to learn?
3. Where does learning take place in your courses?
4. What do you do to motivate students to learn?
5. What do you do to help students learn?
6. What challenges do students have in learning in your classes?
7. What challenges do you have in helping them learn?

TEACHING

8. How do you prepare to teach? What questions do you ask yourself as you prepare?
9. What are your primary teaching methods?
10. What are your key assignments?
11. What do students find exciting in your course(s)?
12. How do you start each course? End it?
13. Are there any good metaphors for your approach to teaching?

RELATIONSHIPS

14. How would you describe your relationship with students?
15. What do you like *most* about your students?
16. What do you like *least* about your students?

ASSESSMENT

17. How do you provide feedback to students during the course?
18. How do you evaluate students?
19. How do you check your progress and evaluate your own efforts?
20. How do you know when you have done a good job in teaching a class?
21. How do you know when you have done a good job in teaching a course?

GLOBAL

22. Do you have any evidence of the success of your students in learning what you wish them to learn?
23. Do you have any evidence that your teaching methods contribute significantly to that learning?
24. What is a good metaphor for your courses (a game, a journey, a tragedy, an obstacle course)? How does that metaphor illuminate something about your teaching?
25. How has your teaching evolved over time?

APPENDIX C
QUESTIONS FOR STUDENTS AND ALUMNI

1. What does (did) the teacher do that fosters your learning?
2. How would you characterize the nature of your learning in the class(es)?
3. What changes in the way this teacher conducts (conducted) the class(es) would better foster your learning?
4. How is this teacher different from other teachers you have (have had)?
5. What things (if any) that you learned from this teacher have stayed with you? What did this teacher do that caused those things to stay with you?

List of Subjects' Works Related to Teaching and Learning

PATTI ALLEVA

"Seeking Integrity: Learning Integratively from Classroom Controversy," with Laura Rovner, 42 Sw. U. L. Rev. (forthcoming).

"The Personal as Predicate," 81 N.D. L. Rev. 683 (2005).

Law through Literature: Using Non-Traditional Sources to Study Law and Develop Professional Identity. Reflective Report and Portfolio, Bush Teaching Scholars Program, University of North Dakota, 2004 (on file with the author).

RORY BAHADUR

"Idea of the Month: Teaching Statutory/Rule Interpretation." Institute for Law Teaching and Learning, July 2012, http://lawteaching.org /ideas/index.php.

"Idea of the Month: Using Formative Assessment to Speed Up Doctrinal Coverage." Institute for Law Teaching and Learning, January 2012, http://lawteaching.org/ideas/index.php.

ROBERTO CORRADA

"Formative Assessment in Law School Doctrinal Classes: Rethinking Grade Appeals," J. Legal Educ. (forthcoming).

"'Ill-Structured' Simulations in Law School" (article in progress).

"Simulations in Two American Law School Classes: Labor Law and Administrative Law." In *Simulation and the Learning of the Law*, edited by Strevens, Grimes, and Phillips. Farnham, UK: Ashgate (forthcoming).

Administrative Law: A Casebook (coauthor), 7th ed. New York: Aspen, 2010.

Employment Discrimination Law: Cases and Materials on Equality in the Workplace (coauthor), 8th ed. New York: Thompson Reuters, 2010.

Labor Law in the Contemporary Workplace (coauthor). New York: Thomson West, 2009.

"Introduction: Toward an Ethic of Teaching: Class, Race, and a Pedagogy of Community Engagement," 50 Vill. L. Rev. 837 (2005).

"Comment on the Ethics of Comparison: A Statistician Wrestles with the Orthodoxy of a Control Group." In *Ethics of Inquiry: Issues in the Scholarship of Teaching and Learning*. Stanford, CA: Carnegie Foundation for the Advancement of Teaching, 2002.

"Using Technology to Support Active Learning in a Labor Law Classroom." In *Wayfarer: Chartering Advances in Social Sciences and Humanities Computing*. CD-Rom. Chicago: University of Illinois Press, 2002.

"A Simulation of Union Organizing in a Labor Law Class," 46 J. Legal Educ. 445 (1996).

BRIDGET CRAWFORD

Federal Taxes on Gratuitous Transfers (coauthor). New York: Aspen, 2011.

"Daughter of Liberty Wedded to Law: Gender and Legal Education at the University of Pennsylvania Law Department 1870-1900," 6 J. Gender Race & Just. 131 (2002).

MEREDITH DUNCAN

Advanced Torts: A Lawyer's Perspective (coauthor). Durham: Carolina Academic Press (forthcoming).

Pedagogical Solutions to Teaching Prosecutorial Ethics in Law School (work-in-progress).

Tort Law: A Contemporary Approach (coauthor), 2nd ed. New York: Thomson West, 2012.

PAULA FRANZESE

A Short and Happy Guide to the Law of Sales. New York: Thomson West, 2013.

Strategies and Techniques of Law School Teaching: Property. New York: Aspen, 2012.

"From Tragedy, Hope: The Good Lawyer and the Pursuit of the Public Interest," 32 Seton Hall L. Rev. 451 (2011).

A Short and Happy Guide to Property. New York: Thomson West, 2011.

"The Good Lawyer: Finding Meaning through Service," New Jersey Lawyer (Dec. 2007).

Property Law and the Public Interest (coauthor), 3rd ed. New York: LexisNexis, 2007.

"To Be the Change: Finding Higher Ground in the Law," 50 Me. L. Rev. 11 (1998).

"Mother Teresa's Legacy to Lawyers" (coauthor), 28 Seton Hall L. Rev. 765 (1997–1998).

Throw Your Fears Out the Window: A Book of Wisdom, Inspiration and Guidance for Law Students and Lawyers. Newark, NJ: Seton Hall Law School, 1997.

"The Community of Law Teachers and Scholars Expands: Guideposts for New Faculty" (coauthor), 22 Seton Hall L. Rev. 1375 (1992).

STEVEN FRIEDLAND

Criminal Law: A Context and Practice Casebook (coauthor). Durham: Carolina Academic Press (forthcoming).

Criminal Procedure: Cases and Materials (coauthor), 4th ed. New York: West, 2012.

Evidence Problems and Materials, 4th ed. New York: LexisNexis, 2012.

"Outcomes and the Ownership Conception of Law School Courses," 38 William Mitchell L. Rev. 947 (2012).

Techniques for Teaching Law 2 (coauthor). Durham: Carolina Academic Press, 2011.

"Trumpeting Change: Replacing Tradition with Engaged Legal Education," 3 Elon L. Rev. 93 (2011).

Acing Constitutional Law (coauthor). New York: Thomson Reuters, 2010.

Bar Prep Workbook. Revised. Exam Pro Series. New York: West, 2010.

Evidence Law and Practice (coauthor), 4th ed. New York: LexisNexis, 2010.

"Reversing the Norm: Promoting Student Questioning Proficiency," The Law Teacher (Fall 2010).

Inside Constitutional Law (coauthor). New York: Wolters Kluwer, 2009.

"Portable Learning for the 21st Century Law School: Designing a New Pedagogy for the Modern Global Context" (coauthor), 26 J. Marshall J. of Computer & Info. L. 371 (2009).

Sum and Substance Quick Review of Criminal Law, 5th ed. New York: Thomson West, 2008.

Teaching the Law School Curriculum (coauthor). Durham: Carolina Academic Press, 2004 (parts translated into Japanese by the Japan Legal Foundation, 2005).

"A Critical Inquiry into the Traditional Uses of Law School Examinations," 23 Pace U. L. Rev. 147 (2002).

"Teaching Property: Some Lessons Learned," 46 St. Louis U. L. J. 581 (2002).

Techniques for Teaching Law (coauthor). Durham: Carolina Academic Press, 1999 (translated into Japanese and Vietnamese), http://lawteaching .org/teaching/index.php.

"Test Builder," The Law Teacher (Fall 1999).

"How We Teach: A Survey of Teaching Techniques in American Law Schools," 20 Seattle U. L. Rev. 1 (1996).

"Challenging Tradition: Using Objective Questions in Law School Examinations" (coauthor), 41 DePaul L. Rev. 143 (1991).

"Towards the Legitimacy of Oral Examinations in American Legal Education," 31 Syracuse L. Rev. 627 (1988).

INGRID HILLINGER

Commercial Transactions: Secured Financing; Cases, Materials, Problems (coauthor), 3rd. ed. New York: LexisNexis, 2003.

Teacher's Manual, Commercial Transactions: Secured Financing; Cases, Materials, Problems, 3rd ed. New York: LexisNexis, 2003.

NANCY KNAUER

Property Law: A Context and Practice Casebook (coauthor). Durham: Carolina Academic Press, 2013.

LAWRENCE KRIEGER

"The Most Ethical of People, the Least Ethical of People: Proposing Self-Determination Theory to Measure Professional Character Formation," 8 U. St. Thomas L. J. 169 (2011).

"Ten Commandments of Field Placements and Creating Intimacy in Large Classes." In Gerald F. Hess et al., *Techniques for Teaching Law* 2. Durham: Carolina Academic Press, 2011.

"Human Nature as a New Guiding Philosophy for Legal Education and the Profession," 47 Washburn L. J. 247 (2008).

"Understanding the Negative Effects of Legal Education on Law Students: A Longitudinal Test of Self-Determination Theory" (coauthor), 33 Pers. Soc. Psych. Bull. 883 (2007).

A Deeper Understanding of Your Career Choices. Tallahassee: Fla. St. Univ. Coll. of Law, 2006.

The Hidden Sources of Law School Stress. Tallahassee: Fla. St. Univ. Coll. of Law, 2005.

"Does Legal Education Have Undermining Effects on Law Students? Evaluating Changes in Values, Motivation and Well-Being" (coauthor), 22 Behav. Sci. & L. 261 (2004).

"Institutional Denial About the Dark Side of Law School, and Fresh Empirical Guidance for Constructively Breaking the Silence," 52 J. Legal Educ. 112 (2002).

"Psychological Insights: Why Our Students and Graduates Suffer, and What We Might Do about It," 8 J. Ass'n L. Writing Directors 259 (2002).

"What We're Not Telling Law Students—and Lawyers—That They Really Need to Know: Some Thoughts-in-Action toward Revitalizing the Profession from Its Roots," 13 J. Law & Health 1 (1998-99).

SUSAN KUO

"Culture Clash: Teaching Cultural Defenses in the Criminal Law Classroom," 48 St. Louis U. L. J. 1297 (2004).

NANCY LEVIT

The Happy Lawyer: Making a Good Life in the Law (coauthor). New York: Oxford Univ. Press, 2010.

"Expository Writing across the Curriculum—Legal Storytelling: The Theory and the Practice," 15 Legal Writing: J. Legal Writing Inst. 253 (2009).

"Happy Law Students, Happy Lawyers" (coauthor), 58 Syracuse L. Rev. 351 (2008).

"Dismantling Hierarchies in Legal Education," 73 UMKC L. Rev. 231 (2004).

Jurisprudence—Classical to Contemporary: From Natural Law to Postmodernism (coauthor), 2nd ed. New York: West Group, 2002.

Teacher's Manual to accompany *Jurisprudence—Classical to Contemporary: From Natural Law to Postmodernism* (coauthor). New York: West Group, 2002.

"Separating Equals: Educational Research and the Long-Term Consequences of Sex Segregation," 67 Geo. Wash. U. L. Rev. 451 (1999).

"If It Can't Be Lake Woebegone . . . A Nationwide Survey of Law School Grading and Grade Normalization Practices" (coauthor), 66 UMKC L. Rev. 819 (1997).

PAULA LUSTBADER

"One Size Does Not Fit All: Designing an Academic Support Program that Fits Your School, Part I: Factors to Ensure Success," Web/podcast for the LSAC-sponsored website on Academic Support Programs, 2009, http://lawschoolasp.org/eLearning/designing_asp _that_fits_your_school_part1/viewer.swf.

"One Size Does Not Fit All: Designing an Academic Support Program that Fits Your School, Part II: Components of Successful ASPs," Web/podcast for the LSAC-sponsored website on Academic Support Programs, 2009, http://lawschoolasp.org/eLearning/designing _asp_that_fits_your_school_part2/viewer.swf.

"One Size Does Not Fit All: Designing an Academic Support Program that Fits Your School, Part IV, Staffing," Web/podcast for the LSAC-sponsored website on Academic Support Programs, 2009, http://lawschoolasp.org/eLearning/designing_asp_that_fits_your _school_part4/viewer.swf.

"An Overview of ASP Pedagogy," Web/podcast for the LSAC-sponsored website on Academic Support Programs, 2009, http://lawschoolasp .org/eLearning/overview_of_asp_pedagogy/viewer.swf.

"Can the Professor Come Out to Play? Scholarship, Teaching, and Theories of Play" (coauthor), 58 J. Legal Educ. 481 (2008).

"You Are Not in Kansas Anymore: Orientation Programs Can Help Students Fly Over the Rainbow," 47 Washburn L. J. 327 (2008).

"Walk the Talk: Creating Learning Communities to Promote a Pedagogy of Justice," 4(2) Seattle J. Soc. J. 613 (2006).

Principles for Enhancing Legal Education. Teaching manual and video. Institute for Law Teaching and Learning, 2001, http://lawteaching .org/publications/videos/principlesforenhancing.php.

"Conclusion: Adapting the Seven Principles to Legal Education (Seven Principles for Good Practice in Legal Education)," 49 J. Legal Educ. 459 (1999).

"Principle 7: Good Practice Respects Diverse Talents and Ways of Learning, and Conclusion: Adapting the Seven Principles to Legal Education," 49 J. Legal Educ. 448 (1999).

"Teach in Context: Responding to Diverse Student Voices Helps All Students Learn," 48 J. Legal Educ. 402 (1998).

Teach to the Whole Class: Barriers and Pathways to Learning. Teaching manual and video. Institute for Law School Teaching, 1998, http://law teaching.org/publications/videos/teachtothewholeclass.php.

"Construction Sites, Building Types, and Bridging Gaps: A Cognitive Theory of the Learning Progression of Law Students," 33 Willamette L. Rev. 315 (1997).

"From Dreams to Reality: The Emerging Role of Law School Academic Support," 31 U. S. F. L. Rev. 839 (1997).

"A Theoretical Foundation for Academic Assistance Programs and AAP Pedagogy: Theory and Implementation." In *Handbook on Academic Assistance Programs.* Newtown, PA: LSAC, 1997.

"The Role of Academic Assistance in the Law School," The Equalizer (1994).

"Some Tips on Using Collaborative Learning Exercises," The Law Teacher (Spring 1994).

NELSON MILLER

Entrepreneurial Practice: Enterprise Skills for Serving Emerging Client Populations (coauthor). Lake Mary, FL: Vandeplas, 2012.

The Faithful Lawyer: Flourishing from Law Study to Practice. Commerce City, CA: Bridge Publications, 2012.

The Law, Principles and Practice of Ethics Law (coauthor), 3rd ed. Lake Mary, FL: Vandeplas, 2012.

The Practice of Tort Law (coauthor), 3rd ed. Lake Mary, FL: Vandeplas, 2012.

Civil Procedure in Practice. Lake Mary, FL: Vandeplas, 2011.

A Law Graduate's Guide: Navigating Law School's Hidden Career and Professional-Development Curriculum. Commerce City, CA: Bridge Publications, 2011.

"Using a Faculty Inquiry Process to Examine Student Responsibility for Learning" (coauthor), 61 J. Legal Educ. 280 (2011).

A Law Student's Guide—Legal Education's Knowledge, Skills, and Ethics Dimensions. Durham: Carolina Academic Press, 2010.

"Legal Education as a Pie-Maker—Why Michigan Benefits from Accessible Law Schools," 89 Mich. B. J. 42 (2010).

"The Role of Law Schools in Shaping Culturally Competent Lawyers" (coauthor), 89 Mich. B. J. 46 (2010).

Teaching Law: A Framework for Instructional Mastery. Commerce City, CA: Bridge Publications, 2010.

"Teaching Philosophy Statement," The Law Teacher (Fall 2010).

"Meeting the Carnegie Report's Challenge to Make Legal Analysis Explicit—Subsidiary Skills to the IRAC Framework" (coauthor), 59 J. Legal Educ. 192 (2009).

"Preserving Law School's Signature Pedagogy and Great Subjects" (coauthor), 88 Mich. B. J 46 (2009).

"Who Is the Customer and What Are We Selling? Employer-Based Objectives for the Ethical Competence of Law School Graduates" (coauthor), 33 J. Legal Prof. 223 (2009).

"An Apprenticeship of Professional Identity—A Paradigm for Education Lawyers," 87 Mich. B. J. 20 (2008).

"Community Stewards in a Responsible Republic." In *Reflections of a Lawyer's Soul: The Institutional Experience of Professionalism at Thomas M. Cooley Law School.* Buffalo, NY: William S. Hein, 2008.

"Cultural Competence as a Professional Skill" (coauthor). In *Reflections of a Lawyer's Soul: The Institutional Experience of Professionalism at Thomas M. Cooley Law School.* Buffalo, NY: William S. Hein, 2008.

"Demonstrating and Contextualizing Legal Analysis" (coauthor). In *Reflections of a Lawyer's Soul: The Institutional Experience of Profession-*

alism at Thomas M. Cooley Law School. Buffalo, NY: William S. Hein, 2008.

"An Empirical Study of Student Ethical Commitments" (coauthor). In *Reflections of a Lawyer's Soul: The Institutional Experience of Professionalism at Thomas M. Cooley Law School*. Buffalo, NY: William S. Hein, 2008.

"Equality as Talisman: Getting beyond Bias to Cultural Competence as a Professional Skill" (coauthor), 25 Thomas M. Cooley L. Rev. 100 (2008).

"Extra-Curricular Mentoring and Volunteering" (coauthor). In *Reflections of a Lawyer's Soul: The Institutional Experience of Professionalism at Thomas M. Cooley Law School*. Buffalo, NY: William S. Hein, 2008.

"Instruction in Meta-Ethical Competence." In *Reflections of a Lawyer's Soul: The Institutional Experience of Professionalism at Thomas M. Cooley Law School*. Buffalo, NY: William S. Hein, 2008.

Reflections of a Lawyer's Soul: The Institutional Experience of Professionalism at Thomas M. Cooley Law School (coeditor). Buffalo, NY: William S. Hein, 2008.

"Teaching Faculty How to Learn—Experiences in Faculty Development" (coauthor). In *Reflections of a Lawyer's Soul: The Institutional Experience of Professionalism at Thomas M. Cooley Law School*. Buffalo, NY: William S. Hein, 2008.

"To Think, to Act, to Learn: From Process to Performance" (coauthor). In *Reflections of a Lawyer's Soul: The Institutional Experience of Professionalism at Thomas M. Cooley Law School*. Buffalo, NY: William S. Hein, 2008.

"Meta-Ethical Competence as a Lawyer Skill: Variant Ethics Affecting Lawyer and Client Decision-Making," 9 Thomas M. Cooley J. Prac. & Clin. L. 91 (2007).

HIROSHI MOTOMURA

Immigration and Citizenship: Process and Policy (coauthor), 7th ed. New York: Thomson West, 2012.

Forced Migration: Law and Policy (coauthor). New York: Thomson West, 2007.

JULIE NICE

Sexuality Law. New York: Wolters Kluwer (forthcoming).
Poverty Law: Theory and Practice. New York: West, 1997.

PHILIP PRYGOSKI

Sum and Substance: Constitutional Law, 4th ed. New York: West, 1998.

RUTHANN ROBSON

Constitutional Law Final Exam, 2011 version, http://lawprofessors.typepad .com/conlaw/2011/11/constitutional-law-final-exam-2011-version .html.

Constitutional Law Exam Drafting: The End of Semester Challenge, http:// lawprofessors.typepad.com/conlaw/2010/04/constitutional-law -exam-drafting.html.

"Law Students as Legal Scholars," 7 NYC L. Rev. 195 (2004).

"Critical Challenges: A Conversation on Complicity and Civility in Legal Academia" (coauthor), 1 Seattle J. of Social Justice 601–629 (2003).

"The Zen of Grading," 36 Akron L. Rev. 303 (2003).

"The Politics of the Possible: Reflections on a Decade at CUNY School of Law," 4 NYC L. Rev. 245 (2000).

"Pedagogy, Jurisprudence and Lesbian Sex in a Law School Classroom." In *Lesbian Erotics,* edited by Karla Jay. New York: New York University Press, 1995. Reprinted in *Sappho Goes to Law School.* New York: Columbia University Press, 1998.

TINA STARK

"Contract Drafting: A Prerequisite to Teaching Transactional Negotiation," 12 Transactions, Tenn. J. Bus. L. 162 (Special Report 2011).

"Transactional Education: What's Next?—Opening Remarks," 12 Transactions, Tenn. J. Bus. L. 3 (Special Report 2011).

"My Fantasy Curriculum and Other Almost Random Thoughts," 2009 Transactions, Tenn. J. Bus. L. 3.

"Transactional Skills Training: Contract Drafting—The Basics" (coauthor), 2009 Transactions, Tenn. J. Bus. L. 139.

Transactional Training Resource Guide. Emory Law and Economics Research Paper No. 9–44 (August 17, 2009). SSRN, http://ssrn.com/abstract =1456543.

Drafting Contracts: How and Why Lawyers Do What They Do. New York: Aspen, 2007.

A Business Education for Business Lawyers. Program materials. Spring 2005 Meeting of the ABA Section of Business Law.

"Thinking Like a Deal Lawyer," 54 J. Legal Educ. 223 (2004).

ANDY TASLITZ

Skills and Values: Criminal Law (coauthor). New York: LexisNexis (forthcoming).

Mastering Criminal Procedure. Vol. 2, *The Adjudicatory Stage* (coauthor). Durham: Carolina Academic Press, 2012.

Strategies and Techniques for Teaching Criminal Law. New York: Wolters Kluwer, 2012.

Constitutional Criminal Procedure (coauthor), 4th ed. New York: Foundation Press, 2010.

Evidence Law and Practice (coauthor), 4th ed. New York: LexisNexis, 2010.

Mastering Criminal Procedure. Vol. 1, *The Investigative Stage* (coauthor). Durham: Carolina Academic Press, 2010.

Criminal Law: Concepts and Practice (coauthor), 2nd ed. Durham: Carolina Academic Press, 2009.

"Narrative, Statutory Interpretation, and the Training of Future Trial Lawyers; First Day Exercises; and Five Helpful Evidence Cases." In Hess & Friedland, *Teaching the Law School Curriculum.* Durham: Carolina Academic Press, 2004.

"Exorcising Langdell's Ghost: Structuring a Criminal Procedure Casebook for How Lawyers Really Think," 43 Hastings L. J. 143 (1991).

ACKNOWLEDGMENTS

We are thankful for financial support in the form of writing grants from our home law schools, Washburn University School of Law, University of New Hampshire School of Law, and Gonzaga University School of Law. We also have received a wide variety of administrative support for this project, including web support provided by Martin Wisneski of Washburn, and audiotape transcription services provided by our administrative assistants, Shirley Jacobson of Washburn, Deborah Paige and Kathi Hennessy of the University of New Hampshire, and Barb Anderson of Gonzaga.

This project also was made possible with the support of research assistants. We are grateful to Washburn students Lindsee Acton, Julie Covel, Chris Davies, Jennifer Horchem, Ryan Kilmer, Eileen Ma, Levi Morris, Sarah Peterson-Herr, Rosa Phifer, and Lauren Schultz, and Matthew Burrows from the University of New Hampshire.

Finally, we are grateful for logistical and other support provided by the law schools we visited and where our subjects have taught: Boston College Law School, City University of New York (CUNY) School of Law, Elon University School of Law, Emory University

School of Law, Florida State University College of Law, Howard University School of Law, Lewis & Clark Law School, Pace University School of Law, Seattle University School of Law, Seton Hall University School of Law, Temple University Beasley School of Law, Thomas M. Cooley Law School, University of California, Los Angeles (UCLA) School of Law, University of Missouri-Kansas City School of Law (UMKC), University of Denver Sturm College of Law, University of Houston Law Center, University of Illinois College of Law, University of Iowa College of Law, University of New Mexico School of Law, University of North Carolina School of Law, University of North Dakota School of Law, University of Pacific McGeorge School of Law, University of San Francisco School of Law, University of South Carolina School of Law, Washburn University School of Law, West Virginia University College of Law, and Yale Law School.

INDEX

students, 188, 192–194, 212–213, 222, 227, 233–235, 244, 253–255; providing feedback and assessing students, 265, 283; lasting lessons for students, 310
Friedland, Steve: biographical data, 13, 16; qualities, 44, 46, 50, 63, 73; relating to students, 78, 88, 94, 103, 121; expectations of students, 126, 132–133, 137; preparing to teach, 165, 169, 173; engaging students, 182, 197–198, 202, 215–216, 218, 220, 221, 226, 233, 235, 237, 239, 255–256; providing feedback and assessing students, 281–283; lasting lessons for students, 296, 309–310
Fun, use of. *See* Humor

Games, use of, 226
Gerken, Heather: biographical data, 13, 16; qualities, 39, 42–43, 54, 59–60, 64, 66, 70–74; relating to students, 80, 93, 101, 103, 109, 119, 122; expectations of students, 124, 126, 130, 134–135; preparing to teach, 155, 166, 172–173; engaging students, 181, 184–185, 188, 190–191, 216, 220–222, 226, 235–236, 241–243, 249, 253, 257; providing feedback and assessing students, 266–267, 272, 276; lasting lessons for students, 293, 310
Goldberg, Susan, 29
Gordon, Gregory, 30
Grading: congruence, 21, 280; students' reactions to and teachers' response, 92, 94, 108; appeal, 281; criteria, 278–279; curve, 281; extra credit, 281

Harvard Law School, 10, 15, 108, 325
Hess, Gerry, 10
Hillinger, Ingrid: biographical data, 13, 16; qualities, 45, 47, 49, 54–56, 62, 64, 70; relating to students, 87, 91–93, 113,

118–119, 121; expectations of students, 138; preparing to teach, 152, 155, 165; engaging students, 184, 204, 216, 223, 259; providing feedback and assessing students, 261, 276; lasting lessons for students, 291, 306
Hirabayashi, Gordon, 197
Holistic, 27, 30, 62, 244
Homer, Steven: biographical data, 13, 16; qualities, 39, 43, 46, 48, 51, 53, 65–65, 74; relating to students, 77, 91, 99–100, 105, 109; expectations of students, 124, 129, 131–132, 141–142, 147, 149; preparing to teach, 155, 166, 170; engaging students, 180, 187, 200, 220–223, 238, 258; providing feedback and assessing students, 262, 271, 275–276, 279, 285; lasting lessons for students, 294, 297, 303, 305, 308–209, 311
Hornstein, Don: biographical data, 13; qualities, 50, 59, 62, 67, 70, 73; relating to students, 80, 97, 100–101, 103–104, 109, 118; expectations of students, 133, 138; preparing to teach, 160, 173; engaging students, 179–180, 185–186, 188, 193, 199, 232, 234–235, 252; providing feedback and assessing students, 277–278; lasting lessons for students, 291–292, 299
Humanity, 305–307
Humanizing, 108
Humble. *See* Qualities of Best Law Teachers
Humiliation, 86
Humility, 22, 32, 37, 58–61, 75, 148, 302–305. *See also* Qualities of Best Law Teachers: humble
Humor, 7, 74, 121, 158, 193–194, 206–207, 243, 255
Hypotheticals: ineffective, 38; preparing, 137, 214, 219, 244; use of, 157, 165, 211, 247, 250, 257, 263, 285, 295